Education and the Culture of Print
in Modern America

PRINT CULTURE HISTORY
IN MODERN AMERICA

Series Editors

James P. Danky

Wayne A. Wiegand

Christine Pawley

Adam R. Nelson

Libraries as Agencies of Culture
Edited by Thomas Augst and Wayne Wiegand

*Purity in Print: Book Censorship in America from the Gilded Age
to the Computer Age,* Second Edition
Paul S. Boyer

Religion and the Culture of Print in Modern America
Edited by Charles L. Cohen and Paul S. Boyer

*Women in Print: Essays on the Print Culture of American Women
from the Nineteenth and Twentieth Centuries*
Edited by James P. Danky and Wayne A. Wiegand

Bookwomen: Creating an Empire in Children's Book Publishing, 1919–1939
Jacalyn Eddy

Apostles of Culture: The Public Librarian and American Society, 1876–1920
Lora Dee Garrison

Education and the Culture of Print in Modern America
Edited by Adam R. Nelson and John L. Rudolph

Education and the Culture of Print in Modern America

Edited by

Adam R. Nelson

and

John L. Rudolph

The University of Wisconsin Press

Publication of this volume in multiple formats
has been made possible, in part, through support from
several programs at the University of Wisconsin–Madison:
the **School of Library and Information Studies**,
the **Center for the History of Print Culture in Modern America**,
and the **Libraries**.

The University of Wisconsin Press
1930 Monroe Street, 3rd Floor
Madison, Wisconsin 53711-2059
uwpress.wisc.edu

3 Henrietta Street
London WC2E 8LU, England
eurospanbookstore.com

1   3   5   4   2

Printed in the United States of America

Library of Congress Cataloging-in-Publication Data
Education and the culture of print in modern America / edited by Adam R. Nelson
and John L. Rudolph.
p.   cm.—(Print culture history in modern America)
Includes bibliographical references.
ISBN 978-0-299-23614-4 (pbk.: alk. paper)
ISBN 978-0-299-23613-7 (e-book)
1. Mass media and education—United States—History.
I. Nelson, Adam R.   II. Rudolph, John L., 1964–
III. Series: Print culture history in modern America.
P96.E29E35   2010
302.23´20973—dc22   2009040638

Contents

Preface

Nearly all the chapters in this volume had their origin in papers presented at a conference on Education and the Culture of Print in Modern America held in Madison, Wisconsin, in September 2006. At this conference, in the Pyle Conference Center on the shores of Lake Mendota, a diverse range of scholars came together under the auspices of the University of Wisconsin Center for the History of Print Culture in Modern America to explore the varied intersections of print and education in American history. The rich commentary, discussion, and conversation that unfolded that weekend created a stimulating intellectual environment from which this book emerged. We thank all those who participated.

However, getting from the conference to this book was no easy task, and it was accomplished with considerable help from a number of institutions and individuals. Thanks go to the Center for the History of Print Culture and its outgoing director James P. Danky, who initially conceived the idea for a conference on education and print and provided the organizational structure for its success. We are also grateful to Christine Pawley, the incoming director of the Center, for all her help as we began the behind-the-scenes work of reading, screening, selecting, and editing all the fine submissions we received for possible inclusion in this volume. That task was made easier by the advice and counsel we received from Charles Cohen and Paul Boyer, who edited the recent volume *Religion and Print Culture in Modern America*, which preceded this volume in the University of Wisconsin Press series Print Culture History in Modern America. We are all too aware of the height at which the bar has been set by their diligent work.

We also extend our thanks to each of the chapter authors who endured our efforts to reshape their initial submissions into a coherent book that would display the range of work in the field at the same time it highlighted a set of common themes across the chapters. They truly went above and beyond the call of duty in their good-natured willingness to do additional reading and research and to write and revise their chapters over the course of the past year and a half. Finally, we would like to thank Gwen Walker and her colleagues at the University of Wisconsin Press for their encouragement of this volume and their continued support of the Print Culture History in Modern America book series. Without their generous patronage, this book would not have been possible.

Education and the Culture of Print
in Modern America

Introduction

Education, Print Culture, and the Negotiation of Meaning in Modern America

ADAM R. NELSON

MORE THAN TWO DECADES AGO, historian Lawrence Cremin advanced a famously broad definition of *education*. The field of education, he argued, encompassed any "deliberate, systematic, and sustained effort to transmit, evoke, or acquire knowledge, values, attitudes, skills, and/or sensibilities, as well as any learning that results from that effort, direct or indirect, intended or unintended."[1] This volume honors the spirit of Cremin's expansive definition by exploring the link between education and print across a wide variety of settings both inside and outside schools. From workers' camps to world's fairs, from libraries to legislatures, from rural farmhouses to urban street corners, the range of educative settings represented in these chapters is extraordinary. So, too, is the range of education-related print, from dime novels to devotional books, from communist periodicals to closed-captioned television programs. The result is a collection of unusual breadth and depth.

Of course, in a sense, all print is "educative," even if some forms of print are more "deliberate, systematic, or sustained" in their efforts to educate than others. For historians of print culture, the challenge is to explain *how* print educates. As the historiography in this field has expanded in recent years, scholars have offered different answers to this question. Some, emphasizing the *production* of printed material, stress the ways in which producers of print shape, regulate, influence, or even control what Cremin identified as the "knowledge, values, attitudes, skills, and/or sensibilities" of readers. Others, emphasizing the *consumption* of print, stress the ways in which readers reinterpret texts for their own purposes, redefining or resisting, either overtly or covertly, whatever intentions the producers of print (authors, publishers, distributors) may have had. Starting from different premises, different scholars have reached different conclusions about how print educates.

At stake in this debate is the relative power, or agency, of producers or consumers to determine the *meaning* of texts. Those who stress the production (or regulation) of print suggest that producers have more power to determine meaning; those who emphasize the consumption (or reception) of print suggest that readers, or communities of readers, have equal, if not greater, power. In some ways, two subgroups within the field of print culture studies—one exploring the history of the book, the other pursuing literary analyses of "reader response"—have arisen from opposite sides of this debate. Historians of the book typically stress the power of producers and regulators of print to shape meaning, while literary theorists emphasize the independent agency of readers. Given the overlaps between these subgroups, such distinctions can be exaggerated; nonetheless, a focus on the production/regulation or consumption/reception side of print culture inevitably influences scholars' views concerning the relationship between readers and texts.

Seeking to move past some of the polarities of this debate, this volume connects the history of print culture directly with the history of education. Historians of education have long been working to explain the ways in which institutions of education regulate—or attempt to regulate—meaning. They have also done much to reveal the ways in which students reinterpret the lessons they encounter in schools (and other educational settings) to serve their own purposes and meet their own needs. Just as historians of print culture note the ways in which meaning is a product of *negotiation* between author and audience, between writer and reader, historians of education note the ways in which learning, and hence meaning, is a product of negotiation between teachers and students, "lessons" and "learners." Historians of print culture and historians of education share much in common; by combining their strengths, this volume seeks to explain more clearly how print educates.

In an era now largely past, historians of education, working in a vein of historical revisionism, stressed the power of schools and other institutions of education to "impose" meaning on students. In many cases, these historians implied that students—both young and old—had little power to resist the authority of such institutions, dominated as most were by a hegemonic capitalist state. Meanwhile, historians of print culture, taking a cue from literary deconstructionism and poststructuralism, took a different perspective. Rather than stressing the power of *institutions*, they stressed the power of *individuals* to interpret texts for themselves, reframing or rejecting ideas promulgated by the state, the market, the church, the professions, and so forth. As this volume makes clear, a rising generation of scholars has now begun to forge a middle ground between these overdrawn positions, embracing a more nuanced view of the negotiation of meaning between individuals and the institutional contexts in which reading or learning takes place.

In the end, of course, education and print culture are co-constructed, and neither can flourish without the other. Without an educated citizenry, print culture would falter, and without a diverse supply of print, education would likewise fail. Each chapter in this volume notes this symbiotic relationship between education and print, and each offers its own explanation of *how*, exactly, print educates. Some chapters approach this issue from the production side and stress the power of authors, publishers, librarians, or the state to determine or control meaning. Others approach the issue from the consumption side and stress the power of readers to construct meaning for themselves. However, all recognize that, in the end, the process of reading and learning, and hence the construction of meaning, is a complex process in which various parties exercise power (even if the balance of power is unequal), and distinctions between "producers" and "consumers" of print and/or education ultimately blur.

જ

This volume, like others in this series, began with a conference. In September 2006, the University of Wisconsin Center for the History of Print Culture in Modern America hosted a two-day event featuring a wide range of papers, each exploring some aspect of the intersection of print and education. Seeking to illuminate the interaction of authors, readers, publishers, and printed matter in all forms of education, both formal and informal, from preschool through adult education, the conference explored the history of education and print culture since 1876, paying special attention to the historical sociology of print among individuals and groups on the peripheries of institutionalized power, including racial, ethnic, and religious minorities; women; immigrants; and people with disabilities. With presenters from across the United States as well as overseas, this conference, the Center's sixth biennial gathering, brought together an impressive group of scholars.

The papers presented emanated from a variety of subfields—not just the history of print culture and the history of education, but also the history of literacy, the history of childhood, and the history of print-related technology. The papers addressed such diverse topics as the development of children's librarianship and school-based libraries; the evolution of textbook production and use; the rise of education journals, magazines, and other periodicals; the politics of race, ethnicity, and language in education-related print; the role of print culture in the education and self-education of workers; the rise of educational film, radio, television, and other electronic media and their effects on print culture; the regional differences of schoolbooks published in the United States; the link between print culture and visual culture in educational materials; and others. This volume represents only a sample of the extraordinary range of work shared at the conference.

To highlight the central themes of this volume, the nine chapters have been placed in four parts, arranged in roughly chronological order. Each part examines both the production and consumption of education-related print. The first part, "Librarians as Educators," considers the role of libraries—and professional librarians—as purveyors of print and participants in the construction of print cultures related to teaching and learning. The second part, "Children's Experience of Print," takes on the difficult task of showing how young readers actually *responded* to the various forms of print they encountered as they grew up. "Workers as Readers, Reading as Work," the third part, examines the relationship between print and education in the context of social class and gender. The fourth part, "Print, Education, and the State," considers the complex role that government, at both the state and federal levels, has played in shaping Americans' access to education through print.

Each chapter advances its own explanation of *how* print educates. For instance, in the first chapter, "Which Truth, What Fiction? Librarians' Book Recommendations for Children, 1876–1890," Kate McDowell examines the ways in which members of the newly created American Library Association used their professional authority to shape librarians' book suggestions for children. Often, these book suggestions reflected professional librarians' preconceptions of children's social-class background. Noting that libraries, like schools and other institutions of social control, emphasized individual "'self-government,' or the idea that, ultimately, internalized morality would replace external controls," McDowell explains that reading "was supposed to be the major means of acquiring this internalized morality." And yet, while librarians felt a professional duty to see that children, especially working-class immigrant children, read "good" books, their conception of what counted as "good" changed over time.

The second chapter casts the role of professional librarianship in a different light. In "A 'Colored Authors Collection' to Exhibit to the World and Educate a Race," Michael Benjamin places the work of black librarian Daniel Murray of the Library of Congress in the context of the collective efforts of thousands of African Americans to assemble all the extant publications of black authors into a single collection. This collection—with contributions from donors across the country—was exhibited at the Paris Exposition in 1900, the Pan-American Exposition in Buffalo in 1901, the South Carolina Interstate and West India Exposition in 1902, and the St. Louis World's Fair in 1904.

While professional librarians coordinated the collection's development and display, Benjamin stresses that, in key ways, it "emerged from practices of black Americans themselves to record, collect, and maintain evidence of their intellectual, literary, and civic accomplishments." The Colored Authors Collection was, in short, a form of collective *self*-education through print culture.

This notion of collective self-education through print is the central focus of Ryan K. Anderson's chapter, "Merry's Flock: Making Something Out of Education Reform in the Early Twentieth Century." In an era of expanding high school enrollment and increasingly fierce competition for middle-class jobs, Anderson explains, many American youth at the turn of the twentieth century "found themselves negotiating a tenuous path between what adults told them they needed from school and what they wanted from school themselves." In this broader context, he observes, "adolescent reading *outside* school took on particular significance." Especially popular among teenage readers in 1900 were the adventures of Frank Merriwell, whose lessons for "success" were debated in letters published in *Tip Top Weekly*. The self-fashioning revealed in these letters, Anderson finds, "showed that most young people accepted the need for formal education, yet, at the same time, used *Tip Top* to express their *own* interests and exert their *own* authority as individuals."

The meaning of both print and education is always negotiated, as the next chapter, by historian of American Catholicism Robert A. Orsi, also illustrates. In his chapter, "Printed Presence: Twentieth-Century Catholic Print Culture for Youngsters in the United States," Orsi explores the subtle interplay of "printed things" and spiritual "presence" in Catholic devotional culture. He examines in particular a tension between modernist critiques of "incarnational" belief and Catholic print cultures that encouraged young people to search for experiences of divine presence in print materials. "By interacting with printed things—stories and images of the saints, coloring books of sacred figures—a powerful immediacy was brought to children's experience of the supernatural," Orsi concludes (after providing a truly astounding catalog of printed materials produced for Catholic youth). These items, he demonstrates, both "reflected and contributed to powerful contradictions and tensions in Catholic print culture, opening a space for children's own imaginative and ethical work."

The creative use of print for educative purposes continues—in a different form—in Frank Tobias Higbie's chapter, "Unschooled but Not Uneducated: Print, Public Speaking, and the Networks of Informal Working-Class Education, 1900-1940." Linking print culture to public discussion among workers—especially the unemployed—in the first half of the twentieth century, Higbie identifies the ways in which shared or communal reading "helped to create physical spaces in which workers encountered text and conversation together: workplaces, union libraries, street speaking venues, even boxcars, bunkhouses, and park benches." From immigrant newspapers to the "Little Blue Books"

of the socialist Haldeman–Julius Publishing Company, Higbie shows how
workers' reading intersected with an oral culture built around public lectures,
forums, and debates in a broader environment of learning. "Just as the streets
of industrial cities were awash in text," Higbie notes, "so was the air filled with
talk." This link between text and talk goes far toward explaining *how* print
educates.

The role of print culture in worker self-education is the guiding theme of
Jane Greer's chapter, "'Write as You Fight': The Pedagogical Agenda of the
Working Woman, 1929–1935." In this analysis, Greer examines the various ways
in which the *Working Woman*, a publication of the Communist Party-USA with
a circulation of approximately 11,000 in the early years of the Great Depression, urged women—many of them poor—to share their experiences in writing
and, in doing so, to forge a sense of worker solidarity. Drawing on the dialogic
quality inherent in the periodical form, the *Working Woman* sought to "transform working-class women readers from consumers of print culture into producers who could disrupt the gendered ['masculine'] construction of the
worker-writer and articulate their own interests. The magazine viewed its readers not simply as an audience to be mobilized but as potential authors capable
of manufacturing new textual productions that would represent their concerns
as women and as workers."

The gendered construction of reading and learning during the Great
Depression returns in Catherine Turner's contribution, "'A Gentleman Is No
Sissy': Reading, Work, and Citizenship in the Civilian Conservation Corps."
Looking at the so-called "Camp Life Readers" that were developed for literacy
classes in the all-male Civilian Conservation Corps (CCC), Turner examines
"how government policy during the New Deal encouraged reading and, at the
same time, placed limits on materials and discussion as the government became involved in what and how citizens could read." Even as CCC leaders defined reading as masculine "work" and tied literacy to democratic citizenship,
they carefully regulated enrollees' access to print. Echoing themes from Kate
McDowell's chapter, Turner argues that CCC leaders sought "to provide guidance about what—and how—enrollees read. Just as it was important for camp
leaders to assign work tasks, so, too, was it important for leaders to assign reading tasks. Enrollees needed instruction to make sure they completed the right
projects safely."

This role of the state in both the production and regulation of print and education is the subject of Adam R. Shapiro's chapter on "State Regulation of the
Textbook Industry." Although the debate over statewide textbook adoption
has been a recurrent topic of historical study, Shapiro brings a new perspective
to this debate through an investigation of the eighty-year fight that unfolded
over textbooks in the California legislature. Motivated by the extreme corruption in textbook markets—markets in which publishers "fought ruthlessly,

slandering rival publishers, insinuating sales agents onto local school boards, bribing or arranging kickbacks with local board members"—rather than any concern over textbook content, California legislators amended the state's constitution to allow the state to print its own books. So inefficient was this new system, however, that legislators eventually restored old contacts with commercial publishers. "California was the first state to regulate textbooks at the state level," Shapiro observes, but "it was also the first to suffer from the unintended consequences of that regulation."

Market dynamics and government regulation set the context for the final chapter, Greg Downey's skillful history of the politics of closed-captioned television programs from the 1960s to the 1990s, "Teaching Reading with Television: Constructing Closed Captioning Using the Rhetoric of Literacy." What began as a targeted innovation to foster literacy among deaf and hard-of-hearing children evolved into a mass technology reframed as a service for *all*—from immigrants learning English to students with learning disabilities to general viewers of broadcast television. Along the way, the "purpose" of closed captioning was subject to a series of negotiations. For example, Downey explains how transcriptions for the children's show *ZOOM!* brought a "compromise position on the captioning debate: verbatim for adults, edited for children." Similar compromises led to verbatim captions for "entertainment" shows and edited captions for "educational" shows. Downey finds that, in the end, a print technology intended to improve literacy among the deaf and hard-of-hearing became a technology expected to equalize "broadcast justice" for everyone.

◈

While each contributor to this volume takes a different approach to answering the central question—how does print educate?—each also sheds light on the delicate balance that exists between "producers" and "consumers" of print and education, between those who attempt to regulate, or control, the "knowledge, values, attitudes, skills, or sensibilities" of readers or learners and those who resist, reinterpret, reframe, reappropriate, or reject attempts at regulation or control. Thus, while each chapter in this volume shares the conviction that "all print is educative," each shows that all print educates through a complex and continual process of negotiation—or contestation—between institutions and individuals, writers and readers, teachers and students, "lessons" and "learners." Elucidating these conflicts and the co-construction of meaning that ensues, the nine chapters in this volume offer a more nuanced account of the ways print educates.

In the end, of course, clear-cut distinctions between "producers" and "consumers" of education and print culture are merely tools invented for analytical purposes. Indeed, such distinctions between "producers" and "consumers" of print and/or education surface explicitly in only a few places in this volume. Far more often, distinctions between these categories are blurred, and entities that may be designated as "producers" of print and/or education in one instance quickly become "consumers" in another. For example, in Adam R. Shapiro's chapter, the State of California moves back and forth between these categories, and in a somewhat different sense, in Ryan K. Anderson's chapter, the boys and girls whose letters appeared in *Tip Top Weekly* are simultaneously the "producers" and "consumers" of their own education and print culture. So too are the women whose work appeared in the *Working Woman*, as well as the African Americans who built the "Colored Authors Collection." All were producers *and* consumers of their own education and print culture.

And yet, even if distinctions between producers and consumers of education and print culture blur, these distinctions cannot be dismissed or completely set aside. As the contributions of Kate McDowell, Catherine Turner, Adam R. Shapiro, and Greg Downey make clear, the dynamics of institutionalized power *do*, in fact, shape individuals' access to both education and print and also, therefore, become part of the negotiation of meaning. Whether one examines the professions (e.g., the American Library Association), the state (e.g., the U.S. Army, which oversaw the Civilian Conservation Corps), or large private corporations (e.g., the American Broadcasting Company, which captioned its *Evening News* to great acclaim), power is not evenly distributed in the realms of print or education. Some have more power than others to alter the context in which negotiations over meaning occur—and the historian's task is to expose the relative power, or agency, of the different parties involved.

By exploring these differences of power, this volume provides a more refined and multilayered explanation of how, exactly, print educates (for better or worse). Sometimes parties that appear to "control" the production or regulation of both print and education do not, in fact, have as much control as it seems. For example, as Kate McDowell discloses, professional librarians who objected to children reading fiction in the 1870s shifted their stance by the 1890s because their efforts at regulation simply were "overwhelmed by the availability of cheap fictional books and serials." Over time, power came to rest *not* with professional librarians but with commercial publishers and, ultimately, with consumers' growing demand for pulp fiction. Aided by more accepting views of the imaginative life of children, publishers of new serials (including *Tip Top Weekly*) catered to fast-changing market conditions. McDowell argues: "Steering children toward more 'truthlike' fiction was essentially a compromise necessitated by the popularity of sensational fiction."

Similarly complex dynamics of power surface in other chapters. Catherine Turner notes, for example, that despite the concerted efforts of the Civilian Conservation Corps and its carefully regulated "Camp Life Readers," few young men who received literacy training in the camps developed new or more positive views of democracy or democratic citizenship. "As a way to impart information about democracy," Turner concludes, "the CCC education program evidently did little to change enrollees' attitudes" (even if many believed their experiences in the CCC "made them better people and better Americans"). In this case, the federal government exercised a great deal of control over the *contexts* in which reading, learning, and the negotiation of meaning occurred, but individual enrollees retained the power to interpret texts, including the "Camp Life Readers," for themselves. To explain how print educates, one must consider every aspect of this multidimensional balance of power.

While negotiations of meaning often involve conflict, one must not overstate the adversarial nature of this process. Just as the lines between "producers" and "consumers" of print and education are not perfectly clear (or permanent), the negotiation of meaning is by no means a straightforward process. Those who "produce" education and/or print—including those with institutional power—do not all support a single attempt to regulate or control meaning; indeed, they are frequently in direct competition with one another. Similarly, the readers or learners who "consume" education and/or print seek not only to resist but also, in many cases, to *reinforce* meanings created by, or together with, others. Thus, negotiations over meaning involve both contestation and collaboration, both control and compliance. The voluntary construction of a separate "Colored Authors Collection" to document black achievement *within* a context of Jim Crow segregation is just one example of the intricate negotiations of meaning that fill this volume.

The interplay of individual and institutional power arises in each of these chapters, whether in the bureaucratic hierarchies of the Library of Congress in Michael Benjamin's chapter or the executive suite at *ABC Evening News* in Greg Downey's chapter, whether in the doctrinal authority of the church in Robert A. Orsi's chapter or the legislative actions of the state in Adam R. Shapiro's chapter. The production and consumption, the regulation and reception, the interpretation and reinterpretation of texts for educative purposes inevitably entails a mix of both individual and institutional power, and this distribution of power is rarely, if ever, balanced; instead, the *imbalance* of power is what shapes the negotiation, or contestation, of meaning. Thus, while individual readers—or learners—always retain interpretive agency, the contexts in which their interpretations take place involve various institutional constraints. This volume explores both the individual *and* the institutionalized power that shapes reading, learning, and the negotiation of meaning.

Just as one would not want to overstate the adversarial nature of negotiations over meaning, one also would not want to overstate the autonomy of individuals to construct meaning "for themselves." All readers (and learners) exist within cultural networks or communities of meaning that influence their ideas about the world, including the world represented in texts. These networks and communities take many forms related to race, class, gender, region, religion, political ideology, and other markers of identity, each of which structures and circumscribes the negotiation of meaning (indeed, most individuals are unaware of the effect that such taken-for-granted categories and communities have on their learning or "knowing"). Moreover, these categories and communities change over time: it is not uncommon for parents and their children—and grandchildren—to have different experiences with education and print, particularly if children move to different places, move up (or down) the economic ladder, lose (or gain) religious faith, change political affiliations, and so forth.

Thus, when it comes to negotiations over meaning, individuals have agency, but perhaps not complete autonomy. Higbie's chapter clearly makes this point. Reading and learning, he shows, are rarely "individualized" processes; even when the workers in his chapter called themselves autodidacts, their pursuit of reading and learning did not occur in lonely isolation. These men and women belonged to larger communities in which *text* and *talk* went hand in hand as shared resources of education. Indeed, each chapter in this volume reinforces the idea that print educates by creating (or at least attempting to create) communities of colearners who gather around common texts. Such communities of colearners may be real or imagined, harmonious or contentious— from "Merry's Flock" in Ryan K. Anderson's chapter to the *Working Woman* in Jane Greer's chapter to the "Bug Club" in Frank Tobias Higbie's chapter— yet, the educative power of print would be severely limited without them. Indeed, "print culture" would not exist without these communities.

How does print educate? These chapters answer: *in many ways*. Eschewing the notion that education necessarily brings "enlightenment" or "freedom," each chapter in this volume recognizes that education can also represent a form of discipline or control. While education through print can generate a vital sense of identity and community—say, along lines of race, class, gender (dis)ability, religion, or national citizenship—it can also create enduring divisions in society. For every case in which education through print has provided an occasion for individual or communal edification, one can find parallel cases in which education through print has been (or at least has been construed to be) a form of "indoctrination." *Education and the Culture of Print in Modern America* aims not to celebrate the relationship between education and print but, rather, to explore it. All print educates, but the important question is, how does it educate? The nine chapters in this volume begin to sketch the outlines of an answer to this question.

Notes

1. Lawrence A. Cremin, *American Education: The Metropolitan Experience, 1876–1980* (New York: Harper and Row, 1988), x.

1

Librarians as Educators

Which Truth, What Fiction?

Librarians' Book Recommendations for Children, 1876–1890

KATE MCDOWELL

The character is very largely formed by the books read and not read," proclaimed Kate Gannett Wells, a representative of parents at the 1879 American Library Association (ALA) conference, the first such conference to address the question of how public libraries should engage with the reading of children.[1] From 1876 to 1890, librarians in the United States debated which books were appropriate for public library collections, and therefore what constituted "the best reading" for the public.[2] During these years, public librarians' professional discussions and publications reflected growing acceptance of the idea that public libraries should provide services tailored to children.[3] Librarians harbored fears that crime papers, story papers, dime novels, and other forms of "sensational" fiction growing in popularity at the time would harm all citizens, children and adults. Those fears have been well documented in a number of historical studies.[4]

This chapter analyzes the changing book recommendations made by public librarians during the experimental phase of the development of public library services to children from 1876 to 1890. Over the course of these years, librarians moved from resisting fictional publications to a selective acceptance of imaginative literature that reflected the values of middle-class childhood. In the 1880s, as librarians began to make lists of recommended books especially for children, they promoted "truth-like" books over fiction in their recommendations of reading for the young. By 1890, their recommendations had begun to change, as librarians increasingly favored fiction that depicted middle-class childhood as worthwhile reading for children. Librarians' early book recommendations for children provide evidence for understanding how debates over fiction were interpreted in the emerging field of youth services. In addition, analyzing the rationale for these recommendations reveals how competing ideals about the "best" reading played out in changing collection and book evaluation standards. Changes in valuations of reading materials for children within children's librarianship were also connected to broader social changes in publishing markets, schooling, and middle-class expectations of childhood.

The starting point of 1876 is significant in the history of librarianship in the United States for at least three reasons: it was the year of the formation of the American Library Association (ALA); the inauguration of the first professional journal for librarians, *Library Journal*; and the publication of the first national report on public libraries, *Public Libraries in the United States of America*.[5] Within that report, there were several articles that began to probe the issue of what kinds of books public libraries should provide for children. Other significant publications of the period include youth services pioneer Caroline Hewins's 1882 book of recommendations for children's reading, *Books for Boys and Girls: A Guide for Parents and Children*, which was reissued with a slightly modified title, *Books for the Young: A Guide for Parents and Children*, in 1883. Also in 1882, Hewins inaugurated a series of surveys, published as the Reading of the Young reports, that gathered information from libraries across the United States regarding what books and services they were beginning to provide for children. The Reading of the Young reports were created by women and repeated every few years from 1882 to 1898; those examined here were published in 1882, 1883, 1885, and 1889, and 1890. These sources have received little attention to date, despite their national scope, impact on the development of youth services librarianship, and unusually early use of survey methods.[6] Women were still a minority within this male-dominated group of professionalizing librarians. It is significant that the Reading of the Young reports were authored by women because, although men and women participated in discussions of library service to children, women dominated this specialty within librarianship by 1890.

Interest in Children and Reading

Librarians were interested in children and reading at this time period because they, like members of other middle-class associations and professional groups, believed that one's reading choices were central to the formation of character and could therefore lead to personal success or ruin. Rapid changes in social structures as a result of the industrial revolution created fears about how children would grow to be good adults, especially in expanding urban areas. The weakening of religious establishments, the demise of apprenticeships, and the "fostering out" of children contributed to widespread fears that children lacked proper moral guidance from adults.[7] Young men's associations, mercantile associations, young men's Christian associations, and lyceums were founded in response to these changes to provide young men at loose ends in cities with proper moral bearings.[8] Most of these institutions had libraries of appropriate reading materials for young men.[9] There were also many institutions founded in the nineteenth century to keep children isolated from the perceived dangers of the world.[10] These included orphanages, asylums, reform schools, and common or public schools, and most of these institutions provided children with libraries of "wholesome" reading materials.[11] Sunday Schools were widespread and provided many children with religious tracts and religious fiction.[12] All of these institutions placed great emphasis on "self-government," or the idea that, ultimately, internalized morality would replace external social controls.[13] Reading was seen as the primary means of acquiring this internalized morality.

Historian Steven Mintz described this understanding of the power of reading as "the Victorian belief that self-improvement, respectability, and even entertainment could be obtained at home through the written word."[14] Librarians were attuned to this perception of the cultural power of reading as they formalized their profession. Melvil Dewey wrote in the inaugural issue of *Library Journal* in 1876 that "the largest influence over the people is the printed page."[15] As librarians began to gather books suitable for children, they argued that these collections could be a potent source of moral guidance.

In urban industrial centers, reading materials were available on every street corner. An era of cheap book publishing, begun in the 1840s when the serial *Brother Jonathan* began pirating works of British fiction for American audiences, peaked in the 1880s.[16] Dramatic decreases in the price of paper and increased speed of book-production technology contributed to fierce competition in the bookselling markets, which culminated in the publication of large numbers of cheap books in that decade.[17] Librarians' writings reflected these changes, expressing fears that children were in danger from the increased availability of books. One librarian argued that good reading provided through libraries could "inoculate" children against a preference for bad books available in the marketplace.[18] These discussions echoed those of other reform groups of the period, which were especially concerned with the well being of children who grew up outside of middle-class homes.[19]

Librarians had a role not only in providing the right books, but also in assuring that reading was done in the proper ways. Numerous reading advice manuals published during this period describe the slow and thoughtful absorption that characterized reading when done correctly.[20] In other words, when reading was done the right way, it required work. As one reading advice author wrote: "While the cream of literature undoubtedly rises to the surface, it must be worked over and over by the intellect before it yields its best, most desirable product."[21] Such work required time to yield the best results: "A book is not read with profit in an hour; a language is not learned in a month; nor is the knowledge of all things gained in a year."[22] Among the objections to sensational works of fiction was the notion that they invited quick reading, "skimming," or "skipping."[23] Against these temptations, children had to be taught to select books that required the work of good, careful reading.

Librarians and Children,
1876–1879

In the 1876 report *Public Libraries in the United States of America*, several papers took up questions of how public libraries should serve children. Early discussions began to articulate selection and evaluation criteria in simple terms, as "good" or "bad" for children. William Fletcher's article, titled "Public Libraries and the Young," discussed the issues facing public libraries as they considered serving the young. The second half of Fletcher's paper was devoted to the question of which books to collect. Fletcher wrote that children should receive only books that would "do them good." He explained that books should be "instructive and stimulating to the better nature," not merely "amusing or entertaining and harmless." Fletcher praised a handful of authors, including T. W. Higginson, Peter Parley, Jacob Abbott, Walter Aimwell, and Elijah Kellogg as authors who had "devoted their talents, not to the amusement, but to the instruction and culture of youth."[24] Ideas about the malleability of children were reflected in Fletcher's words, as were ideas about the power of books to have specific effects on children, leading them from "instruction" to "culture."

Fletcher went on to indict bad books for children, although he named no specific authors. Bad books were condemned for their negative effects on children's characters. Particularly pernicious, according to Fletcher, were those "deceptive" books, which appeared to profess excellent morals but actually showed characters engaged in improper behavior: "Many of the most popular juveniles, while running over with excellent 'morals,' are unwholesome food for the young, for the reason that they are *essentially untrue*. That is, they give false views of life, making it consist, if it be worth living, of a series of adventures, hair-breadth escapes; encounters with tyrannical schoolmasters and unnatural parents; sea voyages in which the green hand commands a ship and defeats a mutiny out of sheer smartness; rides of runaway locomotives, strokes of good luck, and a persistent turning up of things just when they are wanted,— all of which is calculated in the long run to lead away the young imagination and impart discontent with the common lot of an uneventful life."[25]

Although he named no particular titles, Fletcher was almost certainly referring to the works of Oliver Optic, Horatio Alger, and other adventure writers whose books were extremely popular at the time. These adventure books featured fantastic stories, in which young heroes emerge triumphant from unlikely situations, rewarded with riches or glory. Similar opinions were expressed by reading advice author Noah Porter: "There is a very abundant class of writings that are sometimes denominated cheap literature, which, only by courtesy, deserve to be called literature at all. . . . Much of this sort of literature is open to the more serious objection that it stimulates and inflames the passions, ignores or mislead the conscience, and studiously presents views of life that are fundamentally false."[26] Both Fletcher and Porter referred to "falseness" as a negative characteristic. Throughout the 1880s, librarians would repeatedly grapple with the question of whether certain kinds of reading, especially that which was deemed "untrue," had specific harmful effects on the young, and, if so, how libraries could provide reading that would not cause such harm.

The 1879 ALA conference on Fiction and the Reading of School Children was the first national opportunity for professional librarians to discuss their role in serving children. In a paper, titled "Sensational Fiction in Public Libraries," Samuel Swett Green of Worcester, Massachusetts, argued that different kinds of books should be provided to different people, based on their social class. He argued that "different classes of citizens" required specific kinds of books: higher-class citizens would be satisfied with more intellectual material, while lower-class citizens required a "considerable proportion of exciting stories" to be induced to read at all.[27] He included both children and adults when describing his proposed differentiation by class: "There are many uneducated boys who need sensational stories. . . . There are classes in the community of grown-up persons and of children who require exciting stories if they are to read at all. . . . It is certainly better for certain classes of persons to read exciting stories than to be doing what they would be doing if not reading. . . . They will thus be saved from idleness and vice."[28] Green identified no particular income level that marked these "classes of persons," but he did give as an example those towns and neighborhoods where a "great shoe-shop or cotton factory" were located as places where people were likely to need sensational literature. In other words, he identified the working poor in industrial centers as "needing" bad books. At no point did Green claim that these books were actually worthwhile reading. He simply considered them a necessary evil.

Others at the conference disputed Green's class-based generalizations. For instance, T. W. Higginson challenged Green, arguing that class did not make "such an enormous difference," especially among children.[29] Green's arguments are significant because he brought a new element into the discussion of what books were "good" or "bad." According to Green, determining the right kind of book was not only a matter of the content of the book, but also involved knowing something about the person who would be reading that book. Whether a book was "good" or "bad" depended in part upon the class of the reader, child or adult.

Throughout the 1880s, some librarians echoed the idea that class made a difference in children's reading, but they did not share Green's conclusion that "exciting stories" were sometimes necessary. Instead, when class was mentioned, poor children were described as being in *more* danger from reading sensational fiction. For example, Miss Stevens of Toledo, Ohio, argued in 1883 that the young "street Arab" was in particular danger from reading books such as "Six-fingered Jack, the Border Ruffian" because such a child was "not protected in a measure by healthy influences" of the home, and therefore such reading was "doing an incalculable amount of mischief" to his character.[30] Other librarians, both male and female, echoed Stevens' assertion that poor children were most vulnerable to the negative influences of sensational fiction, and therefore, in need of most protection from bad reading.[31] However, most of the librarians represented in the Reading of the Young reports categorized books as good or bad without explicit reference to class differences among readers. Instead they focused on what constituted wholesome reading for children as a special group, distinct from adults and in need of library collections suited to their special character vulnerability.

Bad Books in the Reading of the Young Reports, 1882–1889

The Reading of the Young reports were given at ALA conferences and published in the proceedings of the *Library Journal*. Caroline Hewins of Hartford, Connecticut, published the first report in 1882, and the second report was given by Mary A. Bean of Brookline, Massachusetts, in 1883.[32] Hewins and Bean received twenty-five replies to their respective queries about what public libraries were doing for the young. Hannah James of Newton, Massachusetts, issued the third report in 1885, and received seventy-five replies to her query from librarians in seventeen states.[33] Mary Sargent, of Lowell, Massachusetts, created the 1889 report, which was based on forty-nine replies to her questionnaire hailing from nineteen states.[34] These numbers give a sense of the many librarians who were represented in this series of reports. While the majority was located in the relatively urban Northeast, there was also strong representation from the Midwest and a few from the South and West.[35]

Louise L. Stevenson's analysis of reading advice books from this period shows that, typically, reading advisers "did not specify what books to avoid," and instead used words such as *vulgar, vicious, vapid,* and *flashy* to describe bad books.[36] In contrast, the Reading of the Young reports reflect a remarkably coherent sense among librarians of which books were bad for young readers and therefore for library collections.[37] They named two authors as emblematic of the worst: Horatio Alger and Oliver Optic (pen name for William Taylor Adams).[38] Other books negatively described in the reports included those authored by Harry Castlemon (pseudonym of Charles Austin Fosdick), Martha Finley (author of the Elsie Dinsmore series), Mary Jane Holmes, E. D. E. N. Southworth, and William Henry Thomes. The fact that these titles were often described as books "of the Optic class" shows the primacy of Optic as the exemplary bad author.[39] Because these reports were assembled by librarians for an insider group at their national professional conference, they may have felt comfortable being more forthright than the individual authors of reading advice books that Stevenson surveys.

What did these "bad books" have in common? All of them were fictional. Some were also very popular with children. Optic's books were a veritable publishing empire; he created series after series of juvenile books and also had a successful magazine. Titles by Alger and Southworth were, if not as wildly successful as those by Optic, not far behind. Ironically, Optic was principal of a public school and a Sunday school superintendent, and he intended his books to be a morally uplifting alternative to crime papers and dime novels available on the streets.[40] In other words, Optic himself intended to displace "bad" reading with better reading through publishing these adventure books for children.

Despite Optic's good intentions, public librarians clearly indicated that they considered his works to have harmful effects on child readers. In her 1882 report, Hewins particularly discouraged the kind of sensational adventure fiction that depicted "stories of street-life, poor-house boys who become millionaires, etc.," by which she was certainly referring to stories by both Optic and Alger that concluded with large inheritances for the child protagonists.[41] She elaborated on this description in the preface to her 1883 edition of *Books for the Young: A Guide for Parents and Children,* writing that bad books depicted "little every-day heroes and heroines [who] leap suddenly from abject poverty to boundless wealth."[42] This "rags-to-riches" transformation was the defining trademark of most of Alger's books and some of those by Optic. Such sudden transformations in the economic class of characters was considered harmful because such stories, according to Fletcher, imparted "false views" of what children could expect from life.

A few librarians reported discarding books by Optic and Alger from library collections. One librarian reported that he had "withdrawn permanently all of Alger, Fosdick, Thomes, and Oliver Optic."[43] Hewins herself, in her response to the 1883 questionnaire, reported to her chagrin that "the boys have not left off their Optic, Alger, and Castlemon, or the girls their Elsie and Mrs. Holmes."[44] She even went so far as to lament that children had not destroyed their "idols:" "I wish that I could tell you of great results, and that the children of Hartford had walked in procession to the Park, and there, Savonarola-like, burned their idols, Alger, Optic, Castlemon, and Elsie; but unfortunately, my regard for truth prevents any such statement."[45] The central objection to bad books was that they were "untrue," and following this logic, some librarians discouraged fiction reading altogether. Several librarians argued that children would enjoy "truthful" books if they were given them. As one librarian wrote, by recommending true books, "we believe the love for the *fiction*, which is so demoralizing to the youthful mind, may be kept in abeyance."[46] There were some similarities in contemporaneous debates over fiction reading for adults.[47] However, children were seen as more susceptible to the influence of "false" books. Debates about adult readers did not have the same recurring theme of "truth" as a measure of good books.

In one case, special tactics were developed to discourage children from reading fictional materials. Librarian Minerva Sanders of Pawtucket, Rhode Island, filled a scrapbook with "cuttings from the daily papers" that detailed crimes committed by boys who had allegedly read bad books and periodicals. Sanders put this scrapbook to use by instructing the boys found reading dime novels and sensational story papers (she does not mention girls doing such reading) to read through the articles, thereby scaring them with the "consequences" of bad reading. She reported success with this method, writing that the boys "seem to grasp the idea quickly, and, without an exception, pass their papers to us, and seem glad to accept something better in exchange."[48] This appeal to children's own rational understanding of their susceptibility to influence was unique in the Reading of the Young reports in that results rested upon each child's ability to choose his or her reading, albeit under pressure from adult beliefs and documentation that the child's life could fall to ruin if such reading did not cease.

Fictional works were also disparaged in many reading advice books because they were too "easy" to read. In the 1870s and 1880s, reading advisers considered the pleasurable escapism of reading some kinds of fiction dangerous because it left the reader "wrapped in the beautiful cloud-land of fancy so fascinating to youth." Advisor John Charles Van Dyke explained this danger, writing, "You may read for hours at a time in such a manner, without a momentary consciousness of your book, without knowing what you are reading about, and without gaining a single idea. . . . Such reading is the laziest kind of laziness: it is useless work."[49] One librarian argued that such books were also mentally damaging. Bean, author of the 1883 report, argued that "the excessive amount of books skimmed by the children weakened their mental power" and that, as a result, they "did nothing thoroughly."[50] This metaphorical understanding of the child's intellect as muscle, which could be properly exercised and strengthened or improperly rested and atrophied, suggests that proper reading, again, required work.

Children's learning was associated with work in other contemporaneous contexts as well. Proponents of the kindergarten movement, which was gaining influence during this period, argued that even young children's learning should be characterized by their own work to gain systematic knowledge by manipulating one class of objects at a time, from spheres to cylinders to cubes and so on.[51] Librarians argued that children's reading should proceed in a similar way, beginning first with the most factual books. These were also the books that were believed to require work in order to be properly understood.

Good Books in the Reading of the Young Reports, 1882–1889

Good books for children were those that were "true." Overwhelmingly, librarians recommended nonfiction books as best for children. They stated that children's reading should be directed toward "works of science, travel, history," "biography," and "geography."[52] Another librarian argued that, when selecting library books for children, one should "give preference to stories with some historical basis."[53] In many similar opinions recorded in the reports, librarians expressed preference for books that had some basis in the truth when selecting books for children. Librarians hoped that guiding children toward reading factual books would slowly begin to "substitute a more useful class of reading for the aimless books which have so long been favorites."[54] While Optic and Alger were commonly decried as bad, there was less consensus among librarians about which authors wrote good books for children. Two authors that received multiple positive mentions in the Reading of the Young Reports were Charles Carleton Coffin, author of *The Boys of '76: A History of the Battles of the Revolution* and other histories for young people and Charlotte M. Yonge, who was recommended for her "Young Folks'" histories.

What most of the approved books had in common was not their authorship but their factual subject matter. One explanation for the recommendation of science and nature books is that these books did not depict adventuresome fictional heroes—or indeed any characters at all—and therefore children were not at risk of mimicking outrageous behavior. A second explanation derives from the context of Victorian culture, which Stevenson describes as characterized by a belief that the natural world was a direct expression of orderly divine laws, and that "scientific discoveries would merely add to their understanding of the divine creation."[55] Children's "mastery of concrete facts" about science and nature was therefore central to their education because such knowledge would help them to understand in greater depth God's plan for the world.[56] History and travel books were recommended for similar reasons, as topics that provided knowledge of the world as it was at different times and in different locales. The idea of "truth" had a moral dimension, related to the idea of the divine order of the universe. One example from a reading advice manual made this connotation of "truth" explicit: "The ground of moral exposure is not the fact that evil is painted, nor that it is painted boldly; but it is in the *manner* in which it is represented,—whether with fidelity to the ordinances of nature, or falsely to her eternal laws as written on the heart of man."[57]

Some biographies were recommended, but they typically appeared at the ends of lists of recommended reading topics. In several instances, librarians argued that children's reading should begin with books of "natural history," and then move on to "juvenile biographies, Charlotte Younge's juvenile histories, and kindred productions."[58] Because biographies written for juvenile audiences at the time typically celebrate the accomplishments of heroic leaders, children were safe in their presumed tendency to imitate the people they read about. Mimicking such positive role models would not cause harm to their developing characters.

While many librarians believed that children should read factual works, some also argued that "little ones prefer *true* stories."[59] One librarian argued that the fact that children asked "Is it true?" after being told a story provided evidence for this basic proclivity.[60] This argument drew on understandings of children that came from the educational philosophy of Jean-Jacques Rousseau, who saw children as naturally innocent and born with a propensity toward goodness.[61] Librarians similarly argued that children's natural preference was for truth, in alignment with the divine order of the universe.

In addition to the recommendation of specific topics, genres, and some authors, a few librarians articulated more abstract evaluation criteria for children's books. In Samuel Swett Green's 1883 edited collection of essays, *Libraries and Schools*, one contributor offered the following criteria for evaluating "a good story for children:" "1. It must be pure in thought, and simple in style and language. 2. It must not be unreal."[62] The awkward double-negative construction of this criterion, that a story should be "not unreal," highlighted the value of true or truthlike books for children, and yet left room for those fictional books that were nonetheless realistic or "true" to the natural order of things.

Truth in Fiction

There were a few occasions in the 1880s when librarians recommended fiction for children. Hewins's 1882 book *Books for Boys and Girls* (reprinted in 1883 as *Books for the Young*) was mentioned frequently in the Reading of the Young reports as a good resource for libraries building children's collections. And while a quick glance at the table of contents shows that she recommended more nonfiction than fiction—with lists of books on travel and adventure organized by geographic region; science; farming, gardening, plants, and trees; arts and manufacture; health and strength; outdoor sports; household arts and amusements;

drawing and painting; and music—some works of fiction appeared in her sections on home and school life; history, historical biography, novels, and tales; modern fairy tales; and finally a category devoted to myths, legends, and traditional fairy tales.

In the section on home and school life, stories contained the largest proportion of fiction and included several series by Jacob Abbott, Elijah Kellogg, and Charlotte M. Yonge. Other familiar recommended authors were Mary A. Dodge (editor of the *St. Nicholas* magazine), Maria Edgeworth, Louisa May Alcott, Samuel L. Clemens, Washington Irving, George MacDonald, Frank R. Stockton, and Harriet Beecher Stowe. The books Hewins recommended from the oeuvre of these authors were "truth-like" stories about the everyday lives of child characters.

Accompanying descriptions of some books reveal that the "truth" was an important consideration, even in evaluating fictional works. For instance, among the books recommended in the history sections, she included such fictional but historically informative books as *A Tale of Two Cities* by Charles Dickens, *The Prince and the Pauper* by Samuel Clemens, *Ivanhoe* by Sir Walter Scott, and *Uncle Tom's Cabin* by Harriet Beecher Stowe. Each recommendation was accompanied by a descriptive phrase clarifying the time period or element of history about which the book provided information. Thus *A Tale of Two Cities* was accompanied by the parenthetical descriptor "French revolution," and *Uncle Tom's Cabin* by "Slavery."

Hewins did include some imaginative works, including modern fairy tales by Hans Christian Andersen, George MacDonald, and Frank R. Stockton. Among recommended myths, legends, and traditional fairy tales were stories collected by the Grimms, Thomas Bulfinch, Joel Chandler Harris, and Nathaniel Hawthorne, as well as several traditional collections without author attribution, such as the *Arabian Night's Entertainments*. Several excerpts from Hewins's 1883 "Literature for the Young" columns are extremely useful for understanding how such imaginative literature was seen as being wholesome for the young in a milieu that valued truth over fiction. In recommending a book titled *Classic Mythology* by C. Witt, Hewins wrote that it was "a useful introduction to the study of comparative mythology," thereby highlighting a hypothetical intellectual approach that child readers could adopt, although it is debatable whether any child readers did so.[63] She also recommended a book titled *The Golden Lotus and other Legends of Japan*, arguing that it would give young people an understanding of "how the children of Japan think, dream, and play."[64] In another case, she recommended *The Bodley Grandchildren and their Journey in Holland* by Horace E. Scudder by quoting a review from the magazine *Literary World* that lauded the "filling instructive fact" contained in this fictional story.[65]

In these instances, even explicitly imaginative fictional works were framed as being important because of the historical or geographical factual content

they offered children. However, myths or fairy tales were also acceptable because they would not give children "false views of life," as Fletcher wrote. Children would not be likely to confuse these stories with reality. Myths, legends,
and fairy tales were full of explicitly magical occurrences, events that were so
far removed from everyday reality as to be clearly made-up. Books by Alger
and Optic, on the other hand, placed children in realistic settings where wildly
improbable but nonetheless possible events took place.

Rather than being filled with fantastical happenings or outrageous adventures, the best fiction consisted of realistic stories about "everyday" children. In
the Reading of the Young Reports, several librarians credited Jacob Abbott's
works with being among the best fiction or "stories" written for children, citing
in particular his *Rollo* and *Franconia* series. These fictional works were described
as wholesome because they were "truth-like" fiction for children.[66] However,
the reality that such fiction depicted was very selective, reflecting middle-class
ideals of protected childhood. The Rollo series, for example, followed the life of
a young boy named Rollo in his middle-class household where he was read to
by his mother and instructed in reading by his father. Rollo learns the names of
farm animals and games, such as playing at driving hoops with sticks, from the
comfort of his mother's lap.[67] Maternal protection and leisure time to play and
explore were ideal activities for middle-class children, activities that were not
available to children in families where the parents and perhaps the children
themselves were engaged in materially productive labor.

An excerpt from the second book in the series, *Rollo Learning to Read*, illustrates a connection between acceptable imaginative play and fiction. The book
opens with a fireside scene as Rollo's father is giving him basic reading instruction.[68] Later in the story, Rollo discusses the difference between fiction and
"deception" with his father. Rollo's father asks him:

> "Suppose you were coming along the yard, and were riding on my cane,
> and should come up to me and say, 'Papa, this is my horse. See what a noble
> horse I have got.' Would that be wrong?"
> "No sir."
> "Would it be true?"
> "No sir, — It would not be a real horse."
> "Now do you know why it would be right in this case for you to say it was a
> horse, when it was not?"
> Rollo could not tell.
> "I will tell you," said his father. "Because you would not be trying to
> deceive me. I could see your horse, as you call him, and could see that it was
> nothing but a cane. You would not be trying to deceive me, to make me think
> it was a real horse when it was not."
> "No sir," said Rollo.
> "If you should say any thing which is not strictly true and want to make me
> think it is true, that would be very wrong. That would be telling a lie. So it

would be very wrong for me to tell you any thing which is not true, and try to make you think it is true. But it is not wrong for me to make up a little story to amuse you, if I do not try to deceive you by it."[69]

In this passage, the intent to deceive differentiates lies from pleasant fiction. Librarians' recommendations of fiction books reflected a similar logic, albeit inflected with class values. Good books for children included works that were "realistic" depictions of ideal middle-class households where children's work was, as in Rollo's house, tasks such as learning to read and playing games. Tales of historical children and some fairy tales were also permitted, as the previous examples demonstrate, as long as they were "not unreal" and did not show children engaged in activities that were too fantastic, such as running away or becoming independently wealthy. Librarians and other adults feared the potential "deception" of fictional realism outside of middle-class childhood. As one librarian wrote: "We discourage applications for stories of street-life, poor-house boys who become millionaires, etc."[70]

Which Truth, What Fiction?

The 1890 Reading of the Young report showed a change in overall professional orientation to the value of fiction for children. Report author Minerva Sanders explicitly endorsed providing such work for children and offered, for the first time in these reports, negative appraisals of some factual books. This was the same Minerva Sanders who had created the scrapbook in her Pawtucket, Rhode Island, library, to discourage the reading of dime novels and story papers. Though her position in 1890 was not an indiscriminate embrace of all fiction, she did argue that fiction could be among the best literature for children.

In prescribing selection principles, Sanders condemned with equal vigor books of preachy and pious Sunday school fiction, books of sensational adventure fiction, and books of "cold, dry fact unrelieved by a single scintillation of imagination." Of this last category she wrote: "The Society for the Prevention of Cruelty to Children should confiscate such books, make one grand bonfire, and let the children dance around it."[71] This represented a departure from the opinions of librarians during the 1880s who promoted nonfiction without reference to any drawbacks that such books might present in terms of appeal. What Sanders promoted as good reading for children were any books, fiction or nonfiction, that would "awaken the imagination, sharpen the observation, develop the humanities, and cultivate in them a respect for the English language pure and simple."[72] Instead of arguing that books for children should be true, "truthlike," or "not unreal," Sanders now argued that appeal to young readers was a more important criterion. However, she also retained a solidly middle-class orientation in her recommendation through reference to "English language pure and simple." This stands in opposition to books that reproduced "street slang" in written form, such as those found in the Jack Hazard series by J. T. Trowbridge and many others.

Sanders's report also showed that, by 1890, some librarians were collecting even "sensational" fiction depicting lower-class children. One librarian described his more permissive selection policy: "I don't consider some books bad that other librarians do. I put Oliver Optic into the library freely. We have some of Castlemon's books, and I have found these will attract young readers when better books will fail. If they do not go from these to better reading, they have at least not be harmed by the brief time spent reading these little tales; and if they do drop them for better, we can score a point gained."[73] While librarians in the 1880s fixated on guiding children away from fiction, in the 1890s more librarians accepted that fiction might lead readers to better reading. Public declarations of a pro-Optic stance indicated that librarians' attitudes about such books were slowly changing. Librarians' were losing their apprehensions about what harm reading could cause and instead began to focus on pleasure, play, and enjoyment through reading.

This shift in librarians' selections reflected several broader trends in late nineteenth-century American culture, including widespread availability of public schooling and of newly popular forms of entertainment that competed for children's attention. Though public schools were widely available by 1860, their cultural role was still developing. During the 1880s, librarians expressed some concern that teachers were not properly attentive to their pupils' reading choices and worked to inform educators of the importance of reading selections.[74] However, as the century drew to a close, public schooling became more widespread and expanded cultural expectations that the institution would foster both the intellectual and the moral development of children. The influence of schools grew as teachers and principals came to be seen as "managers of virtue" for the young.[75] Schools were understood to serve as a corrective measure to bad character development, and librarians had reason to believe that children's reading, whether "good" or "bad," would be balanced by the moral training they would receive in school.

Like other reform groups that had attempted to regulate social activities in the 1880s, librarians in the 1890s were overwhelmed by the emergence of mass commercial amusements of many kinds. Attempts to reform American culture were floundering as new forms of amusements competed for attention with reading. Historian Francis Couvares argues that the abandonment of upper-class attempts to create a morally appropriate public culture in Pittsburgh was indicative of a more general American "failure of leisure reform."[76] Kathy Peiss defines what reformers were up against in her descriptions of compelling and attractive "cheap amusements," from dance halls to shows, that were available to the working classes in urban settings.[77] David Nasaw further documents the culture of consumption associated with "going out" at the turn of the twentieth century.[78]

During the 1880s, there were numerous mentions of the particular danger that the marketplace of print materials presented for children. The main problem that the expanded print marketplace posed was that it made print materials indiscriminately accessible, even to children with limited economic means. As one librarian wrote: "Poor, indeed, in resources must be the child who cannot now buy, beg, or borrow a fair supply of reading of some kind; so that exclusion from the library is simply a shutting up of the boy or girls to the resources of the home and the book-shop or newspaper."[79] Other librarians similarly decried the marketplace, citing the immense amounts and low quality of juvenile publishing: "Bookmaking, and especially of the juvenile and fictitious class, has become gigantic, if not alarming. Far better if we had one-fourth the amount, improved fourfold in quality. . . . Too many feel that they must write a book; hence the *flood*, doing more damage, I fear, than those of wind and water, which are physical and temporary."[80] Still others argued that, because librarians could not control the markets, they had to work with the "flood" of printed materials being sold to children in order to offer effective reading guidance. Although librarians were wary of the dangers of the print marketplace, by the 1890s their efforts to control children's reading were overwhelmed by the availability of cheap fictional books and serials. Mary Bean, one Reading of the Young report author, compared the burgeoning publishing markets to an "afrite," a powerful spirit, released from imprisonment like the genie in *Tales from the Arabian Nights.*

> Like the Afrite of Eastern story, which arose from the fisherman's casket, the genie of letters, released from its long imprisonment, has developed into such sudden and enormous proportions, has become in some respects so unmanageable a fact, it is not surprising that occasionally we find the thoughtful man and the ignorant man alike regarding this wonderful power with dismay. Still, as letters are an acknowledged power, it is evident that, as communities and individuals, our responsibility is to adapt these means to their destined ends. And while those parents and guardians who have the selection of reading for their youthful charges under their own control are in such small minority, it seems all the more necessary that public sentiment should conspire to do the work which indifferent and injudicious parents and guardians do not attempt.[81]

Like other reform-minded groups, librarians risked marginalizing their roles as reading guides if they held to their most conservative ideas. Librarians continued to make efforts to regulate the reading of the public, "adapting" what was published in order to guide children from bad books to better books, but they gave up fighting the flood of published fiction.

In this burgeoning marketplace of amusements, librarians began to emphasize the importance of leading children to the "*pleasure* of reading" in the books

they recommended.[82] Some librarians, Sanders among them, began to explicitly embrace playful, imaginative fiction as centrally important to the reading
of the young. In a similar vein, many of the women who became leaders in the
formal establishment of children's librarianship in 1900 were, in the 1890s, beginning to provide entertaining activities for children in libraries. They created
children's reading clubs, included games in children's rooms in public libraries,
and inaugurated that most enduring institution of children's librarianship, the
story hour, which was and is marked by the reading or telling of fictional stories
to children. Still, in both collections and activities, public libraries reflected and
reproduced middle-class values in their services to children.

Conclusion

Librarians' debates over the right kind of reading for children reveal their
immersion in an economy of middle-class childhood that deemphasized children as "useful" economic contributors to their families through paid or un-
paid work. Instead, children were to be "useless," protected, and educated, but
valued for sentimental and emotional rather than economic reasons.[83] In the
1880s, librarians promoted nonfiction over fiction in their book recommendations for children. By the 1890s, the landscape had changed, and as publishers
continued to make dime novels and other fiction cheaply available, librarians
began to accept some of this material as appropriate for children. When it
came to choosing which fiction belonged in libraries, librarians' argued for
"truthlike" or "realistic" fiction, but they recommended books that depicted
only middle-class childhood, not that of poor or working children.

Fiction was deemed "good" when it took the form of realism about the
everyday lives of middle-class children. Some folklore and fairy tales were also
recommended because they represented the kinds of escapist fantasies that
posed no challenge to the ideals of middle-class childhood. These fantasies
were sometimes justified as learning experiences, as when children learned the
folklore of other lands, or as pleasurable "little stories" of amusement for the
imagination. Children's reading about fantasy lands could be a kind of mental
play, as long as those fantasies were clearly demarcated as fantasy, unmarred
by poor or working-class characters or setting.

In the late nineteenth century, childhood in the United States became
middle-class childhood, enforced by laws mandating schooling and banning
child labor. This ideal of childhood was not all-inclusive, as evidenced by
working-class resistance to child-labor legislation. In addition to protecting children from harsh industrial work environments, these laws also prevented poor
families from earning income.[84] With the success of Progressive Era social institutions, such as playgrounds, settlement houses, and juvenile courts, more children were required to be in school and out of the labor market. Middle-class

protections became childhood norms. John Dewey and others had begun defining "play" as a significant aspect of children's environments and an activity that made positive contributions to their learning.[85]

As real children were prohibited from working, play came to be understood as the "work" of the child, and imaginative reading became part of that play. Optic's stories of bad children redeemed and Alger's tales of street children who underwent rags-to-riches transformations only became marginally acceptable as fantasy for children because the independent, wage-earning, fictional lives they depicted became socially inappropriate for real children. Librarians' book recommendations retained a lingering bias toward "truth" that became a bias toward middle-class reality in fiction for children.

In contemporary contexts where "children's literature" is sometimes used synonymously with "fiction" or even "fantasy," it can be easy to overlook the past, when "truth" was valued over fiction in writings for children. Librarians' book recommendations during the late nineteenth century evince a transformation in values regarding children's reading. Librarians moved from valuing "truth" to valuing some limited forms of imaginative fiction, particularly fictional realism that narrated the everyday lives of middle-class children. Analyzing librarians' changing book recommendations illuminates some of the ways that print culture in public libraries reflected the emerging ideal of middle-class childhood in the late nineteenth century. Which truth was called "realism" and what fiction was permitted as fantasy depended upon the particular expression of middle-class values in public libraries.

Notes

1. Kate Gannett Wells, "The Responsibility of Parents in the Selection of Reading for the Young," *Library Journal* 4, nos. 9–10 (September–October 1879), 325–330.

2. Wayne A. Wiegand, *The Politics of an Emerging Profession: The American Library Association, 1876–1917* (Westport, CT: Greenwood Press, 1986), 14–39.

3. Dee Garrison, *Apostles of Culture: The Public Librarian and American Society, 1876–1920* (Madison: University of Wisconsin Press, 2003), 173–217; Sybille A. Jagusch, "First among Equals, Caroline M. Hewins and Anne C. Moore: Foundations of Library Work with Children" (PhD diss., University of Maryland, 1990), 28–204; Gwendolen Rees, *Libraries for Children: A History and a Bibliography* (Ann Arbor, MI: University Microfilms, 1968), 85–138; Fannette H. Thomas, "The Genesis of Children's Services in the American Public Library, 1875–1906" (PhD diss., University of Wisconsin–Madison, 1982), 28–307. My use of the term "public library" is deliberately broad, including all libraries that were available to the public, regardless of whether they charged membership fees. This definition is consistent with the contemporaneous definition in the 1876 report of the U.S. Bureau of Education, Public Libraries in the United States of America.

4. Esther Jane Carrier, *Fiction in Public Libraries, 1876–1900* (New York: Scarecrow Press, 1965), 458; Evelyn Geller, *Forbidden Books in American Public Libraries, 1876–1939: A*

Study in Cultural Change, Contributions in Librarianship and Information Science 46 (Westport, CT: Greenwood Press, 1984), 234; Michael Denning, *Mechanic Accents: Dime Novels and Working-Class Culture in America* (London and New York: Verso, 1987), 259; Thomas Augst, "Faith in Reading: Public Libraries, Liberalism, and the Civic Religion," in *Institutions of Reading: The Social Life of Libraries in the United States*, ed. Thomas Augst and Kenneth Carpenter (Amherst: University of Massachusetts Press, 2007), 148.

5. Wiegand, *The Politics of an Emerging Profession*, 3–13.

6. Kate McDowell, "Surveying the Field: The Research Model of Women in Librarianship, 1882–1998," *Library Quarterly* 79, no. 3 (July 2009), 279–300.

7. Steven Mintz, *Huck's Raft: A History of American Childhood* (Cambridge, MA: Belknap Press of Harvard University Press, 2004), 138–139; Steven Mintz, *A Prison of Expectations: The Family in Victorian Culture* (New York: New York University Press, 1983), 28–29; Joseph F. Kett, *Rites of Passage: Adolescence in America, 1790 to the Present* (New York: Basic Books, 1977), 86–108.

8. Charles Howard Hopkins, *History of the Y.M.C.A. in North America* (New York: Association Press, 1951), 818.

9. Carl Bode, *The American Lyceum: Town Meeting of the Mind* (New York: Oxford University Press, 1956), 275; Cephas Brainerd, "The Libraries of Young Men's Christian Associations," in *Public Libraries in the United States of America: Their History, Condition, and Management*, Part 1, ed. U.S. Bureau of Education (Washington, D.C.: Government Printing Office, 1876), 386–388; Hopkins, *History of the Y.M.C.A. in North America*, 818; F. B. Perkins, "Young Men's Mercantile Libraries," in *Public Libraries in the United States of America*, 378–385.

10. Mintz, *Huck's Raft*, 156.

11. Ibid., 75–93; David B. Tyack and Elisabeth Hansot, *Managers of Virtue: Public School Leadership in America, 1820–1980* (New York: Basic Books, 1982), 15–104; Kenneth Cmiel, *A Home of Another Kind: One Chicago Orphanage and the Tangle of Child Welfare* (Chicago: University of Chicago Press, 1995), 243; U.S. Bureau of Education, "School and Asylum Libraries," in *Public Libraries in the United States of America*, 38–59; U.S. Bureau of Education, "Libraries in Prisons and Reformatories," in *Public Libraries in the United States of America*, 218–229.

12. F. Allen Briggs, "The Sunday-School Library in the Nineteenth Century," *Library Quarterly* 31, no. 2 (April 1961), 166–177; Frank Keller Walter, "A Poor but Respectable Relation—The Sunday School Library," *Library Quarterly* 12, no. 3 (July 1942), 731–739; Anne M. Boylan, *Sunday School: The Formation of an American Institution, 1790–1880* (New Haven, CT: Yale University Press, 1988), 225; Robert W. Lynn and Elliott Wright, *The Big Little School: Sunday Child of American Protestantism* (New York: Harper & Row, 1971), xiii, 108.

13. Mintz, *A Prison of Expectations*, 30–32.

14. Ibid., 22.

15. Melvil Dewey, "The Profession," *Library Journal* 1, no. 1 (1876), 5.

16. Frank Luther Mott, *Golden Multitudes: The Story of Best Sellers in the United States* (New York: MacMillan, 1966), 76.

17. John William Tebbel, *A History of Book Publishing in the United States* (New York: R. R. Bowker, 1972), 482–484.

18. Melvil Dewey, "The Public Library and the Public Schools," *Library Journal* 1, no. 12 (August 1877), 439.

19. Cmiel, *A Home of Another Kind*, 243; LeRoy Ashby, *Endangered Children: Dependency, Neglect, and Abuse in American History* (New York and London: Twayne Publishers; Prentice Hall International, 1997), xiii, 258; N. Ray Hiner and Joseph M. Hawes, *Growing Up in America: Children in Historical Perspective* (Urbana: University of Illinois Press, 1985), xxv, 310.

20. Louise L. Stevenson, *The Victorian Homefront: American Thought and Culture, 1860–1880* (New York: Twayne Publishers, 1991), 31–47.

21. Amelie V. Petit Child-Mathews, *How to Read, and Hints in Choosing the Best Books* (New York: S. R. Wells, 1878), 20.

22. John Charles Van Dyke, *Books and How to Use Them: Some Hints to Readers and Students* (New York: Fords, Howard, & Hulbert, 1883), 23.

23. Christine Pawley, *Reading on the Middle Border: The Culture of Print in Late Nineteenth-Century Osage, Iowa* (Amherst: University of Massachusetts Press, 2001), 61–62.

24. William Fletcher, "Public Libraries and the Young," in *Public Libraries in the United States of America*, 416.

25. Ibid., 417.

26. Noah Porter, *Books and Reading: Or, What Books Shall I Read and How Shall I Read Them?* (New York: Scribner's, 1871), 97–98.

27. Samuel Swett Green, "Sensational Fiction in Public Libraries," *Library Journal* 4, nos. 9–10 (September–October 1879), 349–350.

28. Ibid., 348–349.

29. T. W. Higginson, "Address of T. W. Higginson," *Library Journal* 4, nos. 9–10 (September–October 1879), 357.

30. Mary A. Bean, "Report on Reading of the Young," *Library Journal* 8, nos. 9–10 (September–October 1883), 225–226.

31. Hannah P. James, "Yearly Reports on the Reading of the Young," *Library Journal* 10, no. 8 (August 1885), 290.

32. Caroline Maria Hewins, "Yearly Report on Boys' and Girls' Reading," *Library Journal* 23, no. 8 (1882), 182–190; Bean, "Report on Reading of the Young," 217–227.

33. James, "Yearly Reports on the Reading of the Young," 278–291.

34. Mary Sargent, "Reading for the Young," *Library Journal* 14, nos. 5–6 (1889), 226–236.

35. While the state of Massachusetts was perhaps over-represented—forty-one of the seventy-five replies in 1885 were from that state alone—replies from librarians in Louisiana and California were also recorded in these reports.

36. Stevenson, *The Victorian Homefront*, 37.

37. Public librarians were far from alone in their fears of harm to children being caused by reading in the 1880s. Among other voices raising similar concerns were the teachers of the National Educational Association (NEA). At the NEA conference in 1881, a speaker described a boy in prison as having been corrupted by dime novels, stating that "the immediate cause of his committing his horrible acts was the class of reading in which he indulged." Also included were other detrimental effects of dime novel reading, including "slang language," "disrespect for parental authority," poor treatment of the "aged," "wrong ideas of life," and a "general spirit of insubordination."

Four years later, in 1885, the NEA board passed a resolution against "demoralizing literature," urging teachers to cultivate children's tastes for good literature in order to displace the bad. Many newspapers and magazines published accounts of individual children, usually boys, who attributed their descent into lives of crime to the reading of too many adventure stories, in story papers and dime novels. Anthony Comstock published his famous book *Traps for the Young* in 1883, which compiled many of these anecdotes together, hoping to induce parents to look out for the reading and thereby the moral health of their children. J. B. Beaslee, "Moral and Literacy Training in the Public Schools," *National Educational Association Proceedings* 20 (1881), 115–116; Thomas W. Bickness, "Resolutions," *National Educational Association Proceedings* 24 (1885), 21.

38. Hewins, "Yearly Report on Boys' and Girls' Reading," 185, 187; Bean, "Report on Reading of the Young," 218, 221, 222, 224; James, "Yearly Reports on the Reading of the Young," 280.

39. Hewins, "Yearly Report on Boys' and Girls' Reading," 187, 189; Bean, "Report on Reading of the Young," 221, 224.

40. Geller, *Forbidden Books in American Public Libraries*, 20–22; Carrier, *Fiction in Public Libraries*, 188.

41. Hewins, "Yearly Report on Boys' and Girls' Reading," 218. For one of many examples, see Horatio Alger, *Ragged Dick; Or, Street Life in New York with the Boot-Blacks*, Ragged Dick series, vol. 1 (Boston: Loring, 1868), 296.

42. Caroline Maria Hewins, *Books for the Young: A Guide for Parents and Children* (New York: F. Leypoldt, 1883), 3–9.

43. Hewins, "Yearly Report on Boys' and Girls' Reading," 187.

44. "Elsie" referred to the series featuring the character Elsie Dinsmore by Martha Finley. Elsie was a pious Christian heroine who berated herself for any untoward thoughts she had toward her harsh guardians and eventually made the adults around her feel the error of their ways and embrace a Christian path.

45. Hewins, "Yearly Report on Boys' and Girls' Reading," 221.

46. Ibid., 223.

47. Carrier, *Fiction in Public Libraries*, 458.

48. James, "Yearly Reports on the Reading of the Young," 289; Providence Journal, "The Pawtucket Free Public Library and the Dime Novel," *Library Journal* 10, no. 5 (May 1885), 105.

49. Van Dyke, *Books and How to Use Them*, 1.

50. Bean, "Report on Reading of the Young," 218.

51. Marilynn Strasser Olson, "Little Workers of the Kindergarten," *The Lion and the Unicorn* 26, no. 3 (September 2002), 353–373.

52. Bean, "Report on Reading of the Young," 221, 223, 224.

53. Sargent, "Reading for the Young," 233.

54. Ibid., 226.

55. Stevenson, *The Victorian Homefront*, 77.

56. Ibid.

57. Porter, *Books and Reading*, 83.

58. Bean, "Report on Reading of the Young," 223.

59. Ibid., 222.

60. Ibid.

61. Jean-Jacques Rousseau, *Emile* (La Haye, Amsterdam: Chez Jean Neaulme, 1762).

62. Samuel Swett Green and others, *Libraries and Schools* (New York: F. Leypoldt, 1883), 76.

63. Caroline Maria Hewins, "Literature for the Young," *Library Journal* 8, no. 5 (May 1883), 84.

64. Ibid.

65. Caroline Maria Hewins, "Literature for the Young," *Library Journal* 8, no. 2 (February 1883), 37.

66. Hewins, "Yearly Report on Boys' and Girls' Reading," 222–223.

67. Jacob Abbott, *Rollo Learning to Talk* . . . , a new ed. (Boston: Phillips, Sampson; New York: J. C. Derby, 1855), 44–46.

68. Jacob Abbott, *Rollo Learning to Read* . . . , a new ed. (Boston: Phillips, Sampson, 1855), 3.

69. Ibid., 96–97.

70. Bean, "Report on Reading of the Young," 218.

71. Minerva A. Sanders, "Report on Reading for the Young," *Library Journal* 16, no. 11 (November 1890), 58–59.

72. Ibid.

73. Ibid., 60–61.

74. Bean, "Report on Reading of the Young," 227.

75. Tyack and Hansot, *Managers of Virtue*, vii, 312; Lawrence Arthur Cremin, *The Transformation of the School: Progressivism in American Education, 1876–1957* (New York: Vintage Books, 1964), xi, xxiv, 387; Carl F. Kaestle and Eric Foner, *Pillars of the Republic: Common Schools and American Society, 1780–1860* (New York: Hill and Wang, 1983), 266.

76. Francis G. Couvares, *The Remaking of Pittsburgh: Class and Culture in an Industrializing City 1877–1919* (Albany: State University of New York Press, 1984), 120–126.

77. Kathy Lee Peiss, *Cheap Amusements: Working Women and Leisure in Turn-of-the-Century New York* (Philadelphia: Temple University Press, 1986), 244.

78. David Nasaw, *Going Out: The Rise and Fall of Public Amusements* (New York: Basic Books, 1993).

79. Hewins, "Yearly Report on Boys' and Girls' Reading," 186.

80. Hewins, *Books for the Young*, 223, emphasis in original.

81. Bean, "Report on Reading of the Young," 225.

82. Electra Doren, "School Libraries," *Library Journal* 22, no. 4 (April 1897), 190 emphasis in original.

83. Viviana A. Rotman Zelizer, *Pricing the Priceless Child: The Changing Social Value of Children* (Princeton, NJ: Princeton University Press, 1994), xvi, 277; Mintz, *Huck's Raft*, xi, 445.

84. Joachim Liebschner, *A Child's Work: Freedom and Play in Froebel's Educational Theory and Practice* (Cambridge, MA: Lutterworth Press, 1992), xv, 153; Walter I. Trattner, *Crusade for the Children: A History of the National Child Labor Committee and Child Labor Reform in America* (Chicago: Quadrangle Books, 1970), 319; Zelizer, *Pricing the Priceless Child*, xvi, 277.

85. Jay Martin, *The Education of John Dewey: A Biography* (New York: Columbia University Press, 2002), 562; Neil Coughlan, *Young John Dewey: An Essay in American Intellectual History* (Chicago: University of Chicago Press, 1975), xii, 187.

A "Colored Authors Collection" to Exhibit to the World and Educate a Race

MICHAEL BENJAMIN

IN 1900 AT THE LIBRARY OF CONGRESS in Washington, D.C., Daniel Murray, a black American and an assistant librarian since 1881, embarked on a collection development plan to exhibit black authorship to the world and circulate print culture's educative force among black Americans. To reach black Americans both within and beyond the nation's common schools, colleges, and universities, Murray relied on a broad network of teachers, civic leaders, and ordinary individuals who were driven to educate as many people as possible about the dignity and humanity of black lives. In a period when many white Americans questioned black humanity's worth, Murray and his collaborators made it their mission to exhibit the literary achievements of black Americans to international travelers, common school students, and the casual and astute observer, alike. With Murray as their agent, black Americans, during what historian Rayford Logan has termed "the nadir" of the African American experience, helped to form and exhibit a collection of books for the world to see. This collection came to be known as the "Colored Authors Collection of the Library of Congress."[1]

In the 1910s, a collection of books and pamphlets by black authors was cataloged, labeled, and physically segregated for shelving at the Library of Congress. One might readily think of this classification scheme as a product of the *de jure* and *de facto* racial segregation policies that shaped twentieth-century American race relations. Indeed, in the late 1970s, within the Library, this classification scheme created anxiety as librarians recalled the role that libraries marked "for whites" and "colored only" played in practices of racial segregation in the American South. If only out of political necessity, managers of the Library of Congress decided after the civil rights movement to rename the collection and reframe its cultural function in relation to America's troubled racial past.

Renaming the collection the "Daniel A. P. Murray Collection" in the 1970s, the Library recovered a sense of its institutional memory about Murray's fifty-two years of professional service. At the same time, however, this recovery obfuscated more than it illuminated the historical process that had shaped the collection's development and the evolution of its identity. Jim Crow segregation practices during this low point certainly influenced both; still, the collection's identity as "colored" resulted from actions taken by African Americans themselves to include their literary achievements in the American story, not merely actions taken by others to exclude them from that story. The emergence of the "Colored Authors Collection" for books and pamphlets written by people of African descent was more nuanced than our present understanding of the twentieth-century label of "colored only" suggests.

African Americans created much of the material culture and the collection identity of the books and pamphlets that came to be called the "Colored Authors Collection." The collection emerged from practices of black Americans themselves to record, collect, and maintain evidence of their intellectual, literary, and civic accomplishments. Through their collection practices, African

Daniel A. P. Murray. (Library of Congress, Rare Book and Special Collections Division, Daniel A. P. Murray Pamphlets Collection)

Americans refuted the ideologies of racial inferiority that undergirded early-twentieth-century racial discrimination and segregation. The collection's identity was not merely the result of institutionally endorsed policies in the context of Jim Crow. Neither was the collection itself the result of an exceptionalism that might be said of Murray's work. Both the collection and its identity were much more the product of tactical and strategic decisions made by a number of African Americans that also shaped Murray's course. As a result of these efforts, the "Colored Authors Collection" exhibited an extraordinary range of public sphere performances that black folks could claim as their own—not only to educate themselves and other Americans about their capacity for productive citizenship, but also to educate the world about their common humanity.

Historians John Hope Franklin and Alfred Moss have reminded us that in the early decades of the twentieth century, libraries were among the various "means of education" in which African Americans took an interest. This was true even as the South—where 90 percent of the African American population continued to live—lagged in extending library resources to black citizens. In the period between 1900 and 1910, Franklin and Moss note that African Americans gained access to libraries only through "restricted privileges at the main library" or through the establishment of segregated "black branches." For example, the Cossitt Library of Memphis, Tennessee, made available a librarian and books to its city's black patrons as long as the black Lemoyne College provided a reading room. Library historian Cheryl Knott Malone recounts the Jim Crow challenges libraries faced between 1907 and 1925 in Louisville, Nashville, Charlotte, and Houston. In Louisville and Nashville, Malone has found that black librarians struggled to create reading audiences among black children using collections of books that derided black culture, such as the works of Joel Chandler Harris and Thomas Nelson Page. Meanwhile, Jim Crow practices also provided the setting for the Carnegie Public Library in Charlotte, North Carolina, established as a separate library for the city's black citizens. In Houston, by contrast, at least for the decade from 1911 to 1921, the city's Carnegie-supported library had an all-black board of trustees and achieved relative autonomy in its collection development.[2]

It is no surprise that Jim Crow practices profoundly influenced black citizens' access to library collections, services, and educational resources through the first decades of the twentieth century. Since the decision of the United States Supreme Court in *Plessy v. Ferguson* (1896), the practice of racial separation in public facilities was the law of the land. Moreover, in the South at least, enforcement of Jim Crow customs came with the extra-legal proceedings of lynching. Between 1900 and 1910, as Murray planned for the development of the Library's collection of books by black authors, 962 people were lynched, 858 of them black. Although crimes were often alleged, including the charge of rape, in justification for the lynchings that occurred, an objective observer would have recognized a lynch mob's purpose to intimidate Southern black citizens to live within the social spaces and places authorized by Jim Crow.[3]

Moreover, if not enforced by lynchings or given the authority of the Supreme Court, post-Reconstruction federal education policies had fostered racially segregated schools. The Freedmen's Bureau had built racially segregated schools throughout the South, and the system of segregation was reinforced by philanthropic foundations such as the General Education Board and the Phelps Stokes Fund. By 1913, as Murray's plan for the Library's collection of works by "colored" authors matured, he did not even need to leave his place of employment to feel Jim Crow's sting. Newly elected President Woodrow Wilson issued an executive order to segregate all federal offices, presumably including the Library of Congress. Yet, as we shall see, the Colored Authors Collection's development and identity had more to do with the needs of black citizens to exhibit their works to the world and educate themselves and other Americans about their lives than with the legalized segregation practices of American society, and Murray was just one of a number of historical actors involved.[4] This chapter examines African American print culture practices during the nadir of American thought about their lives. Forming, exhibiting, and shaping the identity of the Library of Congress's collection of books concerned with black Americans, African Americans educated themselves about their literary achievements, other Americans about their shared citizenship, and the world about their common humanity.

Call for Books and Pamphlets

At the request of the Library of Congress, in January 1900, Murray had circulars printed "to acquaint the public" with the Library's intention "to compile a bibliography of all books and pamphlets" published at any time by "Colored authors." He was assigned the task by David Hutchinson, the supervisor of the Library's reading room, who was preparing to exhibit the "industrial and intellectual progress of the Negro race" as part of the United States' contribution to the Paris Exposition of 1900. Murray started with a list of 153 titles prepared for the United States Bureau of Education in 1893 and 1894. These titles were contained in a report that U.S. Commissioner of Education Ferdinand Peck published in 1894. After adding 117 titles, Murray attached the list to his circular and called for assistance from all who could supply information about books, titles, or publishers of any book written by an author of African descent. Peck, as Commissioner General of the U.S. Commission to the Paris Exposition, expected that items "selected from the books in the Library" would be exhibited in Paris. However, Murray solicited the public to form a collection that, assembled from their contributions, would "be installed in the Magnificent Library of Congress, to be on exhibition and for consultation for all time."[5]

Murray's circular was accompanied by his letter with letterhead from the "United States Commission to the Paris Exposition of 1900" at the "Library of Congress, Washington, D.C." Murray wrote, "You are doubtless aware of the effort being made to present to the world at the Paris Exposition what the Negro has contributed to the harvest of literature." Soliciting his correspondents, he wrote, "A collection of books by Negro authors is now being made" under the "auspices of the Librarian of Congress." He asked, "Will you not contribute, as an exhibition, all you have written and published, books or pamphlets, or such books and pamphlets written by others as it may be in your power to solicit and send?"[6]

The response to Murray's circular was encouraging, though he was frustrated with the "imperfect recollection of individuals" who responded with accounts of books "seen or heard" and thus only believed to have been published by a "colored author." However, he succeeded in generating interest among his correspondents in the Library's project, even if tracing "every rumor" was a task that seemed to offer "scarcely a prospect of success." In addition to individuals, Murray sent requests for works to schools and libraries, such as the Boston Public Library. Even with books from libraries, however, he recognized that it would be difficult "to separate books or pamphlets by black authors from the general mass." He hoped the circular he sent to "one hundred and eighty educational institutions devoted to Negro youth" in the South might result in titles or information about black authors and their publications.[7]

It is not clear whether Murray expected the schools and libraries he contacted to merely identify books and pamphlets from their collections, provide knowledge from their faculties and librarians, or both. From 180 schools, he received only twelve responses, with "five of them from white men presiding over Colored schools." To his supervisor Hutchinson, he reported that, "The white people took hold of the matter with an enthusiasm to me truly astonishing." Their response, he wrote, justified "beyond question" his belief in the "deep interest" of that group. However, of black Americans Murray—who "had pictured the race eager, anxious and appreciative" of what he considered "a golden opportunity"—wrote that he was "discouraged and disappointed."[8] Yet a careful reading of Murray's report to his supervisor suggests that he found the best support for this effort to build a collection of books by black authors among black folks themselves.

At the close of his report to Hutchinson, Murray acknowledged the contributions of four groups that had responded to his circular: libraries, universities, book publishers, and individual citizens. Two libraries were identified by name, the American Antiquarian Society and the Lenox Society Library, as were two universities, Harvard and the University of Pennsylvania. In addition, Murray listed seven book publishers in his report: American Publishing Company, L. C.

Pope and Company, Lippincott and Company, G. P. Putnam Sons, Lea and Shepard, Small Maynard and Company, and Funk Wagnall and Company.[9]

The institutional missions of the libraries, universities, and publishers explain their interest in the project, but Murray also listed the names of eighteen individual citizens who had responded to his request. Fifteen of these individual respondents were of African descent. Of these, seven of them held leadership positions in black churches, and five of those were denominational bishops. Although acting as individuals, the black ministers, as church leaders, also represented the broader communities of black Americans whose churches they pastored. In addition, Murray noted the assistance he received from unnamed "colored men, who actively ferreted out" information about black authorship. Quantitatively and qualitatively, black folks provided Murray significant support in identifying books and pamphlets authored by writers of African descent.[10]

Among the black ministers, Bishop Benjamin William Arnett responded enthusiastically to Murray's call. Born in Brownsville, Pennsylvania, in 1838, Arnett was entirely self-taught. He moved to Washington, D.C., after being certified as a teacher. However, when licensed to preach by the African Methodist Episcopal (AME) Church, Arnett relocated to Walnut Hills, Ohio, near Cincinnati, where he also taught school. Ordained as a deacon in the AME Church in 1868, he became an elder and later general and financial secretary of the AME. General Conference. His rise to prominence extended beyond the black community. In the 1880s, as a member of the Ohio legislature, he secured funds for the AME-owned Wilberforce University and sponsored the Ohio Civil Rights Act of 1886, which repealed Ohio's notorious "Black Laws." Arnett was a staunch Republican and also advised President William McKinley about his black political appointments.[11]

Arnett responded to Murray's call for black publications with a collection Murray later cataloged as "Arnett's Collection of Pamphlets by Negro Authors." With this collection Arnett sent AME church-related financial reports, addresses, journals, and sermons that he and others had given and published. For example, he included an address titled "Character and Constitution of Tawawa Sunday School Assembly," given in Xenia, Ohio, in 1883. Arnett sent issues of the *Repository of Religion and Literature* that had been published by the AME Church since 1838. Along with lectures he gave to the faculty and staff of Clafin University and the Georgia State Industrial School, Arnett sent published lectures that he had presented to the Chicago Parliament of Religion. He also included pamphlets that were published for special occasions, such as the *Historical Oration: Jubilee of Freedom* published in 1888. In all, Arnett donated more than 200 pamphlets to the Library of Congress, which he intended as a permanent addition to the Library's collections.[12]

J. Clement White Jr. also responded to Murray's request. In 1864, White, then a teacher at the Institute for Colored Youth in Philadelphia, was appointed to the all-black Robert Vaux Elementary School where he served as the city's only black teacher and later as the school's principal. As principal, White helped to set the agenda in Philadelphia's public schools for African Americans. Moreover, in the 1860s, he organized the black Pythians Baseball Club. Throughout his life, he was able to maintain a role as an educator, a social leader, and a business entrepreneur. He retired from education in 1896 but remained active in public life, chairing the board of the Frederick Douglass Hospital that was founded by black Philadelphians and opened in 1895, the year before his retirement.[13]

Along with his public endeavors in Philadelphia, White collected and exhibited antislavery memorabilia at public fairs. As scholars have noted, fairs, such as the Philadelphia area's industrial fairs of 1884, 1889, and 1891, brought book collecting and exhibiting as forms of "private recreation" into the public eye. White's collection of antislavery memorabilia was exhibited at one of the fairs in 1891, and there were many others who exhibited at these fairs. They included Edmonia Lewis, a sculptor who showed a bust of her work; Meta Vaux Warrick, another sculptor who won prizes for her work; and book collectors Robert Adger, Jr., and William Carl Bolivar, who also exhibited their collections of watercolors and painting. Both Adger and White with collector William Dorsey founded the American Negro Historical Society in 1897 and later advised William Edward Burghardt Du Bois on his project, *The Philadelphia Negro*, published in 1899. Adger, Bolivar (Murray's cousin), Dorsey, and White were among the "colored men" Murray referred to as actively ferreting out information about black authorship. However, White did more than ferret out black authors; he, like Arnett, also sent Murray copies of their works.[14]

Responding to Murray's request on March 19, 1900, White sent nineteen pamphlets covering a thirty-year span of black print culture. His pamphlet collection included convention proceedings, critical reviews, addresses, appeals, letters, and poems. The earliest was a record of the *Proceedings of the Colored National Convention* from 1855. Other pamphlets included the first publication of the *Proceedings of the Equal Rights Convention* from 1865, as well as the controversial addresses of Edward Wilmot Blyden, essays collected as *Liberia's Offering* and published in 1862. Reviews of proslavery texts, letters by the Pan-Africanist intellectual Alexander Crummell, and orations that celebrated anniversaries of the Declaration of Independence by Philadelphia's Banneker Institute were also sent.[15]

Arnett's and White's broad interpretation of Murray's request for evidence of black authorship reveals a print culture sensibility to the meaning of authorship among black Americans that included public proceedings in print. The public purpose of these proceedings, disseminated in printed publications for discussion by informed citizens, underscored, as it also illustrated, black print culture's agency in the public sphere. Arnett's and White's gifts to the Library of Congress answered Murray's call to exhibit that agency in authorship, and thereafter maintain it "for all time." The black contributors would have found appealing the Library's promise to "rebind and repair all books needing" the work. This promise resulted in the binding of some 60 books and 175 pamphlets by black authors. Based on his solicitation for the Library of Congress, Murray reported that several people, including Arnett and White, gave collections of "many rare" books and pamphlets by Negro Authors to the Library.[16]

To prepare the collection for exhibition in Paris, Librarian of Congress Herbert Putnam suggested the design of a catalog. Under subject headings, 980 titles were classified on sixteen large sheets measuring eighteen by twenty-four inches. These sheets were then encased in frames under hinged panes of glass and attached to a stationary post. Titles were arranged according to headings such as "Books on Education," "Fiction," "Sciences and Arts," "Religion," and "Travels." In all, some 214 volumes with the engrossed sheets were shipped to Paris, along with two bound volumes of miscellaneous newspapers, and installed with the "Negro Exhibit." Eighty additional volumes that Murray reported as "not received in time" were added to the collection upon its return. The titles of 1,400 works received for the June shipment to Paris were typed from manuscript cards and "arranged" by Murray to "be utilized for consultation" in the future. Although sponsored by the Library of Congress with the assistance of Murray, it is a mistake to conclude that the books collected and exhibited at the Paris Exposition of 1900 came from the shelves of the Library or even from Murray himself. Print culture's agency, as seen in collections of published works within the turn-of-the-century African American community, was simply much broader than Murray's efforts as an assistant librarian at the Library of Congress. With contributions like those received from Arnett and White, hundreds of the titles assembled for Paris came from donors as private citizens of African descent, who intended to show what *they* had contributed to the arts, sciences, religion, and education of the United States, while also illustrating their group practice of collecting, preserving, and making that evidence available.[17]

To Curate a Collection

In June 1900 the *Colored American Magazine* publicized Murray's plans to exhibit the books and pamphlets assembled for the Paris Exposition. The announcement, no doubt Murray's but not attributed to him, promised that the exhibit would "provoke" reflection by every "thinking observer" about the progress achieved by black Americans. As the announcement stated, the exhibition was not evidence of blacks' "complete attainment" as authors, nor was it offered as "perfected production." Yet the exhibition was expected to reveal the true

potential for African American achievement by illustrating their progress
"against long injustice." Still, as a Library of Congress exhibit, the notice drew
attention to black achievement as an expression of the American narrative of
exceptionalism. "No country other than the United States could make such an
exhibit," it read. With the observation that "slavery has existed in other countries," the announcement stated that "only in the United States" had there
existed "a large Negro population subject to conditions which furnish an incentive to authorship on so large a scale."[18]

Three months later, in September 1900, Murray was identified with the exhibition for the first time in the pages of the *Colored American Magazine*. In July,
the magazine had taken notice of Thomas Calloway and the exhibition, commenting on his participation in the first Pan-African Conference in London.
The magazine presented Calloway as the agent "in charge of the display of the
work done at the Paris Exposition by the Negroes in the United States." An
African American, Calloway won the position from the United States Commission and, along with Commissioner Peck, had urged Librarian of Congress
Herbert Putnam to authorize Murray's assignment to organize the books and
pamphlets shipped to Paris.[19]

In its September issue, the magazine announced that "Colored men and
women of this country have written at least 1,200 books and pamphlets." This
was a "remarkable" number, readers were told, resulting from "the researches
of Mr. Daniel Murray, assistant librarian of Congress." Readers also learned
that Murray was the librarian-collector who had assembled the books sent to
Paris. The announcement stated that it was "perhaps not an exaggeration" to
say "that no one would have believed that the colored race in this country was so
prolific in the production of literature." From the start, Murray "felt incredu-
lous as to his ability to obtain three hundred titles," the announcement declared.
In the end, however, he located 1,200 titles and identified "the authors of every
one," going to great lengths, readers were told, to confirm authors' identities.[20]

Murray apparently did not travel to Paris with the exhibition, but there was
at least one request that he do so. Murray probably did not know that Commissioner Peck requested his assignment "to accompany the collection" to Paris.
Peck wrote to Putnam in February 1900, suggesting Murray's assignment as
"the special agent in charge of the Negro Exhibit" and his ability to provide an
educational service with "information along the lines of the exhibit." Peck offered to pay for Murray's transportation to and from the Exposition, so long as
the Library would "continue his salary while abroad in charge of the Library's
collection of books."[21] Putnam referred Peck's request to assistant librarian
Ainsworth Spofford and asked him for a recommendation. It does not appear
that Spofford made a recommendation, nor is there evidence that Putnam
acted on one. If Murray was aware of Peck's request, his papers do not reflect
it. Neither Murray's letters to his dear friend and confidant George Myers nor

relevant files of the Librarians of Congress suggest that Murray knew of Peck's request.

In May 1900, Murray reported to Myers that he had met personally with President McKinley and presented arguments to overrule Peck's "stout" opposition to a Negro exhibition. However, Peck's letters inviting the Library of Congress to participate in the exhibition and his explicit request to exhibit a collection of black writing cast doubt on Murray's version of events. It is telling that in this letter to his good friend, Murray presented himself meeting with the president and championing black authorship and the exhibition of a black authors' collection against opposition, when in fact no such opposition seems to have existed. Murray's reworking of his relationship to this emerging collection suggests that he only belatedly came to see its value and only over time came to associate himself more closely with it.[22] Why else would he need to strengthen his ties to a collection in which he held a pre-existing interest with an event that seems not to have occurred? Moreover, Murray's self-fashioning obscures the collective interest in and support for the exhibition by others such as Peck and agent Calloway.

W. E. B. Du Bois reported on the Negro Exhibition's reception in Paris for the *American Monthly Review of Reviews* in November 1900. Without mentioning Murray, Du Bois described the exhibit of "American Negro Literature" as "perhaps the most unique and striking" of those on display. There were four award categories: bronze, silver, gold, and grand prix. The Negro Exhibit won the grand prix, as did the exhibit of the Hampton Normal and Agricultural Institute. Gold medal awards went to Du Bois and Calloway as "compilers" of the Negro Exhibit. The Tuskegee Normal and Industrial Institute and Howard University won gold medals (as did other schools). Fisk University and Berea College won silver medals, and Clafin University, Pine Bluff Normal and Industrial School, and Atlanta University won bronze medals. According to Du Bois, the exhibit Murray organized, as a result of delay, was not installed until after the juries were disbanded and thus could not have been reviewed for prizes. However, the papers of the Librarian of Congress reveal that "in Class 3, Group 1" the Library received "a Grand Prix granted by the International Class and Group Juries" that was "completed and made final by the Superior Jury."[23]

Educational goals were central to the themes that organizers of the "Negro Exhibit" wanted the world to see. As Calloway made clear in the report he submitted to the Exposition's "department of education and social economy," the aim was to "exhibit the progress of the American negroes in education and industry."[24] Detailing this goal, Calloway outlined the extent to which educational themes dominated the exhibition's mission. Along with industrial themes, five of ten goals focused on educational practices. Lessons stressed: (1) the history of Africans and their black American descendants; (2) the education of black Americans; (3) "education's effect" upon African American property

The Negro Exhibit at the Paris Exposition, 1900. (Library of Congress, Prints and Photographs Division, Washington, D.C.)

acquisition; (4) the "mental development" of African Americans as shown by "the books, high class pamphlets, newspapers, and other periodicals written or edited by members of the race"; and (5) the achievements of black Americans seen "particularly in the field of education."[25] As seen here, print culture practices in black Americans' production, distribution, and consumption of text and printed images figured prominently in efforts to achieve educational goals.

The Library of Congress's collection of books by black authors was exhibited alongside statistical charts depicting black progress; photographs of black businesses; tables detailing the black military experience; charts and photos illustrating black religious, civic, and cultural life; and examples of prosperous households maintained by black Americans. These visual aids accompanied records and drawings of educational institutions. Photographs depicted buildings, grounds, classes, and school life, with several examples of libraries displaying book collections and readers at reading tables or in search of books in library stacks. The volumes exhibited by the Library of Congress appeared with "a series of bound volumes of written work by pupils of Fisk University."[26]

However, the educational life on display in the Negro Exhibit was not limited to the work taking place in schools, colleges, and universities. Kindergarten and normal school programs were also on display. For example, the students at Ms. Lucy Laney's Haines Institute in Augusta, Georgia, showed promise of printed productions to come. Even the exhibition's companion theme—the industrial capacity of black Americans—drew on print culture to present that case to the Exposition's audience. On an exhibit case with photographs showing the buildings, grounds, and classes of black schools, Calloway reported, rested "four beautiful bound volumes containing the official patent sheets issued to nearly 400 negro patentees."[27] Print culture practices were not only tools by which educational goals might be realized and inventive genius captured, but also the mechanism by which both were placed on display.

After it returned to the United States, the Negro Exhibit toured cities in venues both north and south of the Mason Dixon Line. In 1901 the entire exhibit was shown at the Pan-American Exposition in Buffalo, New York. Members of the city's African American community looked forward to this exhibit and expected it to "precede all others, from a racial standpoint," including its award-winning Paris show. Encouraging attendance in record numbers, reviewer James Ross told black folks that a lot could be said about the exhibition, as he urged that "it must be seen to be appreciated." He reported that travelers from all around the country were making arrangements to visit the city and see the exhibition. Black social, literary, civic, and fraternal groups planning to attend and inspect the exhibition included the Fortnightly, the Loyal Union, the Phyllis Wheatley Association, the Political Science Club, the Samaritan, and the Elite Circle. African Americans, Ross wrote, were "manifesting great interest in making the Exposition a success."[28]

Murray was among those who traveled to Buffalo for the Exposition. He did not go in an official capacity for the Library of Congress or, for that matter, with any curatorial ties to the collection; rather he planned to take the trip with his son Harold and was at one point uncertain that he could work out the vacation time needed to go. Because library staff members were away or sick, he felt that, as one of "those now on duty," he had to remain. However, Murray did make the trip to Buffalo and was there in September 1901 when President McKinley was assassinated. Of the tragedy, Murray wrote to his good friend Myers, "Because of the distressing news current here in regard to the President," that he was not able to enjoy himself in Buffalo and quickly returned to Washington. Whether Murray actually saw the Negro Exhibit at the Pan-American Exposition before returning to Washington is not clear. If he had in fact seen it, he left no impression of what he had seen.[29]

The collection was next scheduled for exhibition December 1901 through June 1902 at the South Carolina Interstate and West India Exposition, held in Charleston, South Carolina. Booker T. Washington, the Exposition's Commissioner-in-Chief, headed the Negro department. In its September 1901 issue, the *Colored American Magazine* reported that African Americans were expecting a "show by way of tangible illustration" of their "much-talked-of progress." Editorially, the magazine argued that the race as a whole was "looking for results, and results black Americans must have, brought together in one separate building under Negro direction." "Under one roof," the editorial continued "a mere glance or a critical inspection will convince the most skeptical of the real progress" that African Americans had made since emancipation. Since the much reported exhibit at the Paris Exposition, a great deal was expected by and from African Americans in their performances, now on the stage of international, national, and regional expositions.[30]

The article revealed that, at the South Carolina Interstate and West India Exposition, scholar-critic Kelly Miller of Howard University was assigned responsibility for the "American Negro Exhibit which went to Paris." Calloway was also mentioned as the agent in charge of the successful exhibit in Paris. There is no evidence that Murray toured the Interstate Exposition in Charleston. If he did, it does not appear that he acted for the Library. Neither did his name appear in any capacity with the exhibition in the magazine's announcement. However, Murray's wife, Anna Evans-Murray, did participate in the South Carolina Interstate Exposition as a member of the Women's Bureau. She toured the Negro Exhibit with its collection of books from the Library of Congress, and she and Murray certainly discussed the exhibit upon her return.[31]

No evidence survives to reconstruct that conversation. However, we do know that in May 1902—before the Intestate Exposition closed—Murray wrote to commissioners of the Louisiana Purchase Centennial Committee as they prepared for the World's Fair in St. Louis in 1904. There was an "urgent necessity," Murray wrote, to plan for a program he envisioned as "the Afro-American Department of the World's Fair." He advocated early planning to obtain results that could be received "enthusiastically." "A more creditable exhibition can be made by the Afro-American people" he argued, where "time is allowed for the proper preparation." When "detailed by the Librarian of Congress" to "make a collection of the literature (Books and Pamphlets) written and published by Colored Authors" for the Paris Exposition, Murray noted, he had needed time to prepare the exhibit and he was sure his experience would be useful to the Louisiana Commissioners.[32]

No doubt encouraged by keen observations made by his wife Anna Murray from her tour of the exposition in Charleston, Murray added that in Paris he exhibited 250 books and 800 titles of black authors. He felt that the Paris Exposition had improved significantly upon the exhibition of black authors shown at the Cotton States Exposition of 1895. In the years since the Cotton States fair, he wrote, "I have prosecuted my search and identified about eight hundred books and nearly twenty-five hundred titles." To the Commissioners he argued that in Paris the black authors' exhibition had startled "the literary World of two continents in its immature state." Thus, it was critical to recognize "that such a showing could be made by the Negro race in a field" where "the well informed" had prejudged black folks as simply "rank strangers."[33]

"No argument, in my judgment, is needed," Murray summed up, to see the advisability of extending time for preparation so that African Americans would have an "opportunity to make an excellent showing." He felt that any other course was "unfair to the Colored people," who were "expecting this opportunity." Murray received an answer from Howard J. Rogers, Chief of the Department of Social Economy for the St. Louis World's Fair. Rogers had also directed the Department of Education and Social Economy for the U.S. Commission to the Paris Exposition. He wrote that he was expecting legislation that would permit "more thorough and scientific preparation for the exhibit." However, despite Murray's early, urgent appeal and his wife's probable encouragement, as well as Roger's response, Murray did not participate in the St. Louis World's Fair; nor did the fair include a "Negro Exhibition."[34]

As Murray began to envision a curatorial relationship with the black authors' collection, he also set out to develop its potential for research. In 1901 he had announced plans to publish a work that he called, "Bibliographia Africania." A notice for this publication circulated in *The Twentieth Century Union League Directory* that was described by its editor, Andrew F. Hilyer, as "a compilation of the efforts" of "Colored Washington" for social betterment. In the directory, Murray subtitled his proposal a "History of Afro-American Literature," promising sketches of writers and a bibliography of 1,600 books and pamphlets by "Afro-American Authors." For the Paris Exposition in 1900, Hilyer had organized a "Collective Exhibit of Negroes in Merchandise, Factories and Allied Occupations."[35]

Murray continued to pursue his bibliographic plans in 1904 with an essay in the *Voice of the Negro*. In the *Voice*, as in the earlier notice in the *Union Directory*, Murray's public profile as the bibliographer of the "colored race" drew directly on the successful exhibition of the works assembled for Paris. In both publications he informed readers of his identity as a collector who, responding to "the earnest solicitations of friends," agreed to publish a manuscript. In 1904 with his public *persona* as a bibliographer and collector of race literature, Murray needed a collection with an identity that could embrace the curatorial ambitions he was fashioning for himself. But it was not until July 1907 that Murray finally assumed a curatorlike role with the Library's collection of works first assembled for exhibition in Paris.[36]

In 1907, in response to a request made on behalf of the Jamestown Exposition, Murray's supervisor David Hutchinson, head of the reading room at the Library of Congress, sought authority from Herbert Putnam for Murray to travel to Virginia with "the Negro exhibition materials." At Murray's request, Hutchinson recommended that he travel with the collection to Jamestown "to deliver the books" and "bring them back." As "duplicates" maintained for the primary purpose of exhibition, Hutchinson explained, the books had "not been incorporated in the Library" and, therefore, he pointed out, they could be exhibited safely without risk of loss to the Library's researchers. In addition, Hutchinson promised, Murray's travel with the collection would involve "no cost to the Library" other than his absence and would also "ensure the safe delivery and return of the books." Putnam approved the request, and Murray in 1907, for the first time since the collection's formation in 1900, traveled as a representative of the Library of Congress with the books and pamphlets that he, Arnett, White, black bibliophiles, and others had collected.[37]

A Colored Author Copyright Exhibition

In 1912, five years after the Jamestown Exposition, Putnam received a letter from Richard R. Wright, Jr., setting in motion a series of events that would form the future identity of the "Colored Author's Collection." Wright was born to a family of African Americans with influence both north and south of the Mason Dixon Line. His father, Richard R. Wright, Sr., born in Georgia in 1855, led an active life as an educator, journalist, politician, writer, lecturer, and banker-businessman. Wright, Jr., became a bishop of the AME Church and served as editor of *The Christian Recorder*. In 1912 he published his dissertation, *The Negro in Pennsylvania: An Economic Study*. However, for years prior to this publication he researched and published his scholarship on the lives of African

Americans. Wright's articles addressed the social and cultural progress of African Americans and their challenges. His essays in the *Southern Workmen*, for example, included thoughtful analyses and commentary about black communities, businesses, poverty, crime, and home ownership.[38]

In August 1912, Wright wrote Putnam that both Pennsylvania and New Jersey had appropriated funds to commemorate the fiftieth anniversary of the Emancipation Proclamation. At the time of this letter, Wright was the statistician and director of exhibits for Pennsylvania's celebration of the anniversary. Wright wrote that an exposition was under consideration to showcase "the progress of the colored people for fifty years." From Putnam, he requested "a complete exhibition of the books which have been copyrighted by colored people." He was confident that such an exhibition would "be a lasting benefit to the colored people, and inspiration to them and a great good to the nation." By this time, Murray's project, drawn from the books assembled in 1900, had taken on encyclopedic dimensions. The "Bibliographia Africania" he projected in 1901 had been transformed by 1908 into an "Encyclopedia of the Negro" and, in October 1910, was announced as "Murray's Historical and Biographical Encyclopedia of the Colored Race throughout the World."[39]

Preparing to answer Wright's inquiry, Putnam learned that U.S. copyright procedures included no notation indicating whether the author of a work was "white or colored." From Murray, he also learned that it would "not be possible to have a complete exhibit of the books by Colored authors that have been copyrighted" because no separate list was kept. Murray added that the race of authors was not "required by the copyright law." Still, he reminded Putnam that he had "unearthed over 6,000" titles for his bibliography of black authors. Murray suggested to Putnam that Wright might be able to obtain "the cooperation of various collectors" who could possibly confirm the race of different authors, and Murray suggested that the Library aid Wright in this task. Murray told Putnam that he would be "glad to assist Prof. Wright" in both an official and unofficial capacity "in making this feature of this exhibition interesting." As he reported to the Librarian of Congress in 1912, Murray envisioned Wright doing for the emancipation celebration in 1913 what he had been asked to do for the Paris Exposition in 1900. Moreover, when consulted, Murray suggested that Wright obtain the cooperation of collectors to organize his exhibition, not the libraries, universities, or book publishers he had first consulted in 1900.[40]

Putnam answered Wright in September 1912, stating that "copyright records in no way distinguish books by colored authors from those of others." Moreover, he added, "There would be absolutely no way of determining from them the representation of colored authors in our copyrighted material." However, as he also drew attention to Murray's bibliographic work, Putnam advised Wright that Murray thought "an exhibit of at least representative works might be feasible." Further, Putnam validated Murray's collection development practice for the Paris Exposition, reiterating Murray's suggestion that "loan of material already in the hands of collectors" be solicited. He also encouraged Wright to send inquiries to authors directly for copies of their works. Finally, Putnam wrote that, with proper safeguards, the Library would be willing to "lend a selection of books for the exhibition." By the time Putnam sent this letter, Murray also had corresponded with Wright, offering him suggestions toward his development of a collection of books by black authors for exhibition at the Pennsylvania Emancipation Proclamation Exposition.[41]

Murray wrote Wright that aside from the copyright question, it would not "be possible to obtain from the library several thousand volumes by Colored authors." Instead, he suggested "that the authors and publishers might be in-duced to put on exhibition and sale twenty-five copies." In Jamestown, Murray said he was able to exhibit several thousand books supervised by an attendant who was "paid the difference between the cost and the selling price." Accord-ing to Murray, when Wright requested the books, the Library of Congress had "about twenty-five thousand books of colored authors." However, he alerted Wright that, "it would require a special act of Congress to enable the Librarian to deplete the shelves of such books and use them as an exhibit." The Library, Murray wrote, was prepared to send "nearly seven hundred books together with 170 charts" to support Wright's project. These books must have included the works collected for exhibition in Paris, along with the charts ordered by Putnam to illustrate the collection. To the books and charts, Murray added that he would also send a small bronze statue of Frederick Douglass designed to stand on a pedestal in front of the exhibit. On September 13, 1913, just a few days before the Pennsylvania Exposition was to open, Murray inventoried what he called the "Loan Collection of books by Colored Authors" that he then boxed and shipped with the charts and statuette of Douglass.[42]

A "Colored Author's Collection"

Before this day, the collection of books and pamphlets assembled for exhibition in Paris had not had an established identity to reflect its origins, meaning, and purpose. However, from this day forward, the collection that Murray called for in 1900 was known as the "Colored Authors Collection." In the next month, the State of New York with Du Bois, chair of its programming for the anniver-sary of the Emancipation Proclamation in New York, issued its request for the "Collection of books by Colored Authors." As the representative of the Library of Congress in Philadelphia, Murray had earlier observed that the Philadelphia "exhibition was a success and the Library exhibit an important feature." Its success had reached Du Bois, who was anxious to have Murray "come and act as Curator for the ten days of the Exposition" in New York and offered him "$50.00 as an honorarium." Murray accepted Du Bois's invitation to curate the collection's exhibition in New York, adding titles from his "own collection of books by Colored authors" to round out the exhibit.[43]

When Du Bois invited Murray to curate the "Colored Authors Collection" for the New York Emancipation Celebration, Murray had already decided on alternate uses to which the collection might be put. Three years earlier, on October 19, 1910, in a letter addressed to black intellectuals, community leaders, and activists, Murray had solicited contributions to his plan for an encyclopedia, and in 1912, circulated his prospectus for the encyclopedic work he planned to publish. During the emancipation celebrations in Washington, D.C., Murray had broadly promoted his encyclopedia proposal, which would result in a work containing a bibliography of some 6,000 books and pamphlets—a bibliography that would no doubt have supplied the raw material for many of the 25,000 biographical sketches his encyclopedia would contain.[44]

Without question, Murray's commitment to his ambitious enterprise of bibliographical, biographical, and historical documentation of the lives and culture of African descendants preserved for future scholars an extraordinary array of information that might otherwise have been lost. However, as shown here, Murray's relationship to the "Colored Authors Collection" largely resulted from the activism and inspiration of countless other named and unnamed black Americans who formed the basis of a vibrantly activist black print culture. The collection emerged from a collectivist narrative through the agency of those close to the needs of ordinary black citizens in activists like Arnett, White, and Wright, rather than from a narrative of exceptionalism such as said to exist in the figure of Murray. Murray's exceptionalism resulted from his culture's collectivism. Influenced by other culturally active preachers, teachers, and civic leaders who were both self-taught and academically trained (not to mention Anna Murray, his astute wife), Murray came to see his role at the Library of Congress in a new way. He came to realize an opportunity to help fill the Library's shelves with black voices that could educate the world, the United States, and African Americans as well.

Just as black activists, teachers, ministers, and others close to the lives of black folks gave collections for exhibition to the world in Paris, black folks also framed the discourse shaping the collection's identity as one of "Colored Authors." Dialogues among patrons that were looking for copyrighted books and librarians in a position to know informed the identity of the "Colored Authors Collection" because African Americans themselves wanted to know whether such a collection existed. After its successful 1900 showing in Paris, the "Colored Authors' Collection" toured the country in exhibits, expositions, and celebrations, and African Americans came out to see the collection in large numbers. Much of the collection that was shown in Paris materialized because African Americans collected and donated it. The collection was neither formed by Murray alone nor created merely at the behest of the Library of Congress nor generated simply as a result of segregationist American policies. With the agency of black print culture, African Americans, *through* Murray and their Library of Congress, shaped the "Colored Authors Collection." When they gathered materials, donated them to the library, and called for a special collection, they demonstrated their commitment to educating themselves, their country, and the world about their capacity for literacy, intellectuality, citizenship, and shared humanity.

Notes

1. Robert Harris, "Daniel Murray and the Encyclopedia of the Colored Race," *Phylon, the Atlanta University Review of Race and Culture* 37, no. 3 (1997), 281, 287; Billie E. Walker, "Daniel Alexander Payne Murray (1852–1925), Forgotten Librarian, Bibliographer, and Historian," *Libraries & Culture: A Journal of Library History* 40, no. 1 (Winter 2005), 25.

2. John Hope Franklin and Alfred Moss, *From Slavery to Freedom*, 7th ed. (New York: Alfred Knopf, 1994), 413; Cheryl Knott Malone, "Books for Black Children: Public Library Collections in Louisville and Nashville, 1915–1925," *Library Quarterly* 70, no. 2 (2000), 179–200; Cheryl Knott Malone, "Autonomy and Accommodation: Houston's Colored Carnegie Library, 1907–1922," *Libraries and Culture* 34, no. 2 (1999), 95–122.

3. *Plessy v. Ferguson*, 163 U.S. 537 (1896); Robert L. Zangrando, *The NAACP Crusade against Lynching, 1909–1950* (Philadelphia: Temple University Press, 1980), 6.

4. James D. Anderson, *The Education of Blacks in the South, 1860–1935* (Chapel Hill: University of North Carolina Press, 1988), 130, 132–134.

5. Daniel Murray, Washington, D.C., to David Hutchinson, autographed letter signed (ALS), October 3, 1900, Murray Papers, Reel 1, 84–87; Ferdinand W. Peck, Commissioner-General, United States Commission to the Paris Exposition of 1900, New York, New York, to Herbert Putnam, Librarian of Congress, Washington, D.C., February 17, 1900, typed letter signed (TLS), Manuscript Division, The Records of the Library of Congress, The Central File Macleish-Evans, Box 765, Folder Exhibition 46–2, 1899–1939.

6. "Letter Requesting Gift of Books," typed letter (TL), 1900, Murray Papers, Reel 1, 111.

7. Murray to Hutchinson, October 3, 1900, 88–89.

8. Ibid., 90–91.

9. Ibid., 99–100.

10. Ibid.

11. Andre Willis, "Benjamin William Arnett," *Encyclopedia Africana* (New York: Oxford University Press, 2005); Louis R. Harlan, ed., *The Booker T. Washington Papers*, vol. 4 (Urbana: University of Illinois Press, 1975), 259–260.

12. Murray to Hutchinson, October 3, 1900; "Arnett's Collection of Pamphlets by Negro Authors," Murray Papers, Reel 25.

13. Roger Lane, *William Dorsey's Philadelphia and Ours: On the Past and Future of the Black City in America* (New York: Oxford University Press, 1991), 15, 134, 136, 151, 163, 183.

14. Ibid., 316–317; Tony Martin, *Black Bibliophiles and Collectors: Preservers of Black*

History, ed. Elinor Des Verney Sinnette, W. Paul Coates, and Thomas Battles (Washington, D.C.: Howard University Press, 1990), 29.

15. J. C. White, Jr., Philadelphia, Pennsylvania to Daniel Murray, Washington, D.C., typed document (TD), March 19, 1900, Murray Papers, Reel 27, 18–19.

16. Murray to Hutchinson, October 3, 1900, 86–87, 93–94, 99.

17. Ibid., 93–95.

18. *Colored American Magazine*, vols. 1–2, 1900–1901 (New York: Negro Universities Press, 1969), 124–125.

19. Ibid., 227.

20. Ibid., 260; Ferdinand W. Peck, Commissioner-General, New York, New York, to Herbert Putnam, Librarian of Congress, Washington, D.C., December 18, 1899, TLS, Manuscript Division, The Records of the Library of Congress, The Central File Macleish-Evans, Box 765, Folder Exhibition 46–2, 1899–1939; Thomas Calloway to Putnam, December 19, 1899.

21. Peck to Putnam, February 17, 1900.

22. Ibid.; Daniel Murray, Washington, D.C., to George Meyers, Cleveland, Ohio, ALS, May 10, 1900, Meyers Papers, Box 8, Folder 3.

23. Report of the Commissioner-General for the United States to the International Universal Exposition, Paris, 1900 (Washington, D.C.: Government Printing Office, 1901), 475–476; W. E. Burghardt Du Bois, "The American Negro at Paris," *The American Review of Reviews* (November 1900), 575–577; Department of Social Economy, United States Commission to the Paris Exposition of 1900, October 20, 1900, Manuscript Division, The Records of the Library of Congress, The Central File Macleish-Evans, Box 765, Folder Exhibition 46–2, 1899–1939.

24. Report of the Commissioner-General for the United States to the International Universal Exposition, Paris, 1900, vol. 2 (Washington, D.C.: Government Printing Office, 1901), 463.

25. Ibid.

26. Ibid., 464–465.

27. Ibid.

28. *Colored American Magazine*, 124–125.

29. George Meyers, Cleveland, Ohio, to Daniel Murray, Washington, D.C., ALS, August 8, 1900, Murray Papers, Reel 1, 119–121; Daniel Murray, Washington, D.C., to George Meyers, Cleveland, Ohio, ALS, August 29, 1901, Meyers Papers, Box 10, Folder 5; Daniel Murray, Washington, D.C., to George Meyers, Cleveland, Ohio, ALS, September 13, 1901, Meyers Papers, Box 10, Folder 6.

30. *Colored American Magazine*, 333–335.

31. Ibid.

32. Daniel Murray, Washington, D.C., to Commissioners of St. Louis World's Fair, 1904, autograph letter (AL), May 22, 1902, Murray Papers, Reel 1, 143–144.

33. Ibid.

34. Ibid.; Howard J. Rogers, St. Louis, MO., to Daniel Murray, Washington, D.C., TLS, June 16, 1902, Murray Papers, Reel 1, 148; Executive Committee Minutes, October 19, 1901, Louisiana Purchase Exposition Company Collection, Missouri Historical Society Library and Research Center, St. Louis, Box 20, folder 3.

35. Andrew F. Hilyer, *The Twentieth Century Union League Directory* (Washington,

D.C.: The Union League, 1901), i; Robert G. McGuire, "Andrew F. Hilyer," *Dictionary of American Negro Biography* (New York: W.W. Norton, 1982).

36. Daniel Murray, "Bibliographia Africania," *The Voice of the Negro* 1, no. 5 (May 1904), 186–191.

37. David Hutchinson, Washington, D.C., Memorandum of Negro Exhibition at Jamestown, TLS, July 9, 1907, Murray Papers, Reel 1, 209–210.

38. Richard R. Wright, *The Negro in Pennsylvania: An Economic Study* (Philadelphia: University of Pennsylvania, 1912); Richard R. Wright, "Forty Years of Negro Progress," *Southern Workmen* 36 (March 1907), 157; Richard R. Wright, "Home Ownership and Savings among Negroes of Philadelphia," *Southern Workmen* 36 (December 1907), 665; Richard R. Wright, "Negro Communities in New Jersey," *Southern Workmen* 37 (July 1908), 385; Richard R. Wright, "Negro Businessmen in the North," *Southern Workmen* 38 (January 1909), 36; Richard R. Wright, "Criminal Statistics," *Southern Workmen* 40 (May 1911), 291; R. R. Wright, Jr., Augusta, Georgia, to Daniel Murray, Washington, D.C., ALS, November 25, 1910, Murray Papers, Reel 1, 369.

39. R. R. Wright, Statistician and Director of Exhibits, Emancipation Proclamation Commission of Pennsylvania, to Librarian of Congress, Washington, D.C., TSL, August 28, 1913, Manuscript Division, The Records of the Library of Congress, The Central File Macleish-Evans, Box 768, Folder Hist. 7, 1912–1951.

40. Thorvald Solberg, Register of Copyrights, Library of Congress, to the Librarian of Congress, TLS, September 3, 1912, Manuscript Division, The Records of the Library of Congress, The Central File Macleish-Evans, Box 768, Folder Hist. 7, 1912–1951; Daniel Murray, Reading Room Division, Library of Congress, to the Librarian, ALS, September 17, 1912, Manuscript Division, The Records of the Library of Congress, The Central File Macleish-Evans, Box 768, Folder Hist. 7, 1912–1951.

41. Herbert Putnam, Librarian of Congress, to R. R. Wright, Statistician and Director of Exhibits, Emancipation Proclamation Commission of Pennsylvania, TSL, September 20, 1912, Manuscript Division, The Records of the Library of Congress, The Central File Macleish-Evans, Box 768, Folder Hist. 7, 1912–1951.

42. Daniel Murray, Library of Congress, Washington, D.C., to R. R. Wright, Jr., Director of Exhibits, Philadelphia, Pa., ALS [copy], August 25, 1913, Manuscript Division, The Records of the Library of Congress, The Central File Macleish-Evans, Box 768, Folder Hist. 7, 1912–1951; Daniel Murray, Reading Room, Library of Congress, to W. W. Bishop, Esq., Superintendent, ALS, 5 September 1913, Manuscript Division, The Records of the Library of Congress, The Central File Macleish-Evans, Box 768, Folder Hist. 7, 1912–1951.

43. W. E. B. Du Bois, Emancipation Proclamation Commission of the State of New York, to Daniel Murray, Library of Congress, Washington, D.C., TLS, September 25, 1913, Manuscript Division, The Records of the Library of Congress, The Central File Macleish-Evans, Box 768, Folder Hist. 7, 1912–1951; Daniel Murray, Library of Congress, Washington, D.C., to Wm. W. Bishop, Esq., Superintendent, Library of Congress, Washington, D.C., ALS, October 4, 1913, Manuscript Division, The Records of the Library of Congress, The Central File Macleish-Evans, Box 768, Folder Hist. 7, 1912–1951.

44. Daniel Murray, Washington, D.C., to Jesse Max Barber, Esq., New York City, TLS, October 29, 1910, Murray Papers, Reel 1, 318; Daniel Murray, *Murray's Historical and Biographical Encyclopedia of the Colored Race throughout the World* (Washington, D.C.: World Cyclopedia Company, 1912).

2

Children's Experience
of Print

Merry's Flock

Making Something Out of Educational Reform in the Early Twentieth Century

RYAN K. ANDERSON

In 1899 H. R. DENTON of Belmont, California, wrote to Street and Smith, publishers of *Tip Top Weekly* (1896–1912): "[I found *Tip Top*] a clean, healthy, moral, useful tale, of a true American ... [written by] a well educated, moral man, whose writing bore that unmistakable polish of refinement so visibly lacking in many 'stories for boys' and whose aim obviously was to place before the American youth a noble example."[1] Denton's comments, published in the title's "Applause" column, spoke volumes about young readers' relationship with the best-selling juvenile weekly of its time. To Denton and thousands like him, this dime novel did more than provide thrills; it played a central role in his personal development. Its "Stories for Boys," while fun, possessed a fundamental utility for ambitious "American youth." At a time when the American middle classes began viewing formal education—and especially the nation's growing secondary school system—as a tool that prepared adolescents for the opportunities of corporate America, Denton's letter revealed that young readers blazed their own path to success.

Many of *Tip Top*'s young followers combined their favorite dime novel with their formal education as a form of career preparation. Prior to the twentieth century, most middle-class Americans believed that a basic education and a little work experience paved the way to a young man's economic independence and responsible citizenship. The rapid growth of industrial capitalism in the late nineteenth century changed this view. With "the incorporation of America" came a newly educated, white-collared, and salaried middle class. This emergent managerial set saw progress and prosperity as both a birthright and the glue that held "the better sort" together. For this group, a burgeoning consumer economy made possible a new standard of living and let the nation's professionals set themselves apart from "the meaner sort" by accumulating wealth and acquiring a superior education. A new institution, the comprehensive high school, reshaped adolescence. Between 1890 and 1920, the percentage of people enrolled in high schools rose from 7 to 38 percent, and as enrollments grew, the mission of the high school diversified. By the turn of the twentieth century, two curricular tracks had emerged: one college-preparatory, the other vocational.[2]

High school reformers pushed the best and brightest toward preparation for college, while the rest gained the skills they needed for the changing workplace. Thus reformers cast the comprehensive high school as the root of "equal educational opportunity" for all. Yet for students, the expansion of secondary education held both promise and peril. It gave opportunity to as many adolescents as possible but saved special rewards for those deemed the most academically talented. While some educators called for common learning experiences, others maintained that schools should embrace meritocracy and modern management practices: standards, tests, and curricular stratification according to "scientifically" measured abilities. Many high schoolers found themselves negotiating a tenuous path between what adults told them they needed from school and what they wanted from school themselves. In this context, adolescent reading *outside* school took on particular significance. At the turn of the twentieth century, a new youth culture built around consuming leisure goods like *Tip Top* reflected the points where young people agreed with adults about the purpose of formal education as well as the points where they departed from adults' ideas about "success."

"Applause" provides a unique, albeit filtered, look into what American youth thought about the changing relationship between formal education, social class, and economic opportunity at the turn of the twentieth century. Street and Smith's editors realized that a periodical emphasizing "useful" juvenile literature, established as an inexpensive and decidedly virile alternative to *St. Nicholas* magazine and *The Youth's Companion*, would sell if it appealed to young readers' sense of autonomy and, at the same time, presented fictional heroes like *Tip Top*'s Frank Merriwell as paragons of American success.[3] In introducing the title, Street and Smith entered a broader conversation about adolescent—and especially adolescent male—education. They cast themselves as publishers of a respectable, yet inexpensive, magazine that provided a forum where readers—especially boys—debated how a "manly boy" looked and acted. The manly boy demonstrated both intellectual and physical prowess; a

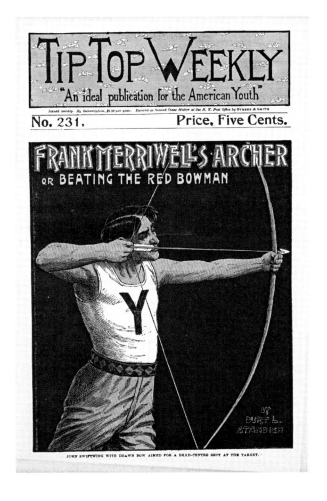

A typical cover of *Tip Top Weekly*, 1900. (image courtesy of Stanford University Library, Stanford, CA)

scholar and an athlete, his personal charm, good manners, and self-reliance always led to success in competitive situations. Yet, as "boyologists" of the day said, "boys will be boys" and the manly boy continued reveling in an updated version of the nineteenth-century's rough-and-tumble boy and youth culture. In classic American form, the manly boy was a self-made individual, one who took an entrepreneurial approach to the development (and performance) of his own character.[4]

The manly boy took shape from letters printed in *Tip Top*'s back pages, chiefly in the "Applause" section. These letters created a literary community, which members called "Merry's Flock."[5] The Flock, a subset of a coalescing new middle-class youth culture, understood the relationship between reading, school, and success in specific ways. In their view, succeeding in the American workplace depended on correctly preparing oneself for work during one's high school years. The new comprehensive high school offered many benefits, but an individual supplemented his formal education through the wise and self-directed use of leisure time. While the Flock agreed with many adults' ideas about formal education and meritocratic success, they also updated middle-class traditions of self-education by combining formal education with literary endeavors, physical culture, and their own culture rooted in consumerism. They asserted that their own culture supplemented the paths to success charted by teachers and parents. In doing so, they demonstrated a belief that their authority as consumers of print gave them the rights in defining their education, broadly construed, toward ends that took shape from both their particular culture and the social expectations adults had for them. In short, in many ways they shared lager society's visions for their education and its ultimate goals but wanted a say in how they prepared for their future. Thus the institutionalization and rationalization of adolescent life did not guide this younger generation into modern America; rather, it set the table for debate and conflict.[6]

Young people recognized that the comprehensive high school, for all its advantages, did not actually help all students succeed equally. Historians, including Lawrence Cremin, William J. Reese, David F. Labaree, David L. Angus, Jeffrey E. Mirel, and others, have revealed the many contradictions that existed in the comprehensive high school: the political compromises embedded in its creation, the mixed messages it conveyed to students, and the near impossibility of fulfilling its diverse pedagogical goals. As Labaree put it, the new American high school represented a "peculiar combination of comprehensiveness and stratification."[7] A high school diploma both proved advantageous in the job market and a prerequisite for college admission.[8] But, dissatisfied with the seemingly clear-cut options laid before them, students resisted efforts that labeled them either "vocational" or "academic" students and began looking for ways they could supplement either their vocation or their academic course of study at school. For instance, when literature classes and school libraries began deemphasizing classic works and pushing modern authors, students responded by including *Tip Top* in their "serious" reading. In the process, they realized that many paths could lead to "success," and they began mixing and matching their formal education, leisure reading, and physical culture and found their own way into the nation's middle class.[9]

"An Ideal Publication for the American Youth"

When Ormond Smith and George Smith assumed control of Street and Smith in the mid-1880s, the firm of Beadle and Adams ruled the inexpensive literature market and had done so since 1860, when they sold 65,000 copies of

Maleska, the Indian Wife of the White Hunter. That title set the model that other houses later imitated. As with *Maleska*, the venerable editor Orville Victor paid writers between $50 and $250, depending on their reputation with the house, for similar tales of heroic adventure. These yarns ran between 30,000 and 60,000 words and sold en masse through mail orders and subscription salesman in their famous salmon-covered editions. Authors did not necessarily produce original work; instead, they rehashed captivity narratives, seafaring tales, and frontier stories, usually in the vein of James Fennimore Cooper's bestselling Leatherstocking Tales series. Beadle and Adams also reprinted stories that they considered sure sellers. Success, most publishers believed, came from buying as much material on the market as possible, recruiting and protecting their best authors (unsuccessfully most of the time), selling as many copies as possible, and imitating or stealing each others' best work.[10]

A series of developments during the late 1880s and early 1890s transformed the dime novel business and shifted power within the industry. First, the cost of producing "cheap" literature dropped. Printing technology, paper, and ink all decreased in cost. Street and Smith capitalized on these savings by building a succession of headquarters that housed all aspects of producing dime novels: acquisition, editing, production, and dissemination. This vertical integration offset the relatively high cost of authors' labor. Second, the International Copyright Act of 1891—together with the panics of the 1890s—ended the days of freewheeling reprinting that had once buoyed the dime novel market. Now houses with a successful story line or author could protect their literary goods, which killed off smaller competitors who relied on "pirating" popular stories. As the number of players declined, the largest publishers—Beadle and Adams, Tousey's, Munsey's, and Street and Smith—consolidated their market share. Street and Smith enjoyed a steady flow of cash through newsstand sales, signed the better freelancers to short-term contracts, began using their weekly publications as a method for constructing book-length manuscripts, reprinted best sellers, and acquired leftover stock from faltering houses.[11]

Meanwhile, the dime novel market changed. In the 1860s, cheap thrillers took aim at a broad, primarily working-class and adult audience. By then readers accepted the idea that they could read for fun and not suffer, and adults embraced the general readership magazines established by Edward Bok and others during the early 1890s, leaving dime novels to youngsters.[12] By the 1880s, children garnered more spending power, which encouraged Street and Smith's focus on them during the 1890s. Over the next two decades, they targeted young readers with thirty-two new titles.[13] Freelance writers pumped out serial stories in weekly formats; if they proved popular, the house reprinted them in a paperback book format in either their *Medal Library* or *Eagle Library*, which sold at newsstands or through second-class mail. As for their adult-directed publications, Street and Smith introduced three general readership magazines:

Ainslee's Magazine (1898), *Popular Magazine* (1903), and *Smith's Magazine* (1905).[14] All sold well.

   Tip Top proved their most successful venture. Advertised as "An Ideal Publication for American Youth," it cost only a nickel and had approximately 150,000 weekly buyers.[15] Each issue contained a 20,000-word story that could be enjoyed on its own or read as a mini-story arc of three stories that, in turn, tied into a larger twelve-story arc. *Tip Top* featured more than just stories. Purchasers received a colored cover, a novelty in those days, depicting a scene from the story. Very little outside advertising appeared in any given issue, but the house loaded the last few pages with descriptions of other Street and Smith titles and premium offers. Two letter columns, the aforementioned "Applause" (devoted to discussing the Merriwell saga), and "Ask Professor Fourman" (focused on questions about physical development and sports) let followers engage each other, the author "Burt L. Standish," and the eponymous "Mssrs. Street and Smith."[16] Despite these bells and whistles, the serial story proved the most important part of *Tip Top*'s success. Gilbert Patten, a Maine-born dime novel veteran, wrote as "Burt L. Standish" between 1896 and 1910; he conceived of his protagonist, Frank Merriwell, as the embodiment of manly virtue. The name said it all: "*Frank* for frankness, *merry* for a happy disposition, *well* for health and abounding vitality."[17] This ruddy youth quickly gained followers because he lived the life they wanted for themselves.[18]

   Readers followed Merriwell through four major story arcs, known collectively as the Frank Merriwell saga. All of the arcs answered questions about how a boy should prepare for success in corporate America, what the proper gender roles in that new environment were, and how one could lead (or follow) as a man. The first story arc followed Merriwell's growth from school boy athlete to fully developed man. Readers met Merriwell just after his mother's death, when he entered Fardale Military Academy and became its greatest cadet, student, and athlete. Friends joined him on adventures around the world and then to Yale, where he became Old Eli's favorite son, leading his teams past cads from Harvard, loafers from Princeton, and other college types.[19] This arc ended with his graduation from Yale and his assumption of adult responsibilities. The second story arc detailed a love triangle with Elsie Bellwood and Inza Burrage, which ended with his eventual marriage to Burrage and the birth of their son, Frank Merriwell, Jr., otherwise known as Chip.

   Discovering and redeeming a long-lost half brother named Dick Merriwell constituted the third story arc and paved the way for the fourth arc. During his college years, Merriwell lost his inherited fortune, worked on a rail line and eventually returned to school, where he set aside the frivolity of student life and made himself into an independently wealthy man with a secure profession. On the eve of his Yale graduation, he discovered that he had a half-brother named Dick, the progeny of an unknown union between his father and an exiled

Spanish duchess, and assumed the task of teaching the youngster virility, control, and leadership by enrolling him in Fardale and Yale, where he replicated his brother's feats and learned his responsibility as a Merriwell. As Dick Merriwell's story unfolded, Frank Merriwell established the Merriwell American School of Athletic Development, and this began the fourth story arc. In this way, Patten could alternate between Merriwell brothers as needed.[20]

Merriwell's "all-American" life appealed to his followers. His physical gifts, wealth, popularity, and intelligence, along with his globetrotting adventures and relative freedom from adult supervision made him the envy of adolescents everywhere. Indeed, life at Fardale and Yale seemed less like work than a manly summer camp. And sometimes Merriwell's fun tested the boundaries of respectability. He joined secret societies, hazed underclassmen, pulled pranks (using his natural talent as a ventriloquist), and played high-stakes poker. Administrators and professors interceded on occasion, but they were either the type of adults who understood that "boys will be boys" or became victims of Frank's fantastic pranks. A wide variety of friends, each with a trademark shortcoming, such as an effeminate nature, a drinking problem, or a southern upbringing that led to backward ideas, surrounded the saga's hero. Frank even had a few non-Anglo-Saxon chums: Germans, Irish, and American Indians figured prominently in this group. And, of course, girls—actresses, power hungry socialites, hillbilly rustics, and spoiled brats—all desired him. In short, Merriwell had options—and decisions to make—about who his associates would be and how he would relate to them. As Merriwell grew into leadership, he accepted his responsibility as the paragon of success by organizing people around him into the right sorts. Most admirably, Merriwell did it his way. He studied hard and played by the rules but never lost his love of rough fun or boyish pranks. Because of this, youths and adults alike recognized him as the ideal American youth.

"A Shining Light for Every Ambitious Lad"

Street and Smith billed the Frank Merriwell saga as a premium quality publication with particular utility to the boy on the make. In one advertisement for Merriwell reprints, which ran in both *Tip Top* and the house's newsdealer catalog, the publishers stated, "Frank Merriwell's example is a shining light for every ambitious lad to follow."[21] The story line saw him develop good working habits, proper leisure pursuits, and a respect for authority.[22] These sentiments did not come wholly from editorial direction or Patten's inspiration; instead, much of the meaning of Merriwell's adventures came directly from readers. Leo Jinks of Houston, Texas, related, "[*Tip Top*] has done a done a great deal towards molding my future life. . . . [I did not] know how to value life or choose the path that leads to fame and success, but since reading the adventures of

Frank Merriwell, I have learned to enjoy the advantages that nature and the world have placed within my grasp."[23] D. W. from Cleveland, Ohio, told others in a letter to "Applause" that, after circumstances forced him from school, his hero's example inspired him to find work as an office boy. He went to college at night, became a stenographer, and "during times when my patience fails me I think of Merriwell—of my model Merriwell. Now, I know I am taking up space, but I cannot help it, my pen will not stop for the enthusiasm for your great *Tip Top* would take a book to express."[24]

Working youth—messengers, bellhops, and others—read and commented on Merriwell's adventures. Having spent their nickel, they grasped "a reader's privilege" and offered up their opinions on Merriwell.[25] Most working readers' letters expressed an admiration of Merriwell's success in the workplace rather than his collegiate career. "The railroad series was the best," Frank Vayo insisted, "I am now a brakeman on the P.C.R.R. out of Bangor, and do not think I would have ever gone on the railroad if I had not read *Tip Top Weekly*."[26] Yet, not every working-class boy shared Vayo's success. One letter writer relayed that, while all his coworkers followed Merriwell, their grueling work schedules kept them from working out or going to night school as their hero suggested.[27] Some people interpreted such obstacles as a test of resolve, like a reader from McKee's Rocks, Pennsylvania, who signaled himself an expert on the Merriwell saga and college life by signing his name "Old Eli." He chastised readers who complained about the struggle to balance work, school, and personal reading, sneering, "look at the letter from OK 2809—I guess he is some messenger boy since goes by a number. . . . [He] just shows his ignorance."[28]

Tip Top's rise in popularity coincided with discussions about job opportunity, social mobility, and the growing pursuit of high school education. Talking about Merriwell in terms of business success, the Flock made sense of what they could achieve in the new century and how they would manage the various influences affecting their daily lives because succeeding seemed less likely than it had been for their fathers. In the late nineteenth century, boys filing into cities found work as clerks, bookkeepers, or typists. Between 1880 and 1900, the number of clerks and clerical workers in America tripled, swelling the ranks of people in junior management positions that had the least opportunity for advancement. Yet most advanced clerical positions and jobs as traveling salesmen were filled not with candidates promoted from within but, rather, through offers to graduates of emerging business schools and engineering programs in the nation's expanding university system.[29] As new layers of professional management emerged in the nation's large corporations, entry-level workers came increasingly from the ranks of blue-collar strivers who saw office work as a way of improving upon their previous stations. As businesses began expecting high school diplomas for entry-level clerkships, school attendance combined with well-chosen leisure reading and self-cultivation became how the Flock understood middle-class mobility.[30]

Tip Top readers associated success with character, and they believed they could develop this trait both inside and outside of formal institutions such as schools. For these young aspirants, reading practices seemed a good way to mark themselves as members of "the choicest youth." By keeping diaries, forming reading societies, and patronizing the swelling number of public libraries, middle-class boys believed they could take control of their own fortunes. Like the nineteenth century go-getters described by Thomas Augst in *The Clerk's Tale*, they believed middle-class status demanded literary effort as part of their self-education and moral progress.[31] Literary pursuits not only provided a network of like-minded companions but also cultivated intellectual abilities. The Flock took this as an opportunity for fashioning a corporate yet vigorous identity. "Good boy" letters in the column might have praised Merriwell's morals, put on display proper correspondence form, and shown off literary criticism skills, but "bad boy" letters demonstrated that not all literary fellows were mollycoddles. Hence, "Applause" featured both letters from Arthur J. A. Charwate, who thought *Tip Top* was "instrumental in molding my career in life . . . [because it] imbued me with the desire to gain an education" and from a group of Indianapolis followers who expelled a member and then had one of their own beat him to a pulp in boxing match for his difference of opinion over the question of who Merriwell should marry. Thus the saga did more than provide an exciting story; it gave young readers a blueprint for becoming the type of man adults desired while allowing them to remain fun-loving boys.[32]

Intellectual and social endeavors, Merry's Flock learned, fostered the development of "the whole person." Conversations about the saga's place in literature, applying its lessons to real life, and matching Merriwell's extraordinary achievements filled page after page of "Applause." The column was a discursive space that all readers could share, even if they did not always concur in their assessments of Merriwell's exploits. As D. N. Platt of Lawrenceburg, Indiana, observed: "It is not often that one finds stories calculated to instruct as well as amuse that are not put up too expensively to reach the class of boys who they should most benefit. . . . [*Tip Top*'s] stories are written with an object, and Mr. Standish has not allowed it to obscure the interest of narration."[33] Matthew Melcher, Leo Melcher, Andrew Weir, and Jarrett Weir of Braidwood, Illinois, agreed. They found the publication singularly "educating, entertaining, and amusing."[34] A reader from Arkansas related, "About five years ago I quit school and read my first *Tip Top*; and today the desire to enter school is again so strong that I cannot wait for next fall."[35]

In a similar fashion, the Flock argued that *Tip Top* redeemed dime novel writing as a literary genre. They drew distinctions between Street and Smith's publication and the yellow-backed blood-and-thunder reading of the last century.[36] One observer thanked the house for saving cheap literature for youngsters by proclaiming, "they [Street and Smith] are invading the Nursery of the Devil, the dime novel, and slowly but surely exterminating the [cancer], and at the same time putting in cheap and attractive form all that is good and manly."[37] Some readers argued that publishers who imitated *Tip Top* provided only sham reading—their literature could not hold up to a discriminating readers' inspection.

Readers put Merriwell, *Tip Top*, and Standish alongside the literature held up as "good" reading. Thomas Hughes's *Tom Brown's Schooldays* (1857), which went through dozens of editions, ranked high among the books recommended for youth. Many Americans found it worthy of emulation because of its realistic portrayal of English school life, which they honored for its success in creating manly leaders who maintained the British Empire. But, according to a reader named Orme Farris, Hughes stood second behind Standish. Ferris wrote, "They say a Rugby game is described in *Tom Brown's Schooldays* the best of any other, but I think Mr. Standish can beat Mr. Hughes all to nothing."[38] Readers held that Standish's abilities ranked him among the better writers in general as well. Elsie Satterfield and Marguerite Morris of Fairmount, West Virginia, admired Conan Doyle, creator of Sherlock Holmes, but Standish outranked Doyle in their list of great living fiction writers. Others placed Standish alongside Dickens, Tennyson, and Hugo. Indeed, the young members of the Manhattan (New York) Literary Club even instituted a rule stipulating that all members must include Frank Merriwell in their libraries and read his adventures regularly.[39]

Who Joined Merry's Flock?

The young people who joined Merry's Flock saw their literary community as one that tied them together and helped them make sense of the lessons they learned both at school and at home. One ardent supporter offered a poem describing what her family thought about *Tip Top* and its message:

> [*Tip Top* is] the best I've ever known.
> It is read by my dear mother,
> By my sisters and my brother,
> It's a blessing to our own sweet home![40]

Parents testified about Merriwell's usefulness in teaching young people the right morals. Mrs. McGregor from Allegheny, Pennsylvania, wrote that she let her eight-year-old son read *Tip Top*, as "there is nothing harmful or luridly impossible in your novel." The stories, she stated, had four chief virtues: they gave a boy an exciting, wholesome, and clean life to emulate, provided good entertainment without undue violence, conveyed sound advice that was easy to swallow, and did all of this without preaching. According to Mrs. McGregor, some of her "narrow-minded friends and neighbors, chiefly among whom is a Presbyterian minister," disapproved of *Tip Top*, but she pointed out that two of the minister's own sons visited her sons and read Merriwell's adventures together.[41] Indeed, George Washington O'Clare of Bangor, Maine, said of the Merriwell stories: "I have heard them endorsed by several ministers and professional men."[42] *Tip Top* followers saw the saga in the same way reformers viewed the comprehensive high school: it both affirmed traditional values and prepared readers for success in the modern world.

This combination of "traditional" and "modern" values placed *Tip Top* in the mainstream of American success manuals. Judy Hilkey's work on success manuals in the late nineteenth and early twentieth centuries argues that small-town Americans in this period remained as wedded to republican virtues and religious faith as they had been before the Civil War. Middle-class parents who worried about their sons running after the brass ring in the big city bought these books for their sons so they could read that small-town life still worked if they developed manly character. Catering to rural and urban readers alike, these success manual authors portrayed the Darwinian "battle of life" as an essential, character-forming experience that rendered American boys self-reliant, moral, and healthy. In effect, historians have shown that the pursuit of manliness created a sense of white brotherhood—a brotherhood that transcended land ownership, the acquisition of capital, or business success. Publishers of periodicals for white boys supplemented this by preaching that manliness came from character, virtue, and will power, not just "narrowly vocational, instrumental, or professional" lessons.[43]

The task of maintaining middle-class ideas regarding the importance of education—and simultaneously making education "work" for individual boys—took place each week in *Tip Top*'s "Applause" column. Readers' letters indicated a self-conscious awareness of how their own progress toward academic and nonacademic success measured up against that of other members of the Flock. For example, for some time, readers differentiated between righteous members of the Flock and boys who were somehow deficient. D. N. Platt, for instance, pointed out, "Here in Lawrenceburg [Indiana] all the right-minded boys admire Merriwell and all the 'cads' envy him. The high principles of life seem as repellant to the mean-spirited in print as well as in real life."[44] As far as Platt was concerned, some boys simply did not possess the moral fiber that Merriwell demanded, and those who lacked these essential qualities would not receive the same opportunities that came to the right sort of boy.

As time passed and the Flock matured, a struggle developed between the people who claimed to have read the Merriwell saga from the first issue and those who picked it up a few years into its life. "Applause" revealed that a generation gap of sorts emerged as the saga carried on. Veteran readers grew into young adulthood and kept following their hero's exploits; they occasionally shouted down the opinions of people who came later to Merriwell and claimed a special right to influence Burt L. Standish and Street and Smith's editors.

"Old Eli," after having sneered at the "messenger boys" who could not use *Tip Top Weekly* correctly, puffed, "Being an old time reader of your weekly, having read from No. 1 to the present [#411], I think it is my duty to write you. . . . I want to go after some of these 'kickers' [who make fun of Frank Merriwell] just to . . . be noticed."[45]

Many readers formed Tip Top Clubs and read their favorite weekly as a group, discussing its finer points. Lynn Hartley, a reader from Connecticut, suggested organizing the clubs with badges and secret passwords established by Street and Smith and managed by local organizations. Hartley hoped that when members met each other on the street they could help each other out, perhaps by "welcoming him into our home, or helping him if in need of help in any way." Street and Smith recognized a tool for increasing readership when they heard one, and they responded with alacrity. "If the boys want such a badge, they shall have it at cost price. So, let us know, boys, what you think of it."[46] Editors printed lists of badge supporters from around the country, and in February 1899 announced the badge's availability, presented an illustration, provided coupons necessary for procuring the medal, and printed a short column on the "Tip Top League" reminding readers that the phrase *true as steel*, announced earlier after a reader contest to choose the password had ended, served as the league password. That week's "Applause" featured a message from Hartley, urging fellow Tip Toppers to "be as 'true as steel' to the *Tip Top* and to each other . . . [and to] show our colors and try our best to uphold and keep our badge from falling into the wrong hands . . . [and] be worthy of such an emblem of purity and manliness; let's fight against liquor and tobacco and make sure that the coming generation will be MEN."[47]

This emphasis on manliness raised a critical question for the Flock. If acquiring *Tip Top* and following Merriwell's advice created opportunity, then who was to say that girls could not also participate? They certainly contributed to "Applause." Some of their letters showed that female fans wanted a softer Merriwell and a greater narrative emphasis on romantic endeavors. These missives fit into the limitations on "women's reading" that Jennifer Phegley notes in her work, *Educating the Proper Woman Reader*—though some male readers made similar requests.[48] For example, Earl Ludlow of York, Nebraska, asked after his hero's love affairs in a letter to the "Applause" column: "I don't want to ask too much for a nickel, but I would like to hear from Elsie Bellwood and Inza Burrage again."[49] Meanwhile, some girls who read the Merriwell saga broke from expected gender roles. "Jake" demonstrated this tendency when she wrote: "I like a bad boy—not bad like Chet A.—but like Dick was before he got civilized. I hope Dick married a girl with a character like Brad. If he gets a good girl like himself, I think he will be unhappy. B. B. also says he liked Frank's flock, and I do too . . . I wish that I. M. Kicking and Will I. B. Right would write and tell us why they are so stuck on Chet A. Ain't they getting it in the neck? I like *Tip Top* most for its sport, even if I am a girl. I can skate and play ball and some other things. Every girl nearby says *Tip Top* is no good, but I think it is the very best thing out."[50] As a governor, boys routinely mocked girls in the Flock who commented on sports, insisting that, while girls made fine reading companions for their gentle features, athletics and rough behavior constituted a boys' realm. But, readers like Jake challenged this idea.

In the athletic school story arc, middle-class boys found the answer to their problems of access to the Flock. Physical training as an integral part of preparation for adulthood gave them a way of excluding girls and enforcing gender norms. In keeping with the physical culture that dominated the Teddy Roosevelt years, preparation for "the battle of life" was construed as something that all boys had to do apart from their feminine counterparts. Yes, girls needed healthy bodies, but for different reasons. And if success remained possible for all boys who made a healthy life despite the intellectually stimulating, but physically stultifying, environment of high school, then those who did not become "generals" in the battle of life had no one but themselves to blame. Life constituted a battle. "We're all soldiers," Merriwell informed them, "some of us may become sergeants, lieutenants, captains, generals."[51] He personally helped track male students into a course of study that combined physical, mental, and dietary plans to help them succeed. He even confronted the prospect that many boys might not ever climb the ranks during the battle of life. Looking out among their numbers, he stated baldly: "It's possible that some of you boys will always remain privates in the ranks. . . . [but] there's a difference among common soldiers. . . . If you must be common soldiers boys, be good ones. I'm going to help you."[52] The mass of boys rose and cheered this speech, after which Merriwell dismissed them from their assembly so they could go to the gymnasium for physical exams.[53]

From Street and Smith's perspective, the problem of audience created a dilemma in that they could not easily satisfy the tastes of male and female readers. In time, the male members of the Flock, together with Patten and his editors, justified excluding girls from doing the sorts of things they needed to do to mimic Merriwell's success, emphasizing instead what his story said about middle-class manly boyhood. Over the course of *Tip Top*'s life span, working-class boys as well as girls argued that Merriwell emboldened their development. The editors accommodated these tastes as much as possible because doing so moved issues, but eventually they privileged middle-class boys' voices because that audience provided the crux of their sales. Street and Smith tried separating their audience by introducing new titles for these different readers, but none did as well as *Tip Top*.[54]

The best example of the publishers' choice of audience came by way of a fitness manual, introduced with the inception of the fourth story arc, entitled *Frank Merriwell's Book of Athletic Development*. Street and Smith advertised the manual by having characters in the saga describe how Merriwell's advice helped them with their physical growth. Bart Hodge, Merriwell's best friend, recalled toppling any boy he wanted during his childhood until butting up against Merry. "This was the first time I had ever had such a thing happen to me," Hodge commented, "So I watched what he did . . . he taught me his methods of training, and, more than that inspired me to follow him.'" Hodge insisted that his improvement came after adhering to Merry's plan for only a few weeks. He added that he never worried about his physical readiness, "I can trust my muscles and strength to pull me through any kind of a struggle."[55] A Troy, New York, reader linked literary endeavors, physical well being, and success when he noted that Street and Smith's *Book of Athletic Development* would help a lot of boys improve their standing in life. *Tip Top*, this and other readers noted, put before them object lessons that gave them the authority over their own development.[56]

Patten and his editors reinforced this emphasis on physical culture with Merriwell's American School of Athletic Development. Readers learned of this new institution and inferred what the manual might do for them when Merriwell explained, "In this country there are numberless free high schools for the education of the mind . . . but I know not of one for the education and upbuilding of the American boy's body. . . . [A] puny body is a handicap for a well-trained mind. . . . Without a strong body, without health, the most brilliant man in the world is incapable of attaining the heights to which he should rise."[57] Merriwell again asserted this belief on the first day of class, when he made "determination and perseverance" institutional watchwords. Every boy there, he knew, could take to the serious task of building themselves physically. The world demanded their dedication in this fundamentally competitive task because the nation's future depended on their success. "The possibility of rising is something that should fill each of you with a fine sensation and a keen ambition," he declared.[58] Room waited at the top, and opportunity existed for every American boy, even if only a few ultimately won.

Conclusion

Merry's Flock found no simple answer to the question of what constituted opportunity and success in turn-of-the-century America. Their conversations about literary endeavors and personal progress in "Applause" showed that most young people accepted the need for formal education yet, at the same time, *Tip Top* let them express their *own* interests and exert their *own* authority as individuals. Even as *Tip Top* readers learned about achieving success in the adult world, they challenged the idea that adults knew what was best for them. When Street and Smith began printing readers' letters, young men often positioned themselves as people confronted with adult authority who drew on

Merriwell's example and exercised power over their own education and their own physical, intellectual, and social development, even as their elders labeled them "adolescents" without the capacity for self-determination.

It was emblematic of the time that the new comprehensive high school, a system designed to offer clear paths to "success," also created a youth culture that, at times, challenged adult definitions of achievement. In many ways, the comprehensive high school provided the children of middle-class professionals with college-preparatory curriculum and at the same time gave children of skilled industrial workers an education that distanced them from unskilled workers. For the children of unskilled workers, including the children of immigrants streaming into the nation's cities, the new comprehensive high school acted as a tool for Americanization—leading, perhaps in future generations, to upward social and economic mobility. Reformers argued that expanding access to secondary school would preserve the democratic nature of public education and ensure that more young people had an opportunity to succeed.[59]

While reformers emphasized democratic opportunity, students realized that high school was an environment fraught with conflict that made grasping opportunity difficult. Within prestigious college-preparatory tracks, a pecking order emerged between the students who took challenging courses and those who viewed a high school diploma as merely a credential and thus a commodity, the value of which was subject to market fluctuation. Of course, students who chose vocational tracks overwhelmingly saw their course of study as job preparation, not edification. These students decided for themselves the value of their formal education, given their own dreams and aspirations. But even as students prepared themselves for the adult world, they had youthful goals and desires, which they could pursue through activities outside of school, such as reading and physical development. These pursuits provided a social education that supplemented their formal education. Because the comprehensive high school did not—and could not—give an equal education to everyone, students educated themselves within and outside of school for their own good.[60]

Merry's Flock wanted stories that helped them understand how their formal and informal educations created more opportunity after school. *Tip Top*, they argued, not only contributed to their mental development but also served the practical end of showing readers how an ideal youth dealt with challenges and made the most of opportunities. It told them how Merriwell got ahead, who he associated with, and what he did with power. They said the saga bolstered educators' emphasis on meritocracy, where potential leaders emerged and thrived. But they also became part of the Flock because it completed the education they pursued at school. In the stratified curriculum of new high schools, these people found the credentials and fundamentals they needed for admission into college and a place within the middle class as adults. In their leisure reading they found intellectual, physical, and social development that they negotiated with the editors of *Tip Top*. They criticized the saga and scrutinized its messages, treating it just as they did any "serious" book. Also they found a group of like-minded individuals willing to converse about the topics that mattered to them. In this way, *Tip Top* acted as a focal point for both formal and informal education.

But in the process, *Tip Top* readers showed that they understood meritocracy in much the same way as their teachers: as a system that opened doors for only the right sort of students. While the print culture created by *Tip Top* let a range of people read, comment, and debate what the story said about preparing boys for adulthood, it did not necessarily democratize the path to opportunity. Like the comprehensive high school, Merry's Flock created a culture that both included a variety of people and granted certain members special privileges and prestige. Middle-class boys ascribed to themselves the greatest degree of talent and authority, even as they claimed to participate in a broader pursuit of success. Working-class boys and girls joined in the conversation about what constituted preparation for success, but found themselves cordoned off by rules prescribed by class, gender, and proper reading habits. Much like the new comprehensive high school, "Applause" reflected that America's transition into a modern nation took shape from a complex negotiation. Middle-class boys, like a lot of other Americans, learned consumerism, education, and class acted as routes to success as long as they found a path different from the ones used by women and working-class boys. In doing so Merry's Flock got its true education.

Notes

1. Burt L. Standish [Gilbert Patten], "Frank Merriwell's Disaster; or, the Hand of the Law," *Tip Top Weekly*, January 21, 1899, 30. All references to Standish hereafter are made with the understanding that this was the pen name of Patten.

2. David L. Angus and Jeffrey E. Mirel, *The Failed Promise of the American High School, 1890–1995* (New York: Teachers College Press, 1999), 1–7, 13, 15; Lawrence Cremin, *The Transformation of the School: Progressivism in American Education, 1876–1957* (New York: Knopf, 1961), 25–26, 28, 34, 36–41, 67, 88–89; William J. Reese, *America's Public Schools: From the Common School to "No Child Left Behind"* (Baltimore: Johns Hopkins University Press, 2005), 182; David Tyack, *The One Best System: A History of American Urban Education* (Cambridge, MA: Harvard University Press, 1974), 180–182, 186, 189–191.

3. Certainly, the venerable *St. Nicholas* and *Youth's Companion* shared a lot in common with *Tip Top*. All of them remained "moral" in their own definitions, all of them targeted juvenile audiences but attracted a certain number of adult followers, they strove for readability and instructiveness, and the young writers who joined the St. Nicholas League (some with more outstanding success later in life than others) saw it as preparation for success in much the same way readers thought of Merry's Flock and "Applause." But some important differences existed as well. *Tip Top*'s five cent price remained

cheaper than the quarter asked for *St. Nicholas* or *Youth's Companion*, and *St. Nicholas* and *Youth's Companion* more closely resembled what readers eventually understood as a "magazine," while Street and Smith's offering was a weekly serial. Most importantly, there existed a difference in tone. The higher-browed *St. Nicholas* and *Youth's Companion* continued espousing traditional republican values into the 1900s, whereas *Tip Top Weekly* expressed a decidedly middle-brow corporate sensibility. Underscoring these dissimilarities was that the Century Company and the Perry Mason Company both saw parents who bought good reading for their kids as their consumers, and Street and Smith saw children who spent their own money as their targets. On *St. Nicholas* and *Youth's Companion*, see Susan R. Gannon, Suzanne Rahn, and Ruth Anne Thompson, eds., *St. Nicholas and Mary Maples Dodge: The Legacy of a Children's Magazine Editor, 1873–1905* (Jefferson, NC: McFarland, 2004); Louise Harris, *None but the Best: or, The Story of Three Pioneers: The Youth's Companion, Daniel Sharp Ford [and] C. A. Stephens* (Providence, RI: C. A. Stephens Collection, Brown University, 1966); R. Gordon Kelly, *"Mother Was a Lady": Self and Society in Selected American Children's Periodicals, 1865–1890* (Westport, CT: Greenwood Press, 1974), 11–15, 23–25. On the tone established by each publication's house, see *"St. Nicholas* Advertising Card Entitled: Make That Youngster Happy," Warshaw Collection of Business Americana, ca. 1724–1977, Collection 60 (Publishers), Box 1, National Museum of American History, Washington, D.C.; *"The Youth's Companion* Announcement for 1906," Warshaw Collection of Business Americana, ca. 1724–1977, Collection 60 (Publishers), Box 14, National Museum of American History, Washington, D.C.

4. I borrow the term "boyologists" from sociologist Kenneth B. Kidd, *Making American Boys: Boyology and the Feral Tale* (Minneapolis: University of Minnesota Press, 2004), 1–2. Boy and youth culture, see E. Anthony Rotundo, *American Manhood: Transformations in Masculinity from the Revolution to the Modern Era* (New York: Basic Books, 1993), 31–74.

5. Burt L. Standish, "Frank Merriwell's Life Struggle; or, a Bluff That Did Not Work," *Tip Top Weekly*, February 9, 1901, 30.

6. My understanding of young people as consumers who clamed authority, even while it unsettled adults, comes from Gary Cross, *The Cute and the Cool: Wondrous Innocence and Modern American Children's Culture* (New York: Oxford University Press, 2004), 10, 34–35; Lisa Jacobson, *Raising Consumers: Children and the American Mass Market in the Early Twentieth Century* (New York: Columbia University Press, 2004), 2, 5–6.

7. David F. Labaree, *The Making of an American High School: The Credentials Market and the Central High School of Philadelphia, 1838–1939* (New Haven, CT: Yale University Press, 1988), 8.

8. This coincided with the creation, dissemination, and maintenance of a "collegiate" culture that came along with a spread in the number of colleges in America during these years. This culture supported the idea that college life differed from "real" life and that one needed to prepare for it by getting the right type of secondary education. John R. Thelin, *A History of American Higher Education* (Baltimore: Johns Hopkins University Press, 2004), 157–162.

9. Angus and Mirel, *Failed Promise of the American High School*, 18, 30–31, 42, 50, 54; Cremin, *Transformation of the School*, x, 133, 142–143, 168–169; Labaree, *Making of an American High School*, 8, 112–117, 150–153, 155–157, 161; Reese, *America's Public Schools*, 102, 121, 151, 186–188, 190, 193.

10. Vicki Anderson, *The Dime Novel in Children's Literature* (Jefferson, NC: McFarland, 2005), 1–6; George Britt, *Forty Years-Forty Millions: The Career of Frank A. Munsey* (New York: Farr and Rhinehart, 1935), 69; "Francis S. Street Obituary," *New York Times*, April 16, 1883; Leslie Gossage, "Street and Smith," in *American Literary Publishing Houses, 1638–1899*, vol. 49, part 2: N–Z, ed. Peter Dzwonkoski (Detroit: Gale Research, 1986), 44; Frank Luther Mott, *A History of American Magazines: 1885–1905*, vol. 4 (Cambridge, MA: Harvard University Press, 1957), 117–120; Russel Nye, *The Unembarrassed Muse: The Popular Arts in America* (New York: Dial Press, 1970), 43, 200–207; Edmund Pearson, *Dime Novels; or, Following an Old Trail in Popular Literature* (Port Washington, NY: Kennikat Press, 1968), 4, 32–33, 47–48; Theodore Peterson, *Magazines in the Twentieth Century* (Urbana: University of Illinois, 1964), 1; Quentin Reynolds, *The Fiction Factory; or, from Pulp Row to Quality Street: The Story of 100 Years of Publishing at Street and Smith* (New York: Random House, 1955), 29–48.

11. "Copyright Progress and Retrogression," *Publishers Weekly* 66 (1904), 1657–1663; Peterson, *Magazines in the Twentieth Century*, 1–6; "The Provisions of the New Copyright Act," *Publishers Weekly* 39 (1891), 561–562; Philip Scranton, *Endless Novelty: Specialty Production and American Industrialization, 1865–1925* (Princeton, NJ: Princeton University Press, 1997), 125; Raymond Howard Shove, *Cheap Book Production in the United States, 1870–1891* (Champaign: University of Illinois Library, 1937), 17–18, 23, 36–37, 42–42; Thorvald Solberg, *Copyright Miscellany: Being Later Contributions concerning the Protection of Literary and Artistic Property with Autobiographical Sketch, Portrait and Bibliography* (Boston: John W. Luce, 1939), 8–9; Robert E. Spiller, Willard Thorp, Thomas H. Johnson, Henry Seidel Canby, Richard M. Ludwig, William M. Gibson, eds., *Literary History of the United States*, 4th ed. (New York: Macmillan, 1974), 963–967; Michael Winship, "The Transatlantic Book Trade and Anglo-American Literary Culture in the Nineteenth Century," in *Reciprocal Influences: Literary Production, Distribution, and Consumption in America*, ed. Steven Fink and Susan S. Williams (Columbus: Ohio State University Press, 1999), 101–102.

12. On audience, see Britt, *Forty Years-Forty Millions*, 73–76; Michael Denning, *Mechanic Accents: Dime Novels and Working-Class Culture in America* (New York: Verso, 1987), 27–46; Robert Peabody Fellows, "The Degeneration of the Dime Novel," *The Writer* 12, no. 7 (July 1899), 97. On general readership magazines, see Peterson, *Magazines in the Twentieth Century*, 1–18.

13. New weekly titles introduced during the 1890s include: *Good News* (1890), *Nick Carter Detective Library* (1891), *New York Five Cent Weekly* (1892), *Diamond Dick Library* (1895), *Diamond Dick Junior Library* (1896), *Red, White, and Blue Library* (1896), *Tip Top Weekly* (1896), *The Yellow Kid* (1897), *Army and Navy Weekly* (1897), *Adventure Library* (1897), *Half-Holiday* (1898), *True Blue* (1898), *Klondike Kit Library* (1898), and *Starry Flag Weekly* (1898). The efforts proved successful, and the house continued the trend through the first decade of the twentieth century with seventeen new titles: *Do and Dare Weekly* (1900), *My Queen* (1900), *Shield Weekly* (1900), *Comrades* (1900), *Boys of America* (1900), *Buffalo Bill Stories* (1901), *Jesse James Stories* (1901), *Brave and Bold* (1902), *Old Broadbrim* (1902), *Young Rover* (1904), *Rough Riders* (1904), *Red Raven* (1905), *Paul Jones* (1905), *All-Sports* (1905), *Bowery Boy* (1905), *Might and Main* (1906), and *Motor Stories* (1909). Taken from Reynolds, *The Fiction Factory*, 272–275.

14. Street and Smith's weekly publications and reprinting habits are more than adequately documented in Edward LeBlanc's well-researched two-part work, *Street and*

Smith Dime Novel Bibliography (Fall River, MA: Edward T. LeBlanc, 1990). All of the second part of LeBlanc's work is devoted to the Merriwell saga; it is the most definitive record of every Merriwell reprinting and use from 1896 through 1990. On Street and Smith, see also Reynolds, *The Fiction Factory*, 121–154; Jean Carwile Marsteller, "*Street and Smith's News Trade Bulletin*: Marketing Popular Literature in the Late Nineteenth Century," *The Papers of the Bibliographical Society of America* 83 (1989), 84–88; John L. Cutler, *Gilbert Patten and His Frank Merriwell Saga: A Study in Sub-Literary Fiction, 1896–1913* (Orono: University Press of Maine, 1934), 60, 62–63; Gilbert Patten, *Frank Merriwell's "Father": An Autobiography by Gilbert Patten (Burt L. Standish)* (Norman: University of Oklahoma Press, 1964), 28, 196; George C. Jenks, "Dime Novel Makers," *The Bookman*, October 1904, 110–111: Mott, *A History of American Magazines: 1885–1905*, 37–38, Street and Smith, *The Greatest Publishing House in the World* (New York: Street and Smith, 1905), n.p. On writing in periodicals during these years, generally, see Ronald Weber, *Hired Pens: Professional Writers in America's Golden Age of Print* (Athens: University of Ohio Press, 1997), 64–84; Christopher P. Wilson, *The Labor of Words: Literary Professionalism in the Progressive Era* (Athens: University of Georgia Press, 1985), 11–13.

15. As is the case with nearly every weekly, accounting for exact circulation numbers is impossible because the house guarded such information closely. John Levi Cutler, after corresponding with both Gilbert Patten and the house in the early thirties, provided three separate amounts regarding weekly circulation: 130,000 (from his house source, likely Frank Blackwell, who was then chief editor at Street and Smith and was almost four decades into his career with the firm), 200,000, and 230,000 (both from Patten!). I use "approximately 150,000" because it is more likely that the house would downplay circulation numbers to a believable amount (a common practice meant to keep authors from arguing for better pay), whereas Patten was, at the time, struggling to get a publishing house off the ground and sell the film, comic, and radio rights to the Merriwell saga. Cutler, *Gilbert Patten and His Frank Merriwell Saga*, 31, 68.

16. Reynolds, *The Fiction Factory*, 85–95. For examples, see Burt L. Standish, "Frank Merriwell's Club; or, Indoor Baseball in Baltimore," *Tip Top Weekly*, February 23, 1901; Burt L. Standish, "Frank Merriwell's Surprise; or, the Contents of the Oil Skin Envelope," *Tip Top Weekly*, July 13, 1901; Burt L. Standish, "Dick Merriwell at Fardale; or, the Wonder of the School," *Tip Top Weekly*, December 7, 1901.

17. Patten, *Frank Merriwell's "Father,"* 177.

18. Cutler, *Gilbert Patten and His Frank Merriwell Saga*, 63; Reynolds, *The Fiction Factory*, 87–91; Weber, *Hired Pens*, 70–74.

19. "Old Eli" was a nickname for Yale used by campus insiders. It referenced the school's namesake, Elihu Yale.

20. I base my outline of the story arcs and my understanding of the narrative on my own reading of *Tip Top*, conducted through three archive collections: The Hess Collection at the University of Minnesota, holdings in the Pat and Ray Browne Popular Culture Library at Bowling Green State University, and the Johannsen Dime Novel Collection at Northern Illinois University.

21. Burt L. Standish, "Frank Merriwell's Eyes; or, Saving an Enemy," *Tip Top Weekly*, May 18, 1901; Burt L. Standish, "Stories in Sets Edited for Cloth Book Department, 1903," Editorial Files, Box 41, Street and Smith Publishers' Archive, Special Collections Research Center, E. S. Bird Library, Syracuse University, Syracuse, New York.

22. See Burt L. Standish, "Frank Merriwell's Misfortune; or, the Start of a New Career," *Tip Top Weekly*, July 9, 1898, through "Frank Merriwell's Reception at Yale; or, a Hot Time in New Haven," *Tip Top Weekly*, April 8, 1899.

23. Burt L. Standish, "Frank Merriwell's First Part; or, the Start as an Actor," *Tip Top Weekly*, October 15, 1898, 34.

24. Burt L. Standish, "Frank Merriwell's Move; or, 13 Pieces of Silver," *Tip Top Weekly*, March 9, 1901, 32.

25. On "a reader's privilege," see Burt L. Standish, "Frank Merriwell's Summer Camp; or, the Athletic School in the Woods," *Tip Top Weekly*, July 21, 1906, 27.

26. Burt L. Standish, "Frank Merriwell's College Chums; or, Bart Hodge's Wonderful Shot," *Tip Top Weekly*, December 17, 1898, 29.

27. Burt L. Standish, "Frank Merriwell's Pluck; or, Never Say Die," *Tip Top Weekly*, February 11, 1899, 29.

28. Burt L. Standish, "Frank Merriwell's Defenders; or, The Strategy of Old Joe Crowfoot," *Tip Top Weekly*, February 27, 1904, 28.

29. I include independent business colleges in this group and in doing so follow the lead of Jerome P. Bjelopera, who explores their social and working worlds in his work *City of Clerks: Office and Sales Workers in Philadelphia, 1870–1920* (Champaign: University of Illinois Press, 2005).

30. On social advancement, see Bjelopera, *City of Clerks*, 14; Cremin, *Transformation of the School*, 36–41; Reese, *America's Public Schools*, 121, 133. On education and entry-level work, see Bjelopera, *City of Clerks*, 9–31; Stuart M. Blumin, *The Emergence of the Middle-Class: Social Experience in the American City, 1760–1900* (New York: Cambridge University Press, 1989), 290–292.

31. Thomas Augst, *The Clerk's Tale* (Chicago: University of Chicago Press, 2003), 15, 31, 111–112.

32. For "good" versus "bad" letters, see Burt L. Standish, "Frank Merriwell in Training; or, the Mystery of the Midnight Prowler," *Tip Top Weekly*, January 22, 1898; Burt L. Standish, "Frank Merriwell's Bosom Friend; or, Making up the Yale Nine," *Tip Top Weekly*, April 13, 1901. Five weeks after the Indianapolis club's letter appeared, "Applause" featured a missive from a female fan chastising the rough treatment they handed their comrade. The editors who answered questions in "Applause" responded by commenting, "[the boys took] heroic measures to punish their offending colleague . . . [but] after all, boys will be boys . . . they are all good friends again; at least we will hope so." Burt L. Standish, "Frank Merriwell's Eyes; or, Saving an Enemy," *Tip Top Weekly*, May 18, 1901.

33. Burt L. Standish, "Frank Merriwell's Great Hit; or, Fighting the Play Pirates," *Tip Top Weekly*, March 25, 1899, 35.

34. Burt L. Standish, "Frank Merriwell's Find; or, the Waif on the Train," *Tip Top Weekly*, March 13, 1897, 31.

35. Burt L. Standish, "Dick Merriwell's Rival; or, Fardale against Farnham Hall," *Tip Top Weekly*, April 21, 1906, 28.

36. Period commentators and later observers referred to dime novels in general as "yellow backed" because the paper publishers used for the covers and interiors was not white (in fact, it was salmon-colored), which spoke to their cheapness. "Blood and thunder" spoke to characterizations of their supposedly violent and overly melodramatic

tones, which were seen as dangerous, in particular to young readers. It is important to note that such designations represent artificial differences that lament the passing of a supposedly idyllic American literature or to legitimize new dime novels' place on a reader's bookshelf. See, for instance, Denning, *Mechanic Accents*, 15–16.

37. Burt L. Standish, "Dick Merriwell at Fardale; or, the Wonder of the School," 27. For praise of *Tip Top* in this vein, see Burt L. Standish, "Frank Merriwell's Club; or, Indoor Baseball in Baltimore"; Burt L. Standish, "Frank Merriwell's Trick; or, His Battle with Himself," *Tip Top Weekly*, June 15, 1901, 254, 270, 495.

38. Burt L. Standish, "Frank Merriwell Stranded; or, the Fate of the First Venture," *Tip Top Weekly*, November 12, 1898, 29.

39. Burt L. Standish, "Frank Merriwell's Great Hit; or, Fighting the Play Pirates," 34, Burt L. Standish, "Frank Merriwell's First Part; or, the Start as an Actor," 36; Burt L. Standish, "Frank Merriwell's 'Brassie' Shot; or, Inza's Difficult Hazard," *Tip Top Weekly*, December 8, 1900, 28.

40. Burt L. Standish, "Frank Merriwell's Judgment; or, the Man Who Won," *Tip Top Weekly*, June 1, 1901, 28.

41. Burt L. Standish, "Frank Merriwell's Athletic Field; or, The Great Meet at Bloomfield," *Tip Top Weekly*, May 12, 1906, 29.

42. Burt L. Standish, "Frank Merriwell's First Part; or, the Start as an Actor," 30.

43. Judy Hilkey, *Character Is Capital: Success Manuals and Manhood in Gilded Age America* (Chapel Hill: University of North Carolina Press, 1997). See also Kelly, *"Mother Was a Lady,"* 76. On whiteness, see Matthew Frye Jacobson, *Whiteness of a Different Color: European Immigrants and the Alchemy of Race* (Cambridge, MA: Harvard University Press, 1998); David R. Roediger, *The Wages of Whiteness: Race and the Making of the American Working Class* (New York: Verso, 1991); Alexander Saxton, *The Rise and Fall of the White Republic: Class Politics and Mass Culture in Nineteenth-Century America* (New York: Verso, 1990). For the appropriation of Darwin's theories in claiming violence lay at the heart of the American male, see David Pettegrew, *Brutes in Suits: Male Sensibility in America, 1890–1920* (Baltimore: Johns Hopkins University Press, 2007), 1–20.

44. Burt L. Standish, "Frank Merriwell's Great Hit; or, Fighting the Play Pirates," 35.

45. Burt L. Standish, "Frank Merriwell's Defenders; or, the Strategy of Old Joe Crowfoot," 27.

46. Burt L. Standish, "Frank Merriwell in Advance; or, Adventures Ahead of the Show," *Tip Top Weekly*, October 22, 1898, 31.

47. Burt L. Standish, "Frank Merriwell's Failure; or, High Hopes and Hard Luck," *Tip Top Weekly*, February 4, 1899, 29.

48. Jennifer Phegley, *Educating the Proper Woman Reader: Victorian Family Literary Magazines and the Cultural Health of the Nation* (Columbus: Ohio State University Press, 2004), 24–28. See also Ellen Gruber Garvey, *The Adman in the Parlor: Magazines and the Gendering of Consumer Culture, 1880s to 1910s* (New York: Oxford University Press, 1996), 80–105; Jennifer Scanlon, *Inarticulate Longings: The Ladies Home Journal, Gender, and the Promises of Consumer Culture* (New York: Routledge, 1995), 137–168; Lynne Vallone, "Introduction," in *The Girl's Own: Cultural Histories of the Anglo-American Girl, 1830–1915*, ed. Claudia Nelson and Lynne Vallone (Athens: University of Georgia Press, 1994), 3–6.

49. Burt L. Standish, "Frank Merriwell's Texas Tournament; or, Sport among the Cowboys," *Tip Top Weekly*, August 14, 1897, 32.

50. Burt L. Standish, "Frank Merriwell on the Trail; or, from Phoenix to Peaceful Pocket," *Tip Top Weekly*, January 9, 1904, 28.

51. Burt L. Standish, "Frank Merriwell's New Idea; or, the American School of Athletic Development," *Tip Top Weekly*, February 3, 1906, 5.

52. Ibid.

53. Ibid., 5–6.

54. Once the house realized that their audience was pulling them in three ways—between middle-class boys, working boys, and girls—they tried creating a title for each group. *Comrades* emerged for working boys and featured blue-collar Merriwell stories, and *My Queen* gave girls all the romance they could handle.

55. Burt L. Standish, "Frank Merriwell's Eyes; or, Saving an Enemy," *Tip Top Weekly*, May 18, 1901, 32.

56. Burt L. Standish, "Dick Merriwell at Fardale; or, the Wonder of the School," 27.

57. Burt L. Standish, "Frank Merriwell's New Idea; or, the American School of Athletic Development," 1–3.

58. Ibid., 5.

59. Angus and Mirel, *Failed Promise of the American High School*, 3–4, 6–7; Cremin, *Transformation of the School*, 88–89, 122; Labaree, *Making of an American High School*, 152–159; Reese, *America's Public Schools*, 190; Tyack, *One Best System*, 189–191.

60. Angus and Mirel, *Failed Promise of the American High School*, 42, 50, 54; Labaree, *Making of an American High School*, 161; Reese, *America's Public Schools*, 193, 197; Tyack, *One Best System*, 198–216, 234–235, 237, 241.

Printed Presence

Twentieth-Century Catholic Print Culture or Youngsters in the United States

ROBERT A. ORSI

*P*RINT CULTURE SEEMS AN ODD RUBRIC for approaching anything having to do with the modern Catholic veneration of Mary and the saints because it was the destruction of images of these figures in the sixteenth and seventeenth centuries that helped usher in the age of print in the first place. Protestant reformers directed Christian attention away from the crowded sensory world of Catholic sacred space to scripture's pages; here in textual form, Protestants could read the narrative of salvation for themselves, in their own languages. Rome has often been wary of print and the control of words and texts has been fundamental to the authority of the Vatican bureaucracy. But in the twentieth century, one of the signs of the church's coming of age in the modern world with the Second Vatican Council (as many at the time saw it) and of the emergence of a new modern laity was the sudden eruption of print in devotional spaces. Where images of the saints once stood now hung banners with words sewn onto them: "PAX!" "REJOICE!" The documents of the Council and then the text of the Mass were translated into all the languages of the modern church (though discussions at the Council itself were in Latin). The American artist who best expressed the ebullient spirit of this transitional moment in Catholic history was Sister Corita Kent, who painted the inspiring words of

religious and political leaders on paper in bright and vibrant colors. As in the
sixteenth century, print was effacing or subsuming the devotional.[1]

An Incarnational Modernity

Printed things do not work the same way in every culture, and the term "reading" or even "looking" does not exhaust what can be done with print. These
historical commonplaces can be illustrated by the example of a common
printed thing in modern Catholic culture: a holy card (also called prayer card)
specifying that if the prayer printed on it is said a certain number of times a day
over a certain period, the person praying will be granted a special request.
Children held these cards while saying the printed prayer and were thus in
touch with the figures printed on them. The child anticipated the result of the
prayer (and so lived in a particular construal of time), clarified his or her deep-
est desires (so that the card got caught up in the child's subjectivity), and looked
at the card for reassurance about the promise. This use of holy cards indicated
a charged engagement of child and print. Modern Catholic children did not
simply read or look at the varieties of printed material available to them. With
these printed objects they *participated* in their world, they did things for and to
themselves. Through print they entered into and experienced the world as the
world was said really to be, and their experience of the world was embodied
and enacted in print.

   Before turning to Catholic children's print culture, it is necessary to say
something about Catholic children's world. According to Jesuit father Walter
Ong, the modern world is characterized by *disincarnation* and by the replace-
ment of dialogic, interpersonal, and experiential ways of knowing with printed
communication. Although Ong's distinction is too sharply drawn, disincarnation names a dimension of modernity that has been policed as normative since
the seventeenth century. Experiences of presence in things or at certain places
on the landscape—in grottoes, on hillsides, and so on—are routinely ridiculed,
recast as pathological or delusional, or dismissed as the province of premodern
outsiders within, or visitors to, modernity. The "thing-ness" of religion, its materiality, is denigrated in the modern era in favor of disembodied "spiritual"
idioms.[2]

   But Roman Catholicism is an embodied and material faith, most
obviously—even antagonistically—so in the modern era. Mary was believed to
have really appeared to youngsters around the world in the nineteenth and
twentieth centuries (and specifically to a boy named Joseph Vitolo in the Bronx
on October 29, 1945). In their devotional practices, Catholics spoke to images
and statues of the saints, pleaded with them, and reprimanded them. Catholics
understood the saints as being both really there in the representations of them
and not there; presence in one venue (*this* statue or place) did not exclude

presence elsewhere. Things, not printed texts or words, provided access to the sacred. Even today, after the profound reorientation of the Catholic imagination by the Second Vatican Council, Catholic statues weep tears of salt and blood, they move, and they incline their heads to petitioners. Jesus and Mary appear to their devout, most recently on the side of a Florida office building, in the bark of a Chicago neighborhood tree, and on a burnt tortilla in New Mexico in 1977. Following Ong, this Catholic way of being in the world could be called "incarnated." Or it could be called "transubstantiational," referring to practices that turn ordinary events and objects into occasions of presence. (An early modern example of a transubstantiational event is the sacramental violence by Catholics against Huguenots; more recent is the famous 1968 protest against the Vietnam War by the Catholic group that came to be known as Catonsville Nine). Anthropologist Stanley Tambiah, writing about the intersection of ways of being in the modern world, suggests "participatory" for the range of phenomena and experience I am calling transubstantiational or incarnational. Whatever the word, the point here is that Catholic modernity included the incarnated supernatural and experiences of real presences.[3]

So Catholics have and have not lived in the modern world. Scholars of modern Catholic culture and history must search for theoretical terms to explicate our subject that are not completely congruent with or exhausted by reigning modern theoretical nomenclature, including terms that are the antitheses of modern ways of thinking and seeing. Because Catholic religious practices and imaginings are often at odds with modernity's limits and boundaries, modern theoretical vocabularies effectively delegitimate and penalize Catholic ways of being in and imagining the world. This is especially so for Catholic experiences of presence in devotional practice—the presence of the saints, the angels, and the Virgin Mary amid the routines of everyday life and the idioms associated with them (for example, holy water, candles, and statues). The genealogies of modern theoretical vocabularies in Anglo-American and Northern European contexts, including—or especially—the language of *Religionswissenschaft* (the critical, comparative study of religion and religions), reach back to an anti-Catholic intellectual past. Modernity was defined initially and then implicitly as "not Catholic." That things instantiate presence, that the material and supernatural worlds interpenetrate and are accessible to each other, that the words of a prayer or ritual are materially efficacious, or that objects associated with heavenly figures make those figures really, not symbolically, present—all this is profoundly anomalous in the modern world. Therefore, scholars of Catholic culture must find words that blur the sharp distinction between the modern and premodern. Recognizing that contemporary people embody features associated with both, they must develop a historiography that does not organize premodern/modern in a normative universal sequence. Scholars of Catholic experience need to invent a terminology for practice and intention that is not encapsulated by modern notions of causality, to discover ways of understanding the social world (and on the workings of the imagination) not premised on a stable distinction between subject and object.[4]

It is as difficult to conceptualize and write Catholic history in modern theoretical language, especially its devotional dimensions, as it is to do subaltern history. Like subaltern history, the study of Catholic idioms in the modern world (including print idioms) teaches us that "historical time is not integral," as historian Dipesh Chakrabarty writes of subaltern historiography, that the human is not "ontologically singular," that "gods and spirits [are] existentially coeval with the human," and that a modern history that attempts to be all-encompassing is "out of joint with itself."[5]

Print and Presence

One of the most striking instances of the out-of-joint phenomena that Chakrabarty refers to is the interplay of print and presence in modern Catholic culture. Modern Catholics have treated printed things as media of presence, even though (or perhaps because) the presumed antithesis of print and presence has been basic to modern culture. Catholics did so most insistently with printed things for children because it was considered especially important for children to be properly formed in the Catholic ethos of presence. *Formation* is the rich Catholic word for the work of shaping and disciplining children's minds, hearts, and bodies in the traditions of the faith. Catholics who did and did not live in the modern world (who lived at an angle askew to the modern world) did and did not want to form their children in relation to its expectations and limits. Children were taught that the Host was really Jesus' body and blood and that Jesus really lived in the tabernacle. The story of a youngster who sneaks into church to set a plate of cookies on the altar beside the tabernacle for Jesus was a widespread tale in mid-twentieth-century United States Catholicism. Tremendous cultural effort was expended to insure that children came to a deeply embodied recognition of the central doctrine of the real presence, which formed the essential boundary between Catholics and non-Catholics. In this world, a holy card was not just a piece of paper with a saint's image printed on it and a missal was more than a manual, just as in this world, especially in the middle years of the twentieth century, Catholic children were prepared for life in modern America—for its workforce, cities, and armies—by the same people who formed them toward presence. This formation toward presence put Catholic children at an odd angle to the modern world for which they were being prepared.[6]

It is to do a kind of historical violence, or at least to risk historical disorientation, to look at print culture and Catholic devotional practice in relation to each other or to treat printed things as devotional media. But it is a risk worth taking because the unexpected alignment of print and devotional practice may be revealing. The uneasiness occasioned by an intersection of print and image is a fundamental feature of Catholic devotional culture in the modern world and of Catholic modernity itself. (It is not too much of a simplification to say that in the 1960s, Catholicism in the United States and elsewhere split into two parties, those who were more oriented in practice and in imagination, who were more comfortable and at home with material devotional culture, on the one side, and those for whom print was more central on the other side. Pope John Paul II bridged the two worlds, but only for a while; in the latter half of his pontificate he had become clearly associated with devotionalism, much to the dismay and suspicion of those more oriented to print, among them his successor).[7] Uneasiness found its way into devotional print, moreover, as Catholics themselves, who after all were living in the modern world, struggled with the incommensurability between devotional idioms and modern ways of being and thinking, and as they contended particularly with the potential hazards of bringing children to devotional practice. The adult religious who were responsible for the religious training of American Catholic children worried intermittently throughout the twentieth century that the print culture intended for youngsters was too graphic, too intense, too demanding. This clash of worlds forces us to question some of the unacknowledged assumptions—and limitations—of the frameworks we use to understand modern history.[8]

Within modern Catholic print culture, the use of printed idioms, the practices associated with them, and the functions and meanings of printed things in relationships between children and adults (both lay and religious adults) were all fundamentally shaped by the orientation of Catholic imaginations to presence. Devotionalism runs as a circulatory system through all of Catholic printed culture, even through print that was not explicitly or primarily devotional. There is a characteristic Catholic dynamic of sacred transference at work in its print culture, just as there are different degrees of holiness and power in relics (a first-class relic comes from the saint's body, a second-class relic is something that touched the saint, while a third-class relic was touched to a first- or second-class relic), so the power of presence most evident in devotional printed matter (which sometimes included relics) touched and inflected other print media in which devotional items appeared or to which devotionalism was proximate. A magazine for boys that juxtaposed a snappy article on sled dogs or baseball with another article on the death of a modern martyr to the faith in Communist Asia and another on the meaning of the Trinity served to bring everything into the imaginative and religious space of the devotional—and thus of the experience of presence.

American Catholic Children

Before cataloging the various forms of midcentury printed idioms for young Catholics (see the following section), there is the question of who these young-sters were. Children growing up Catholic in the United States in the years from 1925 to 1965 were the first American Catholics.[9] Their religious formation was in the hands of increasingly better-prepared adult religious (mostly nuns but priests and brothers too), who were organized into national professional organi-zations during these years to improve religious pedagogy. (There was a general trend toward the formation of national accrediting bodies and bureaucracies in the U.S. church from the 1920s forward.) These religious instructors, who themselves lived dedicated religious lives, held intense spiritual ambitions and high religious expectations for the children in their care. Although Catholic ed-ucational professionals understood children have different needs and capacities at different developmental stages, Catholic culture made no special allowance for children. Children's masses were no different from others. A child who took a sip of water before receiving Holy Communion (thus breaking the require-ment of fasting from midnight) had committed a mortal sin and was at the same risk of eternal damnation as a murderer. (To prevent this grim outcome, some Catholic parents made it a practice to cover the faucets at home the night before Mass and Communion to avoid sleepy mishaps, and children practiced brushing their teeth without swallowing.) Children were expected at least to have memorized the intricate and difficult terminology of scholastic theology, enough to be quizzed on it.

Although not all Catholic children attended parochial schools, a large per-centage did, varying across the country and among different Catholic commu-nities at different times, but steadily increasing around World War II and into the 1960s. The country's bishops put tremendous pressure on parish priests to build schools and on parents to send their children to them. For the others there was religion class on the weekends in their parishes, in vacation schools, or in released time periods. (The national office of the Confraternity of Chris-tian Doctrine, CCD, which oversaw religious instruction for children outside the parochial school system, was established in Washington, D.C., in 1933. By 1943 this organization was at work in 107 dioceses across the country.) The ele-mentary school years were marked by focused sacramental education as chil-dren prepared to go to confession for the first time and to make their first Holy Communion (around ages 6–8) and then to be confirmed (between 8–13). It was between these ages, six to thirteen, that children were most likely to attend Mass regularly.[10] Children were taught the faith in English in this period, even in communities of more recent migrants and immigrants. While most Catho-lics belonged to working-class households, the trajectory of American Catholi-cism over the century was toward the middle class. This included a slow but steady migration out of urban neighborhoods to suburbs, especially after World War II.

To take a sounding of Catholic developmental expectations midway through the years of my study, in a 1946 article in the *Journal of Religious Instruction* (a leading periodical for Catholic religious educators), Benedictine Sister Mary Jane of Mount Saint Scholastica in Atchison, Kansas, asserted that by ages ten to eleven children should be capable of following the (Latin) Mass in their missals. By this she meant that children could read along in the English translation of the Latin Mass, printed side by side, and understand the meaning of what was happening on the altar, specifically the celebrant's many gestures and movements. This would not have been expected a decade earlier, and it would become unexceptional a decade later. Sister Mary Jane also noted that by ages twelve to thirteen, children were likely to reject the Mass as being just for little kids. Religious adults complained throughout the century about this rejection of the Mass among older children, reflecting in part the fact that many fewer children went to Catholic high schools than parochial elementary schools. Indeed, the high school years marked a break between when children were within the reach of adult religious authority and instruction and when they were not, when they were most compliant (in the minds of adults) and when they were most rebellious (again in the minds of adults).[11]

Each age group provoked anxiety. Adult religious were afraid that toddlers were not being adequately prepared at home for their religious duties; that children were memorizing their catechism lessons and the mechanics of the sacraments but failing to come to a deep love of God and neighbor; and that teenagers were forgetting everything they had learned and falling away from the faith. These fears circulate through the print culture for Catholic children in the mid-twentieth century and gave it some of its urgency and even its ferocity.

Mid-Twentieth-Century Print Culture
for American Catholic Children

The world of Catholic print for youngsters can be divided into four major categories: (1) *devotional works* that encouraged prayer and piety among children and introduced them to stories of saints and martyrs, including little theatrical sketches written by nuns; (2) *sacramental guides*, or printed material to help children receive the sacraments appropriately, including the Mass; (3) *popular periodicals* written in a lively American style, replete with typical boy and girl stories and including guides to comportment, style, and manners in public, at school, and in church; and (4) *certificates and commemorations*. These are not discrete categories. Popular periodicals, for instance, almost always included a devotional item or sacramental instruction, and devotional works were offered as sacramental gifts and commemorations. But the broad categories are useful, if only to understand that the interplay among these different categories reflected and contributed to powerful contradictions and tensions in Catholic print culture, opening a space for children's own imaginative and ethical work.

Printed materials for Catholic children took an extraordinary variety of forms, each of which embodied the contradictions of materiality and modernity for children learning a Catholic approach to presence. What follows is a long, but still incomplete, list of items included in mid-twentieth century print culture for Catholic youngsters: (1) prayer books, holy cards, and pamphlets for all ages and for specific occasions, such as novenas, devotions, and holy days; (2) coloring books and picture books with strong devotional and moral content—children could color images of guardian angels, saints, and martyrs, for example, or scenes from the life of the Holy Family, the parts of the Mass, or illustrations of grave moral dilemmas (in the *Angel and Imp at Home Paint Book*, for instance, Jesuit Daniel A. Lord, the most prolific writer and publisher of literature for all age groups under the imprint of his Queen's Work Press in Saint Louis, drew a little girl obediently getting out of bed at her mother's call, her guardian angel sitting approvingly on her bedpost, with the caption: "Says Angel: 'Hop right out of bed; / Get face all washed and prayers all said. / But if you go to Mass, sweet daughter; / Don't break your fast and drink that water.'"); (3) comic book lives of the saints (these tales of ancient or contemporary martyrs and miracle-working holy figures could be almost as thrilling as the secular comics Catholic educators so roundly condemned); (4) children's magazines founded in the twentieth century, such as the *Junior Catholic Messenger*, that combined stories of the saints, descriptions of scenes from the life of Christ, explanations of the Mass, tales of heroic adventurer priests and nuns, exciting stories about far-flung Catholic missions, cowboy yarns, tips for playing sports, animal stories, breathless accounts of new technological and scientific achievements, and, during the war, tales of patriotism and American history, especially the Catholic contribution to American history; and (5) books written specifically for different ages in a style that adults thought children would find attractive, commonly involving lively and popular young priests and nuns as main characters or else gangs of misguided boys and girls, most of whom ultimately learn how to do the right thing, although one of them inevitably dies violently.

The list of items continues with (6) holy cards of Jesus, Mary and the saints; (7) missals, in English and Latin, some with descriptions and little drawings (in red) of what the priest was doing at different times in the Mass and different places on the altar; (8) scapulars (small paper images of holy figures affixed to pieces of felt and worn around the neck); (9) funeral cards distributed at wakes (an image of a saint or of Jesus on the front, a picture of the deceased and a short prayer on the back); (10) picture books about the Mass; (11) the Baltimore Catechism (which was significantly revised in 1941 in its presentations of doctrine

A 1950 comic book depiction of the life of Saint Tarcisius, one of the patron saints of altar boys. ("Saint Tarcisius: Boy Marty of the Eucharist," *The Treasure Chest of Fun and Fact*, 1950. The American Catholic History Research Center and University Archives, the Catholic University of America, Washington, D.C., p. 3)

and ritual to bring it up to date for contemporary children and then issued in
an illustrated version several years later); (11a) other catechisms, in the earlier
years printed in the languages of various immigrant communities and understood as a way of preserving those languages among the young; (12) illustrated
books of Bible stories heavily oriented to the New Testament; (13) workbooks
for teachers with instructions for drawing stick figures to illustrate doctrine and
morals for children; (14) books of Western art depicting scenes from the lives of
Jesus, Mary, and the saints (these were more common before World War II;
among the "pictures" that Catholic children should be familiar with, according
to a prominent Chicago educator in 1931, were Murrilo's "Divine Shepherd,"
DaVinci's "Last Supper," and Doré's "Marriage at Cana," "John the Baptist
Preaching in the Wilderness," and "Jesus Preaching to the Multitude"). Also
among the printed materials for Catholic children were (15) small "vacation
guides" with advice for how to spend the summers in a good Catholic way; (16)
elaborate, colorful certificates offered by the Pontifical Association of the Holy
Childhood documenting American children's adoption, baptism, and support
of their counterparts in Asian, South American, and African mission fields—
the famous "pagan babies"; (17) flash cards printed with the words of prayers or
of the responses to the Mass, in English or Latin; (18) guides to confession to
help children examine their consciences, with numbered questions corresponding to the various commandments; (19) lives of the saints in many different forms for various ages, from picture books for babies to book-length stories
for adolescents, and including comic books; (19a) comic book accounts of
saintly contemporary young people, in the United States and Europe, such as
the Italian martyr Maria Goretti or Jane Bernadette McClory, an Illinois farm
girl who promoted devotion to the Sacred Heart of Jesus; (20) large colorful
certificates commemorating First Communion (this was more common before
World War II); (21) cutout books of, for example, the stable in Bethlehem, cutout priests to be dressed in cutout vestments and then moved around cutout altars, and in one case, a cutout Roman Coliseum complete with little cutout
Christians and wild animals, this last published by the inexhaustible Daniel
Lord; (22) purity guides for teenagers; (23) manuals and periodicals to teach up-
to-date middle-class manners and expectations to teenagers; (24) Catholic high
school yearbooks; (25) dramas, usually written by nuns, most often about either
some incident in the life of a saint or a moral crisis in the life of a Catholic boy
or girl and intended to be performed by boys and girls in Catholic schools or
CCD classes.[12]

I also want to identify a category I will call *unprinted print culture:* this com-
prises children's own copying of prayers and catechetical lessons, petitions to
the saints, children's letters to real or imaginary figures in the Catholic world,
and so on. These were printed materials that children were encouraged to
write, keep, and share with others. Unprinted print culture clearly built on

Cutout book *These Are Our Martyrs* by Daniel Lord. (images courtesy of Midwest Jesuit Archives, St. Louis, MO)

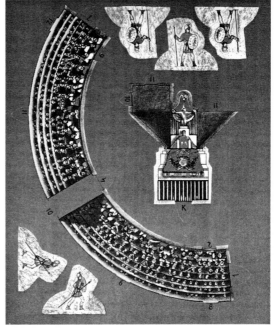

printed matter and was another way for children to bring themselves intimately into a relationship with print, and by the practices of writing and copying, a relationship with the sacred and with their world was created. A common gift for clergy on anniversaries (of their ordination, for example) was a "bouquet of prayers," texts written out and signed by all the children in the parish's school. Catholic Girl Scouts who won the coveted "Marian Award" were responsible for assembling an ambitious "notebook" of prayers, lives of the saints, poems, local Catholic lore, almost all written out laboriously in neat and careful penmanship.[13]

What Catholic Children Did with Printed Things

Printed things were used in various out-of-joint ways by Catholic adults and children and in their relations with each other. Printed things served as conduits of intimacy between children and sacred figures. By interacting with printed things—stories and images of the saints, coloring books of sacred figures—a powerful immediacy was brought to children's experience of the supernatural. Parents were urged by religion writers to put holy cards on the walls near their infants' cribs, to invite their babies to "kiss the piggies" (as one children's author put it in 1958) of the saints on the holy cards. Little children were given holy cards to play with and hold onto. Nuns and priests encouraged children to put themselves within the frame of the images and stories, to imagine playing with the Baby Jesus, for instance, or standing beside Mary on Calvary. The ubiquitous imagery of angels gave form to these invisible beings so that children would come to know their presence. Under the dual inspiration of their Catholicism and the modern educational theories they explicitly rejected but implicitly adopted (about imaginative and tactile learning and play-centered education), Catholic religion teachers emphasized the necessity of appealing to children's emotions and imaginations—as well as their visual and tactile senses—in their religious preparation. Without these printed things, they feared that children would not learn deeply enough and would not become good Catholics. Print was central to this strategy. Printed things drew children closer to the supernatural as it made the sacred proximate to the everyday.[14]

Printed matter associated with the Mass—missals, picture books, cutout and coloring books to teach children the parts of the Mass, and so on—also served as media of intimacy and immediacy. The mid-century Mass was a distant and obscure performance for children (and for adults too). The priest stood way up on the altar in the front of the church with his back to the congregation and murmured the Eucharistic prayers in Latin as he performed a series of complicated movements mostly out of sight of the congregation. The various Mass books were intended to bring the distant liturgy closer, if only to discipline children's restless bodies and minds, but also to enable them to decipher the priest's movements and—if they were especially motivated—to whisper the congregational responses along with the altar boys.

Printed things were incorporated into the networks of association, indebtedness, and commitment that governed the social life of Catholic neighborhoods and parishes. They became embodiments and markers of bonds not only between children and adults but among adults as well, in the medium of children. Nuns rewarded academic achievement or piety by giving children holy cards. Godparents, whose choice was itself often a delicate matter in a family or neighborhood, gave their godchildren prayer books or missals, covered in thick white cloth and embossed with a medal or cross, to celebrate sacramental occasions. Catholics cherished these books throughout their lives. Indeed, the printed matter of mid-twentieth-century Catholicism endures today as powerful media of memory, making present people and events long gone. Missals functioned as a storage place for these holy cards, so that one printed thing—the missal—stuffed thickly with other printed things—the holy cards—became a material expression of a child's environment in the present and in the past.

Finally, Catholic moral teaching was presented to and performed or enacted for children in various print forms, including picture books, confessional aids, and manuals of purity. In *My Jesus and I,* for instance, by the Most Reverend Louis Lavavoire Morrow (who was the Bishop of Krishnagar in West Bengal, India) and published in 1949 in Kenosha, Wisconsin (which gives a sense of the international circulation of Catholic children's printed materials), graphic images show (among other things) bad and good angels struggling over children, good children who have sinned running to Mary, who takes them in her arms, and a child brought by her angel to kiss the feet of Jesus on the cross. These works of ethical instruction made visible the hidden realities and dynamics of Catholic cosmology with all its powerful ethical implications. Images of good and bad angels fighting over a child did not simply endorse virtue. They taught children that the moral life was literally caught up in a grand cosmic struggle that got played out each time they faced a choice. Children's own deaths were often evoked in this literature in a direct way to inspire virtue (though this practice waned in the 1950s and 1960s). Later, as children matured, ethical instruction would become more narrowly verbal, but in the background of older children's moral imaginations were these pictures of warring cosmic powers, wounded holy figures, and the reality of death.[15]

The Historical Challenge of Catholic Modernity

The question at the end now is this: What if we take the interplay of print and presence in Catholic modernity not as the doomed survival of premodern idioms but as a historiographical possibility for modern religious print cultures generally? Perhaps presence has never been quite completely exiled from print.

Perhaps presence continually reasserts itself despite ongoing efforts to expel it. Children lean over to kiss images of favorite figures in books; at night they want to pray for these figures whom they know from printed images or three dimensional representations. How are we trained to stop experiencing this presence-in-print intimacy as we get older? The historical lesson of Catholic modernity may be that modernity in the West may be better characterized by the constant struggle against presence in print (and everywhere else) rather than by its absence, not by "disincarnation" but by the denial of the ubiquity of incarnation. Social commentators work hard to bind the evidence of presence in print with a disciplinary and exclusionary nomenclature that brands those who encounter presence in print as "fundamentalist" or—its most recent version—"religious terrorists." These figures so marked never represent the real, authentic modern version of their respective faiths, we are told. It is as if by these terms, anxious (nonincarnational) moderns may push presence to the margins of the modern world and quarantine it. But what do we fail to understand about our world by this determination to deny the presence in print and the uses to which it is put? What are we afraid of?[16]

A Short Bibliographical Note

Readers interested more generally in the interplay of popular culture and religions in modern American consumer culture might consult the following works. Colin Campbell, *The Romantic Ethic and the Spirit of Modern Consumerism* (Oxford and New York: Basil Blackwell, 1987), establishes a broad historical frame for the subject. A provocative overview of the American context is R. Laurence Moore, *Selling God: American Religion in the Marketplace of Culture* (New York: Oxford University Press, 1994). David Morgan offers an excellent theoretical introduction to religious visual culture in *The Sacred Gaze: Religious Visual Culture in Theory and Practice* (Berkeley: University of California Press, 2005). See also Morgan's edited collection of articles on the artist responsible for the most popular images of Jesus in the modern world, *Icons of American Protestantism: The Art of Warner Sallman* (New Haven, CT: Yale University Press, 1996).

Long neglected as a topic of serious scholarly investigation, the various celebrations, media, practices, and markets of American popular religion became the focus of a number of excellent studies in religious studies and American religious history in the past decade, including Colleen McDannell, *Material Christianity: Religion and Popular Culture in America* (New Haven, CT: Yale University Press, 1995); Leigh Eric Schmidt, *Consumer Rites: The Buying and Selling of American Holidays* (Princeton, NJ: Princeton University Press, 1995); David Morgan, *Protestants and Pictures: Religion, Visual Culture, and the Age of Mass Production* (New York: Oxford University Press, 1999); Bruce Forbes and Jeffrey M. Mahan, eds., *Religion and Popular Culture in America* (Berkeley: University of California Press, 1999);

Daniel Sacks, *Whitebread Protestants: Food and Religion in American Culture* (New York: St. Martin's Press, 2000); and David Chidester, *Authentic Fakes: Religion and American Popular Culture* (Berkeley: University of California Press, 2005). The Bible as artifact of consumption is the subject of Peter J. Wosh, *Spreading the Word: The Bible Business in Nineteenth Century America* (Ithaca, NY: Cornell University Press, 1994). A great study of popular religion in Puritan New England is David D. Hall, *Worlds of Wonder, Days of Judgment: Popular Religious Belief in Early New England* (New York: Knopf, 1989). Hall's edited volume *Lived Religion in America* (Princeton, NJ: Princeton University Press, 1997) played a major role in stimulating subsequent research on popular American religious idioms and media. On the colonial context, see Jon Butler, *Awash in a Sea of Faith: Christianizing the American People* (Cambridge, MA: Harvard University Press, 1990).

Regional popular religious practices have begun to receive scholarly attention again (an earlier generation of American folklorists studied these cultures in the middle years of the twentieth century, but this scholarship seems to have had little impact on historians of American religion, unfortunately). The rich world of Southwestern Catholic material culture is the subject of a number of excellent volumes, including Elizabeth Netto Calil Zarur and Charles Muir Lovell, *Art and Faith in Mexico: The Nineteenth-Century Retablo Tradition* (Albuquerque: University of New Mexico Press, 2001); Eileen Oktavec, *Answered Prayers: Miracles and Milagros along the Border* (Tucson: University of Arizona Press, 1995); and Kay Turner, *Beautiful Necessity: The Art and Meaning of Women's Altars* (London: Thames and Hudson, 1999). An excellent discussion of what happens when regional boosters who are also conservative evangelical Christians get to dreaming of a Vegas-style sacred playground is Aaron K. Ketchell, *Holy Hills of the Ozarks: Religion and Tourism in Branson, Missouri* (Baltimore: Johns Hopkins University Press, 2007). Indiana Christian bikers are the subject of Richard Remsberg, *Riders for God: The Story of a Christian Motorcycle Gang* (Champaign-Urbana: University of Illinois Press, 2000). The world of Southern and Southwestern Pentecostal healing idioms, which included an array of printed and visual media, is described in David Edwin Harrell, Jr., *All Things Are Possible: The Healing and Charismatic Revivals in Modern America* (Bloomington: Indiana University Press, 1975).

The role of popular religion in making modern American Judaism, including an extensive literature for children and teenagers, receives ebullient treatment in Jeanna Weissman Joselit, *The Wonders of America: Reinventing Jewish Culture, 1880–1950* (New York: H. Holt, 2002); see also Jack Kugelmass, ed., *Jews, Sports, and the Rites of Citizenship* (Champaign-Urbana: University of Illinois Press, 2007). The interplay of religious and secular popular idioms has been a consistent, at times explosive, feature of African American religious history and historiography. Recent studies include Jerma A. Jackson, *Singing in My Soul: Black Gospel Music in a Secular Age* (Chapel Hill: University of North Carolina

Press, 2003); Gayle F. Wald, *Shout, Sister, Shout! The Untold Story of Rock-and-Roll Trailblazer Sister Rosetta Tharpe* (Boston: Beacon Press, 2007); Yvonne Patricia Chireau, *Black Magic: Religion and the African American Conjuring Tradition* (Berkeley: University of California Press, 2003); and, most recently, the groundbreaking work by Judith Weisenfeld, *Hollywood Be Thy Name: African American Religion in American Film, 1929–1949* (Berkeley: University of California Press, 2007). A superb study of how African religious idioms became popular forms in the diaspora is David H. Brown, *Santería Enthroned: Art, Ritual, and Innovation in an Afro-Cuban Religion* (Chicago: University of Chicago Press, 2003).

One of the most important recent phenomena of religious print culture in the United States is the vastly popular "Left Behind" series, a sequence of novels by Jerry Jenkins and Timothy LaHaye depicting the exciting events of the Rapture in prose that huge numbers of conservative Christian readers find exciting (perhaps because they anticipate that they will be among the raptured). Good recent discussions of this religious culture include Amy Johnson Frykholm, *Rapture Culture: Left Behind in Evangelical America* (New York: Oxford University Press, 2004); Bruce Forbes and Jeanne Halgren Kilde, eds., *Rapture, Revelation, and the End Times: Exploring the Left Behind Series* (New York: Palgrave Macmillan, 2004); and Jason C. Bivins, *Religion of Fear: The Politics of Horror in Conservative Evangelicalism* (New York: Oxford University Press, 2008).

Notes

1. For an interesting study of Vatican anxiety about print see Owen Chadwick, *Catholicism and History: The Opening of the Vatican Archives* (New York: Cambridge University Press, 1978). The connection between the Protestant Reformation and official Roman Catholic print anxiety is fundamental. The Roman Inquisition was established in 1542 by Paul IV (1555–1559), who also promulgated the first papal Index of Forbidden Books in 1559. The task of supervising print fell officially to several Vatican offices, variously organized and named over time, among them the Sacred Congregation of the Inquisition and the Sacred Congregation of the Index (established in 1571). Paul VI abolished the official list of prohibited books in 1966, following the Second Vatican Council (although this did not end Roman efforts to condemn and prohibit to the faithful particular authors and works). Needless to say, Catholics did not have a monopoly on censorship in the modern era. On Corita Kent, see Harvey Cox and Samuel A. Eisenstein, *Sister Corita/Mary Corita Kent* (Philadelphia: Pilgrim Press, 1968); and Joseph Pintauro and Sister Corita, *To Believe in God* (New York: Harper and Row, 1968).

To make the claim I have here about the disjuncture between Catholic and Protestant practice and imagination in the sixteenth and seventeenth centuries does not require an absolute demarcation. Many great historians have taught us within the last few decades how ways of being denoted "Catholic" characterized Protestant experience, among them Bob Scribner, David Morgan, and David Hall. Still, something changed between the Reformation and the Enlightenment that put sacred things and images in a new cultural place vis-à-vis print.

2. By 1530, writes art historian and theorist Samuel Freedberg, "the main lines of the controversy about images that was to torment the whole of Europe for the rest of the century were firmly drawn." *The Power of Images: Studies in the History and Theory of Response* (Chicago: University of Chicago Press, 1989), 385. Walter Ong's work can be approached through *The Presence of the Word: Some Prolegomena for Cultural and Religious History* (New Haven, CT: Yale University Press, 1967); and *Orality and Literacy: The Technologizing of the Word* (London: Methuen, 1982). My interest in Ong was reawakened by Leigh Eric Schmidt, *Hearing Things: Religion, Illusion, and the American Enlightenment* (Cambridge, MA: Harvard University Press, 2000).

3. A useful reflection on popular devotions as a powerfully experienced and maintained border between Catholics and other modern peoples is Joseph Komonchak, "The Enlightenment and the Construction of Roman Catholicism," *CCICA Annual: Publication of the Catholic Commission on Intellectual and Cultural Affairs* (South Bend, IN: University of Notre Dame Press, 1985), 31–59. On the Bronx apparitions see John T. McGreevy, "Bronx Miracle," *American Quarterly* 52, no. 3 (September 2000), 405–443. I discuss contemporary popular devotions among U.S. Catholics in Robert A. Orsi, *Between Heaven and Earth: The Religious Worlds People Make and the Scholars Who Study Them* (Princeton, NJ: Princeton University Press, 2005). Elaine Peña has researched the Rogers Park apparition; see Elaine A. Peña, "La Virgen de Guadalupe as Apparition and Illegal Alien: Performances of Spirituality and Migratory Histories," http://www .hemi.nyu.edu/eng/seminar/usa/workgroups/theoriesapparition/Papers/paper _elaine_pena.dwt (accessed September 10, 2009). On the "incarnated" aspects of anti-Huguenot violence, I read Mack P. Holt, *The French Wars of Religion, 1562–1629* (Cambridge, UK: Cambridge University Press, 1995); and Barbara B. Diefendorf, *Beneath the Cross: Catholics and Huguenots in Sixteenth-Century Paris* (New York: Oxford University Press, 1991). Stanley Tambiah introduces the notion of "participation" in *Magic, Science, Religion and the Scope of Rationality* (Cambridge, UK: Cambridge University Press, 1990), 86–87, 105–110. On the Catonsville protest, see Daniel Berrigan, *The Trial of the Catonsville Nine* (Boston: Beacon Press, 1970); the protest itself can be viewed at "Fire and Faith: The Catonsville Nine File," http://c9.mdch.org/page.cfm?ID=11.

4. On the anti-Catholic grounds of modern religious scholarship see, for example, Jonathan Z. Smith, *Drudgery Divine: On the Comparison of Early Christianities and the Religions of Late Antiquity* (Chicago: University of Chicago Press, 1990). For an irritating but provocative discussion of the implication of religious theorizing in the project of Western modernity see Daniel Dubuisson, *The Western Construction of Religion*, trans. William Sayers (Baltimore: Johns Hopkins University Press, 2003).

5. Dipesh Chakrabarty, *Provincializing Europe: Postcolonial Thought and Historical Difference* (Princeton, NJ: Princeton University Press, 2000), 16.

6. For a longer discussion of the disciplining of children to the presence in the Communion Host see Orsi, *Between Heaven and Earth*, in particular chapter 3. On teaching children that Jesus *really* lived in the tabernacle and was lonely without them, see Julia Kratovila, "Teaching Children to Pray," *Catholic School Journal* 36 (October 1936), 275–276. "Our ultimate purpose," writes Kratovila, "is friendship with God, communion with the Unseen" (276). Also Henry P. Sullivan, "Instructing Little Children," *Journal of Religious Instruction* 7 (January 1937), 406–410. Baby Jesus "lives in the tabernacle," Sullivan tells children (408).

7. One consequence of this was the clamor for his immediate canonization at his funeral, *Santo Subito!*, which can be translated as "A Saint Right Away!" or "Canonize Him Now!"

8. Examples of this uneasiness are M. V. Kelly, "A Question That Is Never Answered," *Homiletic and Pastoral Review* 31 (May 1931), 874–875; and A School Sister of Notre Dame, "Consider the Lives of the Saints," *Journal of Religious Instruction* 5 (November 1934), 206–212.

9. Charles Morris says the term "American Catholic Church" has real meaning only after World War I, although for Morris this carries the additional connotation of an "emotional withdrawal" of Catholics from secular American life after Al Smith's humiliating defeat. Charles R. Morris, *American Catholics: The Saints and Sinner Who Built America's Most Powerful Church* (New York: Times Books, 1997), 133, 160. I see an ongoing deep engagement with secular modernity but on distinctly Catholic terms.

10. My information on the early development of CCD programs is from Francis Walsh, "The Confraternity of Christian Doctrine and the Present Position of Religious Instruction in the U.S.," *Journal of Religious Instruction* 5 (December 1934), 288–296; William A. Scully, "The Present Status of Released Time in New York," *Journal of Religious Instruction* 12 (March 1942), 624–630; and William A. Scully, "Religion Vacation Schools, Yesterday and Today," *Catholic Action* 5 (June 1943), 14–15, 21. On vacation bible schools, see Edgar Schmiedeler, "The Religiously Under-Privileged Child," *The Truth* 37 (January 1933), 26–31; Paul E. Campbell, "Religious Instruction at the Back Door," *Homiletic and Pastoral Review* 42 (October 1942), 40–45; Paul E. Campbell, "The Use of the Religious Vacation School Manuals," *Journal of Religious Instruction* 10 (June 1940), 867–871; Mary Alma, "Vacation Schools," *Ave Maria* 55 (May 16, 1942), 615–619; Mary Alma, "Religion Vacation Schools," *Ave Maria* 56 (July 25, 1942), 98. On the Catholic Rural Life movement, see J. G. Shaw, *Edwin Vincent O'Hara* (New York: Farrar, Straus and Cudahy, 1957).

11. Mary Jane, "The Sixth Grade Learns the Missal," *Journal of Religious Instruction* 17 (November 1946), 295–300.

12. The coloring book cited in the list is Daniel A. Lord, SJ, *Angel and Imp at Home Paint Book* (St. Louis, MO: Queen's Work, n.d.), n.p. On Lord himself, there is a fulsome autobiography, Daniel A. Lord, *Played by Ear* (Chicago: Loyola University Press, 1956). Lord was an early proponent of Hollywood censorship, an expression of a characteristic modern Catholic anxiety about images beyond church control. The same anxiety charged the Catholic condemnation of comic books; see, for example, Harold C. Gardiner, "If Hatred Is Funny, the Comics Will Kill You," *America* 65 (August 16, 1941), 516–517; and Sister Katherine, "Comics Are Crimes against Our Children," *America* 67 (June 6, 1942), 234–235. The American Catholic History Research Center and University Archives at Catholic University, Washington, D.C., provides online access to most issues of the children's comic book *Treasure Chest*, published between 1946 and 1972 by George A. Pflaum, including full color lives of the saints comics; see Treasure Chest of Fun and Fact, http://www.aladin.wrlc.org/gsdl/collect/treasure/treasure.shtml. Pflaum, based in Dayton, Ohio, also published the *Junior Catholic Messenger*, *Our Little Messenger*, and the *Young Catholic Messenger*. The books I have referenced in number (5) in the text include such titles as Martin J. Scott, *A Boy Night* (New York: P. J. Kenedy and Sons, 1921); Thomas B. Chetwood, *Tony* (St. Louis, MO: Queen's Work, 1933); Thomas B. Chetwood, *St. Peggy's Growing Up*

(A Fictional Saint) (St. Louis, MO: Queen's Work, 1940); and Anthony F. LaBau, *Saint Bill of New York* (St. Louis, MO: Queen's Work, 1945). The suggestions for art that children should know come from Daniel P. Cunningham [diocesan superintendent of schools in Chicago], "A Curriculum in Religion: Grade III—The Public Life of Christ," *Catholic School Journal* 31 (February 1931), 48–51 (the list appears on 49). An example of chalk talk literature is Jerome O'Connor and William Hayden, *Chalk Talks or Teaching Catechism Graphically, Part II* (St. Louis, MO: Queen's Work, 1930). Copies of various cutout books published by Lord can be found in the Father Daniel Lord Manuscript Collection, Pius XII Memorial Library, Saint Louis University. (A note of thanks to Jim Fisher for alerting me to this trove.) On prayer flashcards, see Henry P. Sullivan, "Notes on Teaching the 'Our Father' and the 'Hail Mary' to Small Children," *Journal of Religious Instruction* 7 (November 1936), 265–268. An illustrated edition of the Baltimore Catechism, which had been updated and revised in 1941, *A Catechism of Christian Doctrine, The Illustrated Revised Edition of Baltimore Catechism, No. 1*, was published in 1944 by the New York Catholic house of W. H. Sadlier. The second volume offered more complete discussions of doctrine.

13. Professor Patricia Allwin DeLeeuw, Boston College, allowed me to study her Marian Award Notebook prepared in 1963 in Cuyahoga Falls, Ohio.

14. Encouragement to kiss the saints' piggies is from Richard A. Duprey, "Heroes for Children," *Grail* 40 (November 1958), 34–37 (quote on 34). Summing up more than a decade of ambivalence among American Catholic religious educators toward modern pedagogical theories, one educator proposed in 1943, at last, "a prudent Catholic adaptation of progressive methods," which had actually been going on for years. See Gerald Ryan, "Religious Guidance," *Journal of Religious Instruction* 13 (June 1943), 747–757 (quote on 747).

15. Cited in the text is Louis Laravoire, *My Jesus and I* (Kenosha, WI: My Mission House, 1949). The moral use of death in stories for children is ubiquitous; see, for example, Neil Boynton, *It's Not Worth It: An Adventure That Failed* (St. Louis, MO: Queen's Work, 1931), 22–23; Arthur Tonne, *Talks for Children: Sermons to Children for Every Sunday and Feast of Obligation* (Emporia, KS: Didde Printing, 1948), esp. 12, 36. Father Francis Benz, founder of the Knights of the Altar and editor for many years of *Catholic Boy* magazine, put this bluntly for his readers: "To bring the picture nearer you, if this moment you were to die, would you deserve to go straight to heaven?" Francis Benz, "From the Editor's Pen," *Catholic Boy* 6 (November 1938), 7. For a protest against this use of death in children's education, see Kate Dooley, "Nihil Obstat My Righteous Indignation," *Ave Maria* 84 (August 4, 1956), 22. Dooley's wry comment is to the point: "I doubt that most children have enough spiritual perception to be filled with holy joy should they be reminded, every hour on the hour, of the approach of eternity."

16. Perhaps we are afraid of what becomes of print and of what may be done with print when print becomes a vehicle of presence, as it continues to be in the modern world. In a final list of instructions found in Mohamed Atta's luggage, the 9/11 hijackers are told to bless themselves with verses from the Qur'an, which is done (as Bruce Lincoln explains) "by reading verses into one's hands and then rubbing the hands over whatever is to be blessed." Bruce Lincoln, *Holy Terrors: Thinking about Religion after September 11* (Chicago: University of Chicago Press, 2003), 94. The data about children's relationship with imaginary figures in print comes from my son, Anthony, who is two years old, and earlier from my daughter Claire, who is twenty-three.

3

Workers as Readers,
Reading as Work

Unschooled but Not Uneducated

Print, Public Speaking, and the Networks of Informal Working-Class Education, 1900–1940

FRANK TOBIAS HIGBIE

IN THE SUMMER OF 1921 two men in a North Dakota migrant-worker camp struck up an unlikely conversation. The first was University of Wisconsin economist Don Lescohier, who was leading a study of labor relations in the Great Plains wheat harvest for the U.S. Department of Agriculture. The second man was an Irish immigrant harvest worker, lumberjack, and occasional factory worker by the name of "Doyle." Identifying himself as a Bolshevik and a member of the Industrial Workers of the World, Doyle was saving his harvest wages to pay for tuition at the Socialist Party's Rand School in New York. When the revolution came, as he expected it would, he would be prepared. As Lescohier recounted in his field notes, Doyle was "one of the brainiest and most thoroughly read" migrant workers he had met. "I drew him, or rather he drew me, into an economic discussion. This hobo, this bum, this chap *who had never been inside of a school* could quote fluently from Ely" and other economists. "He reads the daily papers and made me ashamed of my own ignorance on several things," Lescohier concluded.[1]

The professor's shock at being intellectually bested by a hobo says a lot about American intellectual life then and now. It is supposed to take years of formal training to master the kind of knowledge Doyle demonstrated, and the physical space of a migrant worker camp is decidedly not the expected venue for a learned debate. Although American culture celebrates self-taught heroes like Ben Franklin, Frederick Douglas, and Abraham Lincoln, there isn't much space in our national story for post-agrarian, working-class intellectuals, let alone self-identified Bolshevik revolutionaries.

So how did Doyle get so brainy? As Jonathan Rose has argued in *The Intellectual Life of the British Working Classes*, the so-called "self-taught" were anything but isolated hermits. The education they acquired outside of school was embedded in networks of other learners, in community and organizational cultures, and in markets for mass-produced texts.[2] Like the British common readers studied by Rose, American working people sought out knowledge despite their lack of schooling. They pieced together their education though personal experience, reading, political organizing, public lectures, and discussions with others. Unfortunately, we know nothing about Doyle beyond this brief encounter documented by Lescohier. Like many other working-class lives, the specific details are lost to us. But while Doyle was notable in his breadth of learning, his was not a singular experience. To understand Doyle's path to self-education we must turn to a collective biography of men and women like him, pulling together snippets of lives to understand workers' engagement with the world of ideas. These documents offer us clues to the varied paths working people took toward education at a time when many left school by age fifteen. We also can look to a broader context of printed materials aimed at working-class audiences, as well as the social and spatial context of workers' reading practices. Although working people often could not afford books, those with a desire for self-education could find a great deal of inexpensive reading matter ranging from daily newspapers to radical propaganda and religious tracts. Utilizing modern printing technology and promotional techniques, publishing entrepreneurs added greatly to the variety of texts within the budget of workers.

A broad approach of this kind does run the risk of loosing sight of how reading and self-education impacted specific people. Historian Christine Pawley has cautioned that a focus on the "imagined communities" created by audiences for particular texts tells us little about what she terms "known readers and the known texts that they read." I am mindful of this problem, but as Erin Smith argues in her study of detective fiction, the lack of information about working-class readers impels us to cast a wide net. In this chapter I employ a hybrid of methodologies to understand Doyle and his cohort. Like Pawley, Smith, and others, I am particularly interested in the social practices and the contexts of reading and self-education.[3] Just as reading was often a collective practice, the printed word was embedded in a dynamic of speaking and hearing. The conjunction of social movements and cheap printing helped to create physical spaces in which workers encountered text and conversation together: workplaces, union libraries, street speaking venues, even boxcars, bunkhouses, and park benches. Whether the topic was sports, romance, or revolution, printed texts became the occasion for conversations, just as conversations and lectures might lead people to read particular texts. Finally, although I necessarily deal with fragments of peoples' lives, I try to sketch the potential intellectual journeys of self-educated workers that frequently took them in and out of formal education. Engagement with labor colleges and adult education was tempered by workers' economic circumstances, experiences, and personal goals. Theirs was a socially embedded education, highly personal but never singular.

The Print World of Working-Class Readers

Whatever expectations middle-class economists had about the intelligence of the average hobo, urban workers in the early twentieth century were readers. The modern industrial city was literally awash in text to such an extent that they could not have avoided it if they wished to. Signage and advertising covered the facades of many buildings, shop windows announced special sales, and discarded newspapers and handbills littered the streets and park benches. Available statistics also indicate that the vast majority of adult workers had basic literacy skills. For instance, over 90 percent of laborers working in the same kinds of seasonal industries as Doyle were literate, according to statistical samples of the U.S. Census.[4] Literacy rates among foreign-born workers in 1909 ranged from a low of 48 percent among Portuguese to a high of 99 percent among Swedes. Ninety-six percent of Irish immigrants could read.[5] Although Doyle had had no formal schooling at all, most wageworkers had some basic schooling. Although fewer than 10 percent of American 17-year-olds had graduated from high school in 1910, more than three-quarters had at least 5 years of grammar school. Over the first half of the twentieth century an increasing proportion of American young people were attending some high school thanks to compulsory school attendance laws and a school building boom in the 1920s and 1930s. By 1950 a solid majority of 17-year-olds had graduated from high school, and nearly 90 percent had at least 5 years of schooling.[6] The children of working-class families may have been more likely to end their formal education before graduating from high school, but most recognized the economic advantage of basic literacy and they usually left school able and willing to read.

Newspapers were the most accessible and pervasive reading matter for workers in the early twentieth century. On the eve of World War I, there were more than 2,500 daily newspapers in the United States with a total circulation of more than 28 million.[7] In larger cities like New York and Chicago, English-language daily papers competed in part by issuing at different times of the day, a practice that encouraged readers to cast off their used papers and created a great supply of free reading material for the down-and-out, not to mention

improvised blankets for those sleeping outdoors. In addition, every immigrant group of substantial size had at least one, and in many cases several,
newspapers geared toward their language group. Robert Park's 1922 study,
The Immigrant Press and its Control, listed more than 30 language groups with at
least one newspaper in New York City alone. In Chicago in 1930 there were 25
foreign-language daily newspapers publishing in 12 languages, according to historian Jon Bekken. Beyond the mainstream immigrant press, radicals and labor
activists produced a wide array of periodicals ranging from the handwritten
"Fist Press" of Finns in Canada to commercially successful Yiddish language
Forverts.[8]

The simple language of many English-language daily papers that made
them accessible to broad audiences also made them a useful resource for immigrants with limited English language skills. Working as a domestic in Michigan,
the sixteen-year-old Swedish immigrant Mary Anderson learned English by
listening to her employers' dinner table conversations and "by reading the
morning paper over and over again until finally it occurred to me what the
words meant," according to her memoir. Anderson may have been an unusually intelligent domestic servant. She went on to become a union organizer, a
Women's Trade Union League activist, and the first director of the Women's
Bureau in the U.S. Department of Labor. However, her use of English-
language newspapers was common among immigrant workers. For instance, a
survey by the New York City Russian-language newspaper, *Russkoye Slovo*,
found that a quarter of its readers also read English language papers, many of
them simply scanning the headlines in English because "these are easy to
understand, and you know all the news."[9]

In addition to newspapers and periodicals, early-twentieth-century radical
publishers produced an array of books and pamphlets aimed at working-class
audiences, especially those engaged in self-study. Two of the most successful
English-language ventures, and relevant to Doyle's milieu, were Charles H.
Kerr and Company and the Haldeman–Julius Publishing Company. Kerr and
Company of Chicago, Illinois, began as a Unitarian publishing house in 1886
but shifted to Socialism by 1900. Advertising in Socialist Party periodicals and
catering to party and trade union libraries, Kerr published volumes on social
science, literature, and current affairs, including the basic texts of Marxism.
Closely associated with left-wing Socialism and industrial unionism, Kerr also
published the popular monthly magazine *International Socialist Review*, which in
its heyday included colorful covers and dramatic articles on union organizing
and strikes, often illustrated with photographs taken by rank-and-file activists.
In addition, the *Review* published articles of popular science, economics, and
world affairs from a Marxist perspective. Like other radical publishers, the
Kerr Company suffered during World War I and the subsequent Red Scare. In
1918 the postmaster general revoked Kerr's first-class mailing privileges in response to a series of antiwar articles in the *Review* leading to the demise of the

journal. Factionalism among radicals and the costs of legal defense for political prisoners further sapped the finances and personnel of the Kerr Company, and by the 1920s it was a shell of its former self.[10]

Filling the void left by Kerr was the energetic project of the Haldeman–Julius Publishing Company of Girard, Kansas. Emanuel Julius was the self-educated son of an illiterate Russian immigrant bookbinder. He married Marcet Haldeman, daughter of a Kansas banker and niece of settlement house reformer Jane Addams. With Haldeman's money they purchased the presses and mailing lists of the hugely popular Socialist paper, *The Appeal to Reason*. Although Haldeman–Julius published a number of different periodicals and book series, their greatest success was the "Little Blue Books," pocket-sized, paper-covered volumes that sold for five cents each. An early advertisement in a radical journal emphasized the books' convenient size for surreptitious reading: "Many readers have become so enthused that they make a practice of slipping four or five of these books into a pocket before starting the day's work. They do not bulge the pocket and are not noticeable, yet are always available." Among the nearly one thousand titles in print by 1929 were works of European and American literature and drama (among the first titles were those by Oscar Wilde, Voltaire, Hugo, Emerson, and Poe); popular histories, political tracts, and works of science and religion (including debates on Christianity, introductions to Buddhism, Confucianism, Islam, even a book on Yoga); treatises on marriage, sexuality, and birth control; studies of politics including Tom Paine's *Age of Reason*, various popularizations of Socialism, and reprinting of documents from the German and Russian revolutions; how-to books on gardening, baseball, home ownership, psychoanalysis, hypnosis, and writing one-act plays; rhyming dictionaries, joke books, and the like. Haldeman–Julius also published brief synopses by Will Durant of various philosophers, which in 1927 were repackaged by Simon and Schuster as *The Story of Philosophy* to great popular acclaim.[11]

Unlike Doyle, however, most American workers did not make a study of difficult economic volumes. Studies of working-class reading patterns found mass circulation magazines and daily newspapers the most common reading fare, along with popular adventure and romance novels. Although workers read fewer books than middle-class Americans, they were interested in many of the same topics. For instance, the 1931 American Library Association study *What People Want to Read About* found that workers, farmers, housewives and teachers all considered topics like "the next war," "self-improvement and happy living," and "laws and legislation" to be the most interesting for reading.[12] Among Milwaukee vocational students, a slim majority of the over 3,000 surveyed in 1932 were active users of the public library, usually reading one or two books a month. Milwaukee's young working men, like others in the United States, were reading adventure novels, among them *The Call of the Wild, Treasure Island, Tom Sawyer*, and *All Quiet on the Western Front*. Milwaukee's young women favored their own form of romance and drama, including *Rebecca of Sunnybrook Farm, Little Women,* and *Anne of Green Gables.*[13] Although educators hoped to stimulate book reading (which they called "serious reading"), and librarians were developing study guides for adult readers, magazine and newspaper reading was a much more common practice. The sensational literature of *True Story Magazine* and similar story magazines were popular among women and men, as well as *Popular Mechanics* for young men and *Ladies Home Journal* for young women.[14] About 90 percent of the young people surveyed regularly read newspapers, and although the interests of men and women diverged in some predictable ways, the most frequently read sections overlapped quite a bit. "Sport," "theatre and movies," and "criminal" sections were much more popular than world and national news.[15]

Despite the evident despair of middle-class researchers (and of self-conscious radical workers) about the low quality of working-class reading matter, popular fiction and self-help books could have unexpected consequences. As Jonathan Rose argues in his study of British autodidacts, escapist literature had its own logic for those trapped in unpleasant neighborhoods and work routines. Working-class memoirists in the United States often noted a similar dynamic. Jewish garment worker Abraham Bisno taught himself to read with inexpensive Yiddish romance stories and newspapers, which as he recalled in his memoir, "opened my eyes to new worlds." Similarly, as boy growing up in segregated Mississippi, Richard Wright was transported by the novels of Zane Grey. According to Wright, the stories "enlarged my knowledge of the world more than anything I had encountered so far. To me, with my roundhouse, saloon-door, and river-levee background, they were revolutionary, my gateway to the world."[16] Even prosaic reading matter on personal hygiene and "how to get along with people" might lead to deepening social engagement and study. Louise Dieffenbacher wrote to her former teacher at the University of Wisconsin's School for Workers that classes and readings on physical education helped her avoid ill health during the winter, and as a result she had become much more active in her local YWCA. Although she said she was not "doing any systematic studying," she had "been appointed editor of our club paper and in that way try to inspire and encourage the value of choosing good books."[17] These and other examples suggest the need, as Rose argues, to resist drawing conclusions about what particular texts did to working people in the absence of workers' actual responses.[18]

A Collective Engagement with Text

However, the presence of print alone does not tell us the whole story of working-class reading and self-education. As scholars of literacy and print culture demonstrate, reading and literacy are practices rooted in broader cultural, economic, and political dynamics.[19] Working people seeking knowledge oriented themselves around multifaceted networks of informal education that included print, public and private speech and conversation, and community institutions such as unions, churches, and political groups.

Although Doyle's political affiliations placed him in the minority of American workers actively engaged in radicalism, he shared with millions of others the experience of working in North America's booming resource economy. From the 1870s until the Great Depression, it was common for young urban and rural men to work for a number of years as seasonal migrant workers before settling down into family life. Those who were settled sometimes took to the road at harvest time in search of high wages, because they were temporarily unemployed, or just to get out of the city. Women were intimately connected to this seasonal economy as service workers, farm laborers, and homemakers who stayed behind while their husbands, brothers, and lovers took to the road. Nonconformist and radical ideas circulated freely among the so-called "hoboes," spurred on most aggressively by activist members of the Industrial Workers of the World (IWW), a revolutionary union movement founded in Chicago in 1905. Although the IWW, or the "Wobblies" as they were known, successfully organized wheat harvest and oil field workers in the Great Plains region in the World War I years, they were as much an educational and cultural organization as a union. Their weekly English-language newspapers *Solidarity* and *Industrial Worker*, as well as a number of foreign-language papers either directly affiliated or politically oriented toward the IWW, were full of reports from rank-and-file organizers, commentary on current events, theoretical debates about industrial unionism, and book reviews. Never able to institutionalize its power as a union because of employer and government repression, the IWW nevertheless influenced the course of unionism by educating thousands of young workers in a practically oriented Marxism that emphasized the power of workers' direct action over politics.[20]

The years of the IWW upsurge were also the heyday of Progressive reform in America, a time when critics of laissez-faire capitalism grew more assertive and influential across the American political system. The Socialist Party, under the leadership of popular trade unionist Eugene V. Debs, was an open mass political movement that included moderates seeking reforms such as public ownership of water and power, as well as militant industrial unionists and revolutionaries. Although the party and the IWW officially parted ways after 1912, the left wing of the party remained close to the Wobblies and in many local struggles the two groups worked together. Radical workers also came together in a variety of anarchist, Socialist, and reformist organizations, adding to the effervescent nature of radicalism in American cities during the era. The formation of the Workers (Communist) Party in 1919 heralded the splitting up of this fractious coalition into many warring camps, but the fact that Doyle identified

as both a Bolshevik and a Wobbly points to continuing connections of sentiment at the rank-and-file level, at least during the early 1920s. In addition,
while factionalism weakened the left politically, it also stimulated the creation
of independent educational and propaganda initiatives available to workers
interested in self-education.[21]

Collective engagement with text was central to the development of trade
unionism and radicalism, a common theme across the working-class political
spectrum. For instance, Chicago union leader Agnes Nestor treasured an 1881
History of Labor handed down to her from her father who had been in the
Knights of Labor. She recalled her father frequently reading the book, which
also became a resource for their "long talks about labor problems" when she
was involved in a strike shortly after joining the workforce at the age of fourteen.[22] New York union leader Rose Schneiderman, who left school after the
ninth grade to support her brother and widowed mother, recalled reading
aloud to her mother in Yiddish and sharing books with her coworkers.[23] Workplace conversations also frequently centered on what workers were reading.
Spanish-speaking cigar makers, for instance, were known to employ one of
their coworkers to read aloud from a newspaper or book. Although historian
Patricia Cooper doubts that this practice was widespread outside of Cuba and
south Florida, she does note that cigar makers had a reputation for political
debate and conversation in the shop. As one cigar maker recalled, "They
would talk on every subject of the country—what the Congress was doing,
everything. . . . They were very well read people."[24] Similarly, tramps and
hoboes were said to seek out muckraking literature to employ in heated debates
and conversations in lodging houses, work camps, and while traveling in boxcars. As a Chicago bookseller noted, when hoboes could afford to buy books
they "devour them with keen interest. Hunger seems to quicken the senses, and
that may account for their perception in discussing things."[25]

Group photographs of local unions and study groups sometimes offer a
more focused version of the relation between print, reading, and community.
For instance, when the men and women of the IWW's Lumberworkers' Industrial Union in Arlington, Washington, sat for a photograph in 1917 in front of
their union hall, they held up a number of different textual symbols of the common cause, including union pennants, membership cards, song books, pamphlets, and copies of the IWW's national newspapers. A prominently featured
sign above the door of the union hall read "IWW Free Reading Room." Workers in this and similar group portraits may have had several motives. In a world
with many group photographs, they may have wanted simply to distinguish the
particularity of their group. But in the context of the intense repression visited
upon the IWW in during 1917, this image is more a defiant expression of solidarity. During the 1920s the IWW's monthly journal *Industrial Pioneer* published
similar photographs of IWW halls in across the West, each highlighting ample

displays of union literature. For a union battling hostile police and internal factionalism, these images of union halls and the texts they held signaled to migrant members the continued presence of safe places in towns large and small across the continent.[26]

If publicly reading radical books and newspapers was a concrete expression of an ideological community, the same can be said for reading the ethnic press. Reading the immigrant press drew boundaries of language, ideology, and common action, helping to create what Benedict Anderson called the "imagined community" of the nation.[27] The overlay of ethnic nationalism, Socialist sentiment, and self-education was rich in American industrial cities. The industrial working class of the period was comprised predominantly of immigrants and their children, and the majority of immigrants were part of working-class families. When immigrant workers read newspapers in their own languages, they reaffirmed their linguistic bonds with others while engaging in a broad-based process of education and debate. In his study of Polish newspapers in Chicago, Jon Bekken notes the long-running dispute between Catholic and radical papers, each claiming to be the voice of Polish culture and seeing the other as traitors to the Polish people.[28] But the very debate, and the circulation numbers it stimulated, reflected a growing Polish-American reading public. Similarly, in his study of early-twentieth-century New York City, Tony Michels places newspapers at the center of a fervent Jewish radicalism that was distinctly American. Yiddish newspapers reported local and European news and were filled with educational articles on science, health, and politics. The Socialist *Forwerts* (Forward), with a circulation of more than 200,000 in the 1920s (accounting for about half of the total Yiddish-language circulation) was the anchor for what Michels calls a "socialist newspaper culture" that included popular dances, excursions, and educational programs.[29]

According to Michels, "reading a [Yiddish] newspaper was as much a collective endeavor as an individual one." Many immigrant Jews from Eastern Europe arrived with basic, but very limited literacy skills. Few had seen a Yiddish newspaper before arriving in America, and the American papers were written in a local style of Yiddish that was difficult to understand, even for educated readers. As a result, Jewish workers read to each other at home and in public, and they formed a number of self-education societies.[30] The most successful of these, the Arbeter Ring or Workmen's Circle, grew to be the largest Jewish workers' group in the United States by World War I. Begun by rank-and-file Socialist workers in New York City, the Arbeter Ring combined education, mutual aid, and recreation, inviting all to join who were in sympathy with "freedom of thought and aspiration, workers' solidarity, and faithfulness to the interests of their class and its struggle against oppression and exploitation." With thousands of members and a healthy balance sheet, the Arbeter Ring also contributed to many Socialist and union organizing efforts, as well as to left-wing educational initiatives, such as the Rand School for Social Science.[31]

From Open Forums to Adult Education

Reading was a key practice in self-education, but public lectures and open forums represented the easiest point of access to informal education. Just as the streets of industrial cities were awash in text, so was the air filled with talk. The intimate relationship between text and talk was evident even in the founding of *Forverts* in 1897. Completely lacking in funds to publish a physical newspaper, the editors gathered donations by hosting "spoken newspapers" in Rutgers Square that included readings aloud of news, editorials, poetry, announcements, and letters to the editor of the yet-to-be-published newspaper.[32] On street corners, at factory gates, and in public parks, speakers mounted impromptu rostrums to address their fellow citizens. After work, on weekends, and especially on warm summer nights, urban workers stopped to listen to speakers for education, entertainment, and simply as a part of the spectacle of urban life. These open-air forums were vibrant until the 1950s, when they fell into decline, perhaps a victim of the popularity of television, the decline of immigrant working-class neighborhoods, and the suburbanization of workers. In New York, Union Square was well known as a speaking venue, while Rutgers Square was the center of Jewish radical soapboxers. Los Angeles had two major free speech venues, Pershing Square and the Plaza, that were flash points of conflict over public political speech.[33] Two parks in Chicago had long-standing open forums: on the city's south side, Washington Park Forum was known as "The Bug Club," and on the city's north side, Washington Square Park was known as "Bughouse Square." The poet Kenneth Rexroth—self-educated after being expelled from high school—recalled of the Bug Club: "every variety of radical sect, lunatic religion, and crackpot health panacea was preached from a row of soapboxes every night of the week when it wasn't storming." Studs Terkel—who grew up in a working-class neighborhood on Chicago's near west side—recalled that "there was a great deal of 'bull' at Bughouse Square, there was a great deal of all sorts of wild, impassioned talk and conversation of all variety, from all strata of our thought, and to me at least, as a young boy it was a very colorful and very rich area."[34]

Whether on street corners or in public parks, open-air speaking followed certain patterns. After observing an afternoon of speakers on a busy Chicago intersection, the sociologist Nels Anderson noted that the six speakers worked together to attract and hold a crowd, each limiting his talk so that the others could have their turn. After each spoke, he walked through the audience briefly either selling or giving away pamphlets and newspapers. "Regardless of how much they differ in their schemes of reforming the world," Anderson wrote in his field notes, "they are seldom personal in their opposition to each other. Soap-boxers behave toward each other when not on the box, much as lawyers do when they are out of the courtroom, and even while on the box they consider each others' interests."[35]

Outdoor free-speech forums were complemented by a wide variety of indoor forums sponsored by political, religious, ethnic, and reform organizations. By the 1920s there were self-identified "forum hounds," enthusiasts who would spend much of their leisure time attending different forum programs.[36] Many of these forums were associated with the urban bohemian subculture that brought together artists, writers, and working-class activists. In Chicago, probably the best-documented forum was the *Dill Pickle Club*. Located near Bughouse Square, and operating from around 1914 to the early 1930s, the Dill Pickle Club was a mix of open forum, dance hall, tavern, and art studio. The club's founder, Jack Jones, was a Canadian-born miner and organizer for the Western Federation of Miners and the Industrial Workers of the World. He was also a classic autodidact. According to his one-time wife, Elizabeth Gurley Flynn, Jones spent days on end in the Newberry Library researching a plan for a reformed industrial system. Jones worked closely with Dr. Ben Reitman to craft the infamous programming of the Dill Pickle Club. Reitman had been the road manager for anarchist Emma Goldman and had himself organized a series of educational venues for migrant workers wintering in Chicago. Reitman and Jones had a knack for attracting audiences that included workers, academics, and underworld characters. As the journalist Samuel Putnam recalled of the Dill Pickle, "It was fun to listen to the world-famed physicist gravely debating his specialty with a boxcar bum who had wandered in."[37]

Chicago's immigrant communities sponsored a rich educational life including forums on European and American politics, religious and philosophical debates, and discussions of gender and power within the family. Debates often focused on the intellectual and political integration of migrants into American life. For instance, in 1909 the Danish Young Peoples Society sponsored a discussion on "What are the most important interests for Danes entering the U.S.A.?" The main speaker emphasized learning English and adopting American ideals. From the floor, participants objected, insisting that new arrivals should "first of all, join their respective trade unions and the Socialist Party." As reported in a Danish-language newspaper, "So intense did the discussion become that when the president announced 10:00 o'clock and closing time, it was unanimously decided to continue for another hour."[38] Even as immigrants became more grounded in their American setting and learned English, they could maintain community ties through ethnic forums. For instance, Lithuanian forums debated contemporary American political and social issues such as women's suffrage and "Women's Sexual Life." Similarly, Czech-speaking free thinkers chartered a new free thinkers' forum in 1922, naming it after American orator Robert Ingersoll, aiming to organize lectures and publish brochures and books, and to make "the most intimate contacts with other American rationalists." By 1937 there was also a rationalist club for English-speaking Czechs known as the Thomas Paine Club.[39]

Assessments of the quality and character of speakers in these forums varied, usually depending on the political outlook of the observer, and reflected a broader debate about appropriate forms of education and recreation for adults. At issue was not simply radicalism, but also the heterogeneity of audiences and the subject matter. A supportive letter to the editor of the Chicago *Tribune* during the summer of 1921 contrasted the plebian Bug Club to its more elite neighbor, the University of Chicago with its intimidating "medieval towers." The Bug Club, he wrote was "a glorious institution and the man with a craving for knowledge who works all day and cannot afford a university education, if he but listens with an open mind, knowing what to discard as bull (for naturally some of it is) and what to digest, will certainly assimilate a wealth of knowledge in a short summer term." In the opinion of the Chicago Park Commission, however, these open-air meetings were "irreligious, blasphemous, ribald, and revolutionary," and likely to offend the casual passerby.[40] Other critics of the open forums emphasized speakers' profanity, the down-and-out character of the audiences, and the forums' role as venues for sexual encounters.[41] "With the aid of a lecture by an unaware professor from one of the universities, a smutty one-act 'play' or two, some alleged music, and dim lighted dance floors," according to one observer, forum organizers gave "diverse bums from the lodging houses and oldish maidens the thrill of their lives." Homosexuals and lesbians also frequented the forums, the subject of which was "inversion and perversion disguised as a lecture purporting to explain the theories of Freud, Havelock Ellis, Marie Stopes and Margaret Sanger."[42]

Critics' obsession with allegedly bogus intellectual content nevertheless suggested the powerful mixture of print, conversation, and oratory at play in the parks and bohemian forums of American cities. Efforts to institutionalize the self-educational impulses of working-class adults emerged from within the working class itself, as well as from middle- and upper-class reformers. Radicals and labor unions were early innovators in this effort, hoping to train new generations of working-class leaders. Doyle hoped to attend the Rand School for Social Science in New York City, which was founded by the Socialist Party in 1906. Finnish Socialists in northern Minnesota converted a religious school into the Work People's College in 1907, which was soon associated with the IWW and operated until 1941. Among the trade unions, the International Ladies Garment Workers Union (ILGWU) was a leading force, particularly in New York City where it collaborated with the public school system to create a network of workers schools. Activists from the ILGWU like Fannia Cohn and Pauline Newman, along with Mary Anderson of the Boot Workers Union, were also important in directing the educational projects of the Women's Trade Union League (WTUL). In 1921 educational activists from the ILGWU, the United Mine Workers, and other centers of innovation founded the Workers Education Bureau under the auspices of the American Federation of Labor, marking a period of institutional growth for worker-oriented adult education. Building on the WTUL labor school and the YWCA Industrial Clubs, Bryn Mawr College launched its Summer School for Women Workers in the early 1920s, exporting its model to the University of Wisconsin in 1925. At the same time, the Brookwood Labor College in New York and Commonwealth College in Arkansas ran year-round residential schools with highly innovative curricula.[43] There was a similar tendency toward more formal education within the Communist Party. The John Reed Clubs (1925–1934) were a mix of bohemian forums, ethnic clubs, and adult education that drew a number of working-class intellectuals, like Richard Wright, into the Party's ranks. After 1936, reflecting its Popular Front strategy, the party shifted its educational efforts to a system of labor colleges in New York, Chicago, San Francisco and Los Angeles.[44] Perhaps recognizing this flurry of institutionalization as a challenge to its authority, the Carnegie Corporation expanded and diversified its Americanization programs under the aegis of the American Association of Adult Education (AAAE). The AAAE strived to coordinate curriculum and professionalize the teaching staff working in adult education. Carnegie even funded some programs of the American Federation of Labor's (AFL's) Workers Education Bureau, despite the discomfort voiced by left-wing unionists.[45] Spanning the ideological gamut from right to left, these more institutionalized forms of education for workers all sought to surpass the chaos of self-education and the world of the open forums.

Self-Improvement in Social Context

Reading and radicalism sat in a complex relationship with workers' desire for respectability and upward mobility. Many found in self-education a path to less physically taxing work, cleaner living conditions, and higher pay, as well as personal intellectual development. Radical publishers often appealed to workers' desire for the best of culture and linked reading to intellectual independence. For instance, an advertisement for "The Modern Library" book series in the *International Socialist Review* claimed the series included "the best books of recent times in the fields of literature, philosophy, drama, poetry and science. The leaders of modern thought have been iconoclasts in their respective fields, and no Socialist can afford to be ignorant of their best expression." Curiously, the illustration around the border of the advertisement pictures mostly upper-class figures reading books, suggesting that Socialists should aspire to the knowledge already held by elites.[46] Even the classics had lessons for rebels. The Haldeman–Julius Company pushed its edition of Plato's *The Trial and Death of Socrates* as a "valuable book" about state repression of free speech, something much on the minds of Socialists during and after World War I.[47]

Book collecting has often been associated with upward mobility, but workers personal libraries also reflected their status within working-class communities, as well as a worker's lifetime engagement with ideas and social movements. The journalist Stewart Holbrook, who had worked for years as a lumberjack, recounted, "Most loggers like their literary meat red. They want a story with black curly hair on its chest and smoke and fire blowing forth from every chapter." But there were exceptions. During the heyday of the IWW, "every mail brought a large bundle" of newspapers and pamphlets to the camps. And one could still find in many camps well-thumbed copies of Upton Sinclair, Voltaire, and Tom Paine. While the majority killed time with Zane Grey, *Popular Mechanics*, and pornography, Holbrook had found in every camp "at least one man who, all things considered, might well be termed a bibliophile." The cabin of a saw filer he worked with in British Columbia was half-filled with the collected works of Dumas, volumes of Dickens, Bronte, Carlyle, Darwin, and the *Encyclopedia Britannica*. Whether out of boredom or genuine interest, coworkers in the camp availed themselves of this de facto camp library.[48]

Historian Larry Peterson's analysis of his grandfather's personal library provides a good example of this. John Edwin Peterson migrated with his family from Sweden to the United States as a child, settling near the Pullman car works on Chicago's south side just a few years before the famed strike there. Peterson was educated in a Swedish-language parochial school through eighth grade and then went to work at Pullman around 1905. He soon joined the IWW and the Socialist Party, and would be a rank-and-file militant in several unionization efforts over the course of his life. Peterson's library included more than 300 books, many of them multivolume encyclopedias and other reference works. About half of the volumes were nonfiction: current events, social science, history, natural science, and philosophy. Another quarter of the volumes was fiction. Yet, as his grandson argues, the library is not so much a record of consumption as an artifact of engagement with ideas, social movements, and institutions of self-education. The largest number of books dated from his intense engagement with the Socialist Party and the IWW from 1904 to 1924. With the decline of these movements, particularly the IWW, Peterson's book buying slowed, picking up somewhat in the mid-1930s with the revival of industrial unionism. By then he was less involved in unionization, and there were fewer worker-oriented publishers.[49]

Like John Peterson, the working-class men and women who bought Kerr, Haldeman–Julius, and other radical publications were often on a quest to justify their own feeling that all was not right in the world. Many found school curriculum alienating and repressive. In the words of Bethlehem, Pennsylvania, tailor Chris Sproger, the history taught in public schools was "mainly certain events in the lives of conspicuous characters to celebrate their political successes and record their wars. It is given to cultivate good-will toward those now in power. Such educated ignorance leads the mass of the workers to think that the present order of society, with its schemes of things as they are, has been established by some supernatural power and therefore cannot be changed."[50] Roy S. was a middle-aged machinist and Socialist when he began attending Milwaukee's vocational school during the 1930s. He told researchers that as early as age ten "he had started to think." When he asked one of the nuns at his Catholic school "why, if God were almighty, He had to put Abraham's loyalty to Him to such an elaborate test to prove it," her only answer was to give the boy "a sound thrashing." As he grew up he was "very eager to know more and to seek knowledge." He went to the museum, the library, and to lectures. "It was then he began to find himself," researchers noted. "First of all, he read religion exhaustively, then economics, politics, social and labor problems. He thought a great deal on these subjects too, and he has come to hold many views that the world calls radical." So consumed by his desire for greater knowledge, Roy S. attended school five days and two nights a week rather than work.[51]

The impact of the Little Blue Books on their readers is captured in a set of letters excerpted in Dale Herder's 1975 dissertation on Haldeman–Julius. Written by retired workers who read Little Blue Books in the 1920s, the letters recall the convenient size the books—either for hiding from family members or keeping in pockets and lunchboxes—and focused on their power to debunk political and religious orthodoxy. One self-described "autodidact" wrote, "as a kid . . . I was filled full of religious bunk and dark age superstitions, until it drove me mad." "The Little Blue Books brought the first light from out of the darkness for me."[52] A retired railroad worker linked Haldeman–Julius publications to his own political and intellectual awakening in the World War I era Socialist Party: "Little Blue Books were my bible, and account, to a great degree, for my education and what I am today, intellectually."[53] A retired office worker recalled reading his older brother's Little Blue Books. "At the age of 13 this exposure to 'Culture' in a Catholic home was a bit jolting," he wrote. "In retrospect, I firmly believe that my brother's supply of Little Blue Books encouraged me to further home study and self-education. Eight years later I 'broke away' from the church—and have never regretted it."[54]

Other working-class life stories help us connect the educational dots between personal experience, street speaking, organizational cultures, reading, and formal education. Typically, formal schooling provided working people with basic literacy skills, but the need to earn a living and the regimentation of public schooling alienated many from intellectual life. Often as not, it was contact with unorthodox views outside of school that sparked a personal odyssey of self-education, which frequently led the seeker back to formal education.

Philip Taft (1902–1976) grew up in New York City and ran away from home before finishing grade school. His work experience was probably similar to that of Doyle and millions of others. He worked as a sailor, a railroad laborer, a grain harvester, a ditchdigger, and a slaughterhouse worker. Feeling the social stigma of the runaway child worker, Taft recalled that he was attracted to the soapbox speeches of radicals who assailed conventional society. Before he was fifteen years old, he joined the IWW and later was an organizer in the wheat belt and wrote several articles for the union's national newspaper. In the wake of the IWW's factional disputes during the mid-1920s, Taft drifted away from radicalism, finished high school at night in 1928, and went to the University of Wisconsin, eventually completing a doctorate under labor economist Selig Perlman. He lived a long, productive life, ending his career as a scholar of industrial relations at Brown University. In retrospect, Taft considered the IWW a halfway house between the streets and his entry into formal education. As he told an interviewer, "a [union] hall meant that you could talk to someone, and that you didn't have to go into the Skid Row bar. A hall meant that you could read." And so he did. He read Marx, of course, but didn't understand it. Instead it was Jack London that really turned him on to reading.[55]

While Taft found his way to the public university system and a career as an academic, the African American Communist Harry Haywood took an alternate intellectual path. Born in Omaha, Nebraska, in 1898, Haywood's was the only black family in an overwhelmingly Czech immigrant neighborhood. The family got on well with the Czechs, but moved to Minneapolis fleeing threats from an Irish street gang. There Haywood was quickly alienated by his white classmates and quit school in the eighth grade. Like other African Americans who fought in Europe during World War I, Haywood was impressed by the lack of overt discrimination in France. Shortly after his return to the United States, he found himself in the midst of the bloody Chicago Race Riot of 1919. "At the time," Haywood wrote in his memoir, "the racist deluge simply revealed great gaps in my own education and knowledge." His experience growing up in Omaha seemed to refute the idea that white and black could not live as equals, but he longed to find validation for this experience in the more authoritative voices of published authors. His search began with the nineteenth century rationalist Robert Ingersoll, and from there moved on to Darwin. He read *Origin of Species* "armed with a dictionary and *a priori* knowledge gleaned from Ingersoll's popularizations," and found support for his own atheism in its "scientific refutation of religious dogma."[56]

Haywood's personal intellectual development was deeply embedded in his family and organizational connections and reflected the diverse radical milieu of American industrial cities. Like a more famous black Communist, the novelist Richard Wright, Haywood worked in the Chicago Post Office, where he met others seeking knowledge and understanding. He and his coworkers formed a short-lived study group but soon felt "the need for a broader political arena of activity." They went to lectures and forums including the Bug Club and the Dill Pickle Club where they listened to Socialists and anarchists, as well as more mainstream progressives like Clarence Darrow. His older brother, already a Communist, suggested more advanced reading: Henry Morgan's ethnological volume *Ancient Society*, Gustavus Meyer's *History of Great American Fortunes*, John Reed's history of the Bolshevik revolution, *Ten Days that Shook the World*, and Jack London's dystopian vision of American fascism, *The Iron Heel*. By this time he had quit his monotonous job at the Post Office for one as a cook on the Chicago to Los Angeles train. His schedule allowed him time to read and interact with other radicals in both cities, and he soon moved on to a steady diet of Marxist classics until he informed his brother that he wanted to join the Communist party in 1922. Within a few years he was an experienced activist, and in 1925 the party sent him to Moscow to attend the University of the Toilers of the East where he studied with Communists from Asia and Africa. Taking a parallel intellectual path to Philip Taft, Haywood became an important theorist in the Communist Party, articulating its policy on race in the United States that identified blacks in the South as a subject nation with the right to self-determination.[57]

Conclusion

When Don Lescohier met Doyle, he and his colleagues were in the midst of a massive study of labor relations in the Great Plains wheat harvest that surveyed thousands of laborers. Yet Doyle stood out as a unique individual, and Lescohier's notes on their conversation are one of the few documents in his personal papers. As he wrote in an article for *Harper's Monthly Magazine* that likely referred to Doyle, "The 'Red' is on a higher social level than the unorganized hobo. He respects himself, he makes claims for himself, he fights for social justice. However erroneous his theories, he plays a man's part."[58] This essay suggests that however unusual Doyle was, he was not unique. When it came to mastering traditionally defined domains of knowledge and engaging in debate on a high level, workers like Doyle and many others could and did surprise academically trained intellectuals with the scope of their knowledge. Academic's surprise often turned to fear when they realized that these working-class intellectuals aimed to prepare themselves for workers' control of industry. The possibility of revolutionary change (whether one feared or embraced it) hinged on workers' capacity to understand economics, psychology, and technology. Workers like Doyle made claims to the same sets of knowledge as middle-class intellectuals, and in doing so they challenged those intellectuals' claims to social and political leadership.

Of course, Doyle and his comrades were unusual in their radicalism and their taste for difficult economic texts. Many more working people read newspapers and popular magazines simply to pass the time or to be ready to share gossip about movie stars and sports heroes. Yet their life stories point to the importance of overlapping networks of working-class self-education that spread throughout industrial cities and reached isolated labor camps, farms, ships, boxcars, and hobo jungles. Although many working-class men and women had limited formal schooling in the early twentieth century, they could learn from coworkers, street speakers, libraries, and even advertisements. Organizational and cultural networks connected individual workers to others with similar interests. They traded texts and ideas, they argued, and they learned how to speak in public. The wide array of cheap printed material ranging from newspapers and magazines to the Little Blue Books of the Haldeman–Julius Publishing Company offered every type of reader something to think about and discuss.

These networks often grew out of shared political goals, such as Socialism and industrial unionism. In this sense, there were important differences in the content of reading between the highly engaged self-educators like Doyle and average workers. Yet even considering this difference in the content, radicals, rank-and-file unionists, and apolitical young workers shared a set of reading practices that were closely linked to the material conditions of their daily lives. Often financially and socially cut off from mainstream sources of reading, working-class readers frequently encountered text in fragments. Cast-off newspapers, shared magazines and pamphlets, advertisements, and picket signs were common reading fare. Of course, readers from other class communities encountered similar fragmentary texts, but for the formally educated the fragments were anomalous. In addition, working-class readers more often constituted reading communities that intertwined text and the spoken word as they read aloud at home and in the workplace. On street corners and in open-forum lectures, speech and text were further intertwined as speakers peppered their talks with references to books and authors and plied the gathered crowds with pamphlets and newspapers.

The paradox of working-class "self-education" lay in the fact that it was a deeply social education. Certainly, working people read silently to themselves, and they often hoped that education would bring economic and social benefits for themselves and their families. But the world of working-class self-education that flourished in the first half of the twentieth century was tightly bound with a class awareness born of political organizing and the experience of daily life. At the center of this world were men like Doyle and women like Mary Anderson and Rose Schneiderman. They were "class partisans," to use Shelton Stromquist's phrase, people who viewed the Progressive Era social divide from the bottom up, even when they were willing to work with middle-class allies.[59] As the New York garment worker Jennie Matyos, who had left school at age fourteen, told a gathering of worker-educators and students in 1921, "We want education, the real kind, not the taffy, not the sugar-coated stuff. We want the education in regard to the struggle of the worker and how to meet it in an intelligent and practical way."[60] For many of her contemporaries, this was the essence of self-education: the education of workers *as workers*. Certainly, this is what most surprised Lescohier when he met Doyle. Out of a variety of informal practices and networks, a movement was educating itself.

Notes

My thanks to all who made helpful suggestions, especially Adam R. Nelson, John L. Rudolph, Tony Michels, Jim Barrett, Liz Faue, Caroline Merithew, Tim Lacy, Steve Meyer, and Loretta Gaffney. Research for this chapter was supported in part by the University of Illinois Institute for Labor and Industrial Relations and the University of California Labor and Employment Research Fund.

1. Don D. Lescohier Papers, Box 1, Folder 1, State Historical Society of Wisconsin, emphasis in original. See also Don D. Lescohier, "With the I.W.W. in the Wheat Lands," *Harper's Monthly Magazine* 147 (July 1923), 374–375; Frank Tobias Higbie, *Indispensable Outcasts: Hobo Workers and Community in the American Midwest, 1880–1930* (Urbana: University of Illinois Press, 2003), 205–206.

2. Jonathan Rose, *The Intellectual Life of the British Working Classes* (New Haven, CT: Yale University Press, 2001), 1–11.

3. Christine Pawley, "'Seeking 'Significance': Actual Readers, Specific Reading Communities," *Book History* 5 (2002), 144–145; Erin A. Smith, *Hard-Boiled: Working-Class Readers and Pulp Magazines* (Philadelphia: Temple University Press, 2000), 8–9.

4. Higbie, *Indispensable Outcasts*, 102.

5. Harvey J. Graff, *The Legacies of Literacy: Continuities and Contradictions in Western Culture and Society* (Bloomington: Indiana University Press, 1987), 366–368.

6. "High School Graduates, and College Enrollment and Degrees," and "Educational Attainment by Sex," U.S. Census Bureau, The 2008 Statistical Abstract, http://www.census.gov/compendia/statab/hist_stats.html (accessed July 24, 2008).

7. U.S. Census of Manufactures, 1914, vol. 2, p. 653, as cited in Robert Park, *The Immigrant Press and Its Control* (New York: Harper, 1922), 17.

8. Park, *Immigrant Press*, 7; Jon Bekken, "The Chicago Newspaper Scene: An Ecological Perspective," *Journalism and Mass Communication Quarterly* 74 (Autumn 1997), 492. The Chicago Foreign Language Press Survey, a New Deal era translation project, reviewed the pages of more than one hundred ethnic newspapers publishing in Chicago from the 1860s to the 1930s. See Chicago Public Library Omnibus Project, *The Chicago Foreign Language Press Survey: A General Description of Its Contents* (Chicago: Work Projects Administration, 1942), 7–12; Varpu Lindstrom-Best, "'Fist Press': A Study of Finnish Canadian Handwritten Newspapers," in *Essays on the Scandinavian-North American Radical Press, 1880s–1930s*, ed. Dirk Hoerder (Bremen, Germany: Labor Newspaper Preservation Project, 1984), 100–111.

9. Mary Anderson, *Woman at Work. The Autobiography of Mary Anderson as Told to Mary N. Winslow* (Minneapolis: University of Minnesota Press, 1951), 14; Park, *Immigrant Press*, 7–9.

10. Allen Ruff, *"We Called Each Other Comrade": Charles H. Kerr & Company, Radical Publishers* (Urbana: University of Illinois Press, 1997), 160–199. In 1927 Kerr transferred

ownership of the company to the Proletarian Party, a communist group whose leader John Keracher was an autodidact.

11. "World's Famous Books," Appeal Publishing Company advertisement, *Labor Herald* (March 1922); E. Haldeman-Julius, *The World of Haldeman-Julius*, comp. Albert Mordell (New York: Twayne Publishers, 1960); Stuart McConnell, "E. Haldeman-Julius and the Little Blue Bookworms: The Bridging of Cultural Styles, 1919–1951," *Prospects: An Annual of American Cultural Studies* 11 (1987), 59–79; Dale Marvin Herder, "Education for the Masses: The Haldeman-Julius Little Blue Books as Popular Culture during the Nineteen-Twenties" (PhD diss., Michigan State University, 1975). On Durant see Joan Shelley Rubin, *The Making of Middlebrow Culture* (Chapel Hill: University of North Carolina Press, 1992), 231–234. On the *Appeal to Reason* see John Graham, *"Yours for the Revolution": The Appeal to Reason, 1895–1922* (Lincoln: University of Nebraska Press, 1990).

12. Douglas Waples and Ralph Tyler, *What People Want to Read About: A Study of Group Interests and a Survey of Problems in Adult Reading* (Chicago: University of Chicago Press, 1931), 86–92. See also William S. Gray and Ruth Munroe, *The Reading Interests and Habits of Adults: A Preliminary Report* (New York: Macmillan Company, 1929); Rhey Boyd Parsons, "A Study of Adult Reading" (master's thesis, University of Chicago, 1923), 68–71.

13. William Frank Rasche, "The Reading Interests of Young Workers" (PhD diss., University of Chicago, 1936), 44–52; William Frank Rasche, *The Reading Interests of Young Workers* (Milwaukee, WI: Milwaukee Vocational School, 1925).

14. Rasche, *Reading Interests of Young Workers* (1925), 20–42; Rasche, "Reading Interests of Young Workers" (1936), 67–70. Smith, *Hard-Boiled*, 23–32; Ann Fabian, "Making a Commodity of Truth: Speculations on the Career of Bernarr Macfadden," *American Literary History* 5, no. 1 (Spring 1993), 51–76. On nineteenth-century working-class reading see Michael Denning, *Mechanic Accents: Dime Novels and Working-Class Culture in America* (London: Verso, 1987), especially chapter 3.

15. Rasche, "Reading Interests of Young Workers" (1936), 84.

16. Abraham Bisno, *Abraham Bisno, Union Pioneer* (Madison: University of Wisconsin Press, 1967), 49; Richard Wright, *Black Boy (American Hunger): A Record of Childhood and Youth* (New York: HarperPerennial, 2006), 151 (originally published in 1944).

17. Louise Dieffenbacher to Dr. Eliza Edwards, April 13, 1926, University of Wisconsin School for Workers, General Correspondence, Students, Box 1, University of Wisconsin Archives; see also Mary Frederickson, "Citizens for Democracy: The Industrial Programs of the YWCA," in *Sisterhood and Solidarity: Workers' Education for Women, 1914–1984*, ed. Joyce Kornbluh and Mary Frederickson (Philadelphia: Temple University Press, 1984).

18. Rose, *Intellectual Life*, 4–6.

19. Pawley, "Seeking 'Significance,'" 143–160; Christine Pawley, *Reading on the Middle Border: The Culture of Print in Late-Nineteenth Century Osage, Iowa* (Amherst: University of Massachusetts Press, 2001); Cathy N. Davidson, ed., *Reading in America: Literature and Social History* (Baltimore: Johns Hopkins University Press), 1989.

20. Higbie, *Indispensable Outcasts*, chaps. 1 and 4; Nigel Sellars, *Oil, Wheat and Wobblies: The Industrial Workers of the World in Oklahoma, 1905–1930* (Norman: University of Oklahoma Press, 1998). The classic general history of the IWW is Melvyn Dubofsky and Joseph McCartin, *We Shall Be All: A History of the Industrial Workers of the World* (Urbana:

University of Illinois Press, 2000). On the cultural world of the IWW see Salvatore Salerno, *Red November, Black November: Culture and Community in the Industrial Workers of the World* (Albany: State University of New York Press, 1989).

21. Among others, see Shelton Stromquist, *Re-inventing "The People": The Progressive Movement, the Class Problem, and the Origins of Modern Liberalism* (Urbana: University of Illinois Press, 2006); Nick Salvatore, *Eugene V. Debs: Citizen and Socialist* (Urbana: University of Illinois Press, 1982); James R. Barrett, *William Z. Foster and the Tragedy of American Radicalism* (Urbana: University of Illinois Press, 1999).

22. Agnes Nestor, *Woman's Labor Leader. An Autobiography of Agnes Nestor* (Rockford, IL: Bellevue Books, 1954), 43–44.

23. Rose Schneiderman, *All for One* (New York: Paul S. Erikson, 1967), 39–50; Annelise Orleck, *Common Sense and a Little Fire: Women and Working-Class Politics in the United States, 1900–1965* (Chapel Hill: University of North Carolina Press, 1995), 35–41.

24. Gary R. Mormino, "The Reader and the Worker: 'Los Lectores' and the Culture of Cigarmaking in Cuba and Florida," *International Labor and Working Class History* 54 (1998), 1–18; Patricia A. Cooper, *Once a Cigarmaker: Men, Women, and Work Culture in American Cigar Factories, 1900–1919* (Urbana: University of Illinois Press, 1987), 66.

25. Josiah Flynt, *Notes of an Itinerant Policeman* (Boston: L. C. Page, 1900), 216–217; Daniel Horsley, "What the Hobo Reads," Nels Anderson Field Notes, Document 150, Ernest W. Burgess Papers, University of Chicago Library Special Collections.

26. Joyce L. Kornbluh, ed., *Rebel Voices: An IWW Anthology* (Chicago: Charles H. Kerr, 1988), 263. For images of union halls and literature displays see *Industrial Pioneer* (February 1924), 16, and *Industrial Pioneer* (October 1924), 26, 47.

27. Park, *Immigrant Press*, 49–67; Benedict Anderson, *Imagined Communities: Reflections on the Origin and Spread of Nationalism* (London: Verso, 1991).

28. Jon Bekken, "Negotiating Class and Ethnicity: The Polish-Language Press in Chicago," *Polish American Studies* 57 (Autumn 2000), 5–29; Frederick J. Augustyn, Jr., "Together and Apart: Lithuanian and Polish Immigrant Adult Literacy Programs in Chicago, 1890–1930," *Polish American Studies* 57 (Autumn 2000), 31–44.

29. Tony Michels, *A Fire in Their Hearts: Yiddish Socialists in New York* (Cambridge, MA: Harvard University Press, 2005), 3, 104–105; Mordecai Soltes, *The Yiddish Press: An Americanizing Agency* (New York: Teachers College of Columbia University, 1924), 24.

30. Michels, *A Fire in Their Hearts*, 112–113; Orleck, *Common Sense*, 40–41.

31. Michels, *A Fire in Their Hearts*, 181–189.

32. Ibid., 104–105.

33. Ibid., 89–90; Mark Wild, *Street Meeting: Multiethnic Neighborhoods in Early Twentieth-Century Los Angeles* (Berkeley: University of California Press, 2005), 176–199.

34. Kenneth Rexroth, *Autobiographical Novel* (Garden City, NY: Doubleday, 1966), 105–106; interview with Slim Brundage, College of Complexes "Janitor," on the "Studs Terkel Radio Program," WFMT-FM, Chicago, 1967 (audio recording), Chicago Historical Society: Archives and Manuscripts Collections; thanks to Peter Alter for this source.

35. Nels Anderson, "Document 60: Notes on an Afternoon's Series of Talks," Ernest W. Burgess Papers—Other's Work, Individual Students and Collaborators, Nels Anderson, Box 127, Folder 1, Department of Special Collections, University of Chicago, Library.

36. Franklin Rosemont, ed., *Slim Brundage: From Bughouse Square to the Beat Generation* (Chicago: Charles H. Kerr), 93; Sophia Fagan, *Public Forums in Chicago* (Chicago: Works Progress Administration, 1940).

37. Samuel Putnam, "Red Days in Chicago," *American Mercury* 30 (1933), 65. Elizabeth Gurley Flynn, *The Rebel Girl: An Autobiography, My First Life (1906–1926)* (New York: International Publishers, 1973), 86–88; Barrett, *William Z. Foster*, 73. Ben Reitman, "Highlights of Dill Pickle History," Suppl. II, Folder 87, Reitman Papers, University of Illinois at Chicago Library, Department of Special Collections; Roger Bruns, *The Damndest Radical: The Life and World of Ben Reitman, Chicago's Celebrated Social Reformer, Hobo King, and Whorehouse Physician* (Urbana: University of Illinois Press, 1987). On the broader bohemian subculture and its connections to working-class radicalism see Christine Stansell, *American Moderns: Bohemian New York and the Creation of a New Century* (New York: Henry Holt, 2000); James R. Barrett, "Introduction," in *The Spirit of Labor*, ed. Hutchins Hapgood (Urbana: University of Illinois Press, 2004) (original work published 1907).

38. "What Is Most Important for Danish-Americans?" *Revyen*, March 27, 1909, Box 9, Chicago Foreign Language Press Survey (hereafter CFLPS), University of Chicago Library, Special Collections. See also Fred M. Schied, *Learning in Social Context: Workers and Adult Education in Nineteenth Century Chicago* (DeKalb: LEPS Press, Northern Illinois University, 1995).

39. "Plan to Establish Lithuanian Lecture Forum in Chicago," *Lietuva*, August 3, 1917; "Women's Progressive Association Sponsors Lecture," *Naujienos*, April 5, 1916, CFLPS, Box 29; "The Ingersollova Racionalisticka Spolecnost Founded," *Denni Hlasatel*, April 9, 1922; "Thought Is the Thing," *Vek Rozumn*, October 21, 1937, CFLPS, Box 3.

40. Dick Arman, "The Bug Club," *Chicago Tribune*, July 9, 1921, 6; "Park Board File Answer in Suit of the 'Bug Club,'" *Chicago Tribune*, September 15, 1921, 12.

41. "Near North Side. Bug Park, etc.," Box 214, Folder 9, Ernest W. Burgess Papers, Addendum, Department of Special Collections, University of Chicago, Library.

42. Fagan, *Public Forums in Chicago*, 41–42. See also Chad Heap, *Slumming: Sexual and Racial Encounters in American Nightlife, 1885–1940* (Chicago: University of Chicago Press, 2009); Daniel Hurewitz, *Bohemian Los Angeles and the Making of Modern Politics* (Berkeley: University of California Press, 2007).

43. Joseph F. Kett, *The Pursuit of Knowledge Under Difficulties: From Self-Improvement to Adult Education in America, 1750–1990* (Stanford, CA: Stanford University Press, 1994), 352–362; Fred M. Schied, "Labor and Learning: Adult Education and the Decline of Workers' Education," *Journal of the Midwest History of Education Society* 22 (1995), 5–14; Rachel C. Schwartz, "The Rand School of Social Science, 1906–1924: A Study of Worker Education in the Socialist Era" (EdD thesis, State University of New York, Buffalo, 1984); Joyce Kornbluh and Mary Frederickson, eds., *Sisterhood and Solidarity: Workers' Education for Women, 1914–1984* (Philadelphia: Temple University Press, 1984); Orleck, *Common Sense*, chap. 5; Richard F. Dwyer, *Labor Education in the U.S.: An Annotated Bibliography* (Metuchen, NJ: Scarecrow Press, 1977), 1–26; Richard J. Altenbaugh, *Education for Struggle: The American Labor Colleges of the 1920s and 1930s* (Philadelphia: Temple University Press, 1990).

44. Michael Denning, *The Cultural Front: The Laboring of American Culture in the Twentieth Century* (New York: Verso, 1998), 205–211; Randi Storch, *Red Chicago: American Communism at Its Grassroots, 1928–35* (Urbana: University of Illinois Press, 2007), 69–72; Jess

Rigelhaupt, "'Education for Action': The California Labor School, Radical Unionism, Civil Rights, and Progressive Coalition Building in the San Francisco Bay Area, 1934–1970" (PhD diss., University of Michigan, 2005), 3–5.

45. Alan Lawrence Jones, "Gaining Self-Consciousness while Losing the Movement: The American Association for Adult Education, 1926–1941" (PhD diss., University of Wisconsin–Madison, 1991).

46. "The Modern Library," *International Socialist Review* 18 (November–December 1917).

47. Advertisement for "The Trial and Death of Socrates," inside back cover of *De Maupassant's Stories*, People's Pocket Series No. 6 (Girard, KS: Appeal to Reason, n.d.).

48. Stewart H. Holbrook, "What the Loggers Read," *The Bookman* 65 (July 1927), 528–531.

49. Larry Peterson, "The Intellectual World of the IWW: An American Worker's Library in the First Half of the 20th Century," *History Workshop Journal* 22, no. 1 (1986), 153–172.

50. Workers Education Bureau of America, *Workers Education in the United States, Report of Proceedings, First National Conference on Workers Education in the United States Held at the New School for Social Research, New York City, April 2–3, 1921* (New York: Workers Education Bureau of America, 1921), 84–85.

51. Rasche, *Reading Interests of Young Workers* (1925), 143–144.

52. Jesse L. Ralph to Dale Herder, quoted in Herder, "Education for the Masses," 260.

53. Carl Sullivan to Dale Herder, quoted in Herder, "Education for the Masses," 263.

54. Tad Tekla to Dale Herder, quoted in Herder, "Education for the Masses," 258.

55. Maurice Neufeld, ed., "Portrait of the Labor Historian as a Boy and Young Man: Excerpts from the Interviews of Philip Taft by Margot Honig," *Labor History* 19 (Winter 1978), 39–63, 67–70; University of Wisconsin Admission Record for Philip Taft, September 20, 1928, University of Wisconsin Archives.

56. Harry Haywood, *Black Bolshevik: Autobiography of an Afro-American Communist* (Chicago: Liberator Press, 1978), 96–97.

57. Ibid., 98–101, 128–129, 148–175. For a taste of Richard Wright's experiences in the Communist Party, see Wright, *Black Boy (American Hunger)*, 315–328.

58. Lescohier, "With the I.W.W. in the Wheat Lands," 380.

59. Stromquist, *Re-inventing the People*, 3.

60. Workers Education Bureau of America, *Workers Education in the United States*, 96.

"Write as You Fight"

The Pedagogical Agenda of the Working Woman, *1929–1935*

JANE GREER

IN HIS 1929 ESSAY "Go Left, Young Writers," in the *New Masses*, author Mike Gold characterized the emerging proletarian author as distinctly masculine. He was a "wild youth" whose physical prowess would allow him to earn a living as a lumberjack, miner, steel worker, or farm laborer while also sharing his experiences and insights by "writ[ing] in jets."[1] Gold was by no means the only Leftist who constructed working-class authorship as the enterprise of men. The pages of *New Masses* and the *Daily Worker* featured book reviews that commended proletarian novels for their "vigorously masculine style," lauded the songs of black sharecroppers for their "virility," and celebrated poetry for equating male power with both the strength of the American landscape and the promise of industrial advancements.[2] Scholars such as Constance Coiner, Laura Hapke, Barbara Foley, and Paula Rabinowitz have variously noted that the linkage of leftist literary vitality with masculinity created obstacles for any woman who wanted to write revolutionary texts.[3]

However, working-class women writers such as Anzia Yezierska, Agnes Smedley, Tillie Olsen, Leane Zugsmith, Meridel Le Sueur, Grace Lumpkin, Fielding Burke, and Josephine Herbst did overcome these obstacles, and they produced a powerful canon of working-class women's literature. Novels such as *Bread Givers* (1925), *Daughter of Earth* (1929), *Yonnondio* (1934–1937), *A Time to*

Remember (1936), *The Girl* (1978), *To Make My Bread* (1932), *Call Home the Heart* (1932), and *Rope of Gold* (1939) gave voice to a distinctly feminine revolutionary consciousness.[4] A number of fine literary and historical studies have elucidated how these and other radical female writers of the 1930s struggled to bring to light the discrimination women faced in the workplace, the callousness of social service and relief agencies toward the economic needs of women, the spousal abuse and desertion that could result from widespread economic victimization, and the unremitting demands women faced as they juggled their roles as breadwinners and mothers.

Scholars interested in how working-class women disrupted the gendering of the worker-writer as male and articulated their unique concerns in the wider print culture of the early twentieth century have also looked beyond well-known women novelists. They have examined a number of worker-education programs that sprang up in the early part of the twentieth century, providing working-class women with unique opportunities to develop their powers as writers, readers, and labor activists. Karyn L. Hollis has explored how the Bryn Mawr Summer School for Women Workers (1921–1938) enacted a "materialist pedagogy" that acknowledged the lived experiences of women both on the job and on the picket line.[5] Autobiographical writing, poetry, and labor drama were all part of the curriculum as women workers lived and studied together for eight weeks on the lush Bryn Mawr campus every summer. Mary Frederickson has documented the ways in which the Southern Summer School for Women Workers (1927–World War II) "hoped to transcend the reformist goal of improving the lot of individuals" that was common among adult education programs; instead, the school's founders "envisioned regional collective change: a transformation of the lives of Southern working women." As the 1930s saw an increase in labor organization across the South, the Summer School adapted its pedagogy to respond to the 80 percent of attendees who represented local unions and were interested in parliamentary procedure, labor history, and economics.[6] Other important sites for worker education include the Highlander Folk School, Brookwood Labor College, Commonwealth College, and the Affiliated Schools for Women Workers, with programs in Wisconsin, North Carolina, Ohio, and New York.[7]

While these important and pedagogically innovative schools helped to produce labor union leaders and to energize the workers who attended them, such educational opportunities were beyond the reach of the vast majority of working-class women. As Robert J. Altenbaugh notes, these residential labor colleges "succeeded in training a cadre of labor educators, writers, editors, organizers, union officers and other activists," but the working masses were "affected by the schools only indirectly."[8] The working masses would instead need to be educated at the homes, farms, and factories where they worked, and the radical press of the 1930s attempted to do just that. This chapter calls attention to one such effort. From 1929 to 1935, the Communist Party of the United States (CPUSA) used the *Working Woman*, a monthly newsmagazine, to educate working-class women readers.[9]

Selling for five cents an issue (or fifty cents for a year-long subscription), the *Working Woman* provided extensive coverage of women's participation in the labor movement. It featured articles on the militant activities of female workers in Maryland silk mills, the exploitation of black domestic workers by white employers, and the efforts in the Soviet Union to end illiteracy among women and children. Well-known writers and CPUSA leaders such as Harrison George, Grace Hutchins, Myra Page, and Maxim Gorki received bylines when their work appeared in the *Working Woman*. Most articles, though, were unattributed or were authored by "worker-correspondents." As Mary Templin has observed, the early issues of the *Working Woman* physically resembled the *Daily Worker*, the CPUSA's principal news journal. The layout featured four columns per page and small type. Graphic elements included grainy photographs and relatively simple sketches, line drawings, and cartoons. Any available white space at the bottom of columns or ends of articles was filled with appeals to join the CPUSA.[10] In 1933 the *Working Woman* adopted a more reader-friendly, magazine-like format, with a three-column layout, more white space, and more sophisticated graphic elements. Like other CPUSA publications, the primary purposes of the *Working Woman* were to disseminate the Party's political message, to strengthen the allegiance of those already committed to the Communist cause, and to recruit new members. Careful attention, though, to such "propaganda" reveals that even avowedly doctrinaire texts are rarely as straightforward as they seem and can present readers with opportunities to enact a range of interpretive performances. As I will argue throughout this chapter, the *Working Woman* encouraged its readers to view texts as opportunities for critical engagement, not merely as commodities to be traded in the literary marketplace—or the marketplace of ideas—for passive consumption.

More than just informing its readership about the labor movement and the Communist Party's efforts on behalf of the working class, the *Working Woman* attempted to transform working-class women readers from consumers of print culture into producers who could disrupt the gendered construction of the worker-writer and articulate their own interests. The magazine viewed its readers not simply as an audience to be mobilized but as potential authors capable of manufacturing new textual productions that would represent their concerns as women and as workers. Educator and scholar Eli Goldblatt has persuasively argued that authorship is not invested in an individual but is an artifact of that individual's personal and social relationships with a broader culture. "Authorship" thus derives from the extent to which writers feel "authorized" to speak, to fashion their own knowledge into socially meaningful texts to be shared.[11] The *Working Woman* sought to serve as an institution that could educate and authorize working-class women.

The *Working Woman* magazine, issue from 1933. (image courtesy of University of Michigan, Special Collections, Ann Arbor, MI)

In this chapter, I focus particularly on the pedagogical strategies used by the *Working Woman* as it sought to authorize working-class women as writers and to counter the dominant tendency in the discourse of the American Left to construct the category of "worker-author" as male. I will focus on three specific tactics the magazine used to encourage its particular audience—working-class women—to become producers of written texts, not just consumers. First, the *Working Woman* positioned printed texts as a weapon that working-class women could wield to defend themselves, their children, and their coworkers. Second, it offered alternative visions of writing so that working-class women could visualize themselves taking up the pen. And, third, it acknowledged the complexity of women's lives and recognized that even women devoted to working-class causes had multiple, sometimes conflicting, interests. Ultimately, my hope is that this exploration of how the *Working Woman* struggled to transform its working-class female readers into working-class writers may more generally support the argument that expanding our sense of the range of sites where print culture and education intersect can help to uncover the complicated processes by which the authority of authorship can be claimed by members of marginalized populations. To begin, a brief history of the Communist Party in the United States will provide a useful background for understanding the *Working Woman*'s pedagogical strategies.

The CPUSA in the 1920s and 1930s: From Party In-Fighting to Fighting Poverty

The roots of the Communist Party in the United States can be traced to the Socialist Movement in the early years of the twentieth century. Though united under the leadership of Eugene Debs, the Socialist Party was comprised of several blocs, including conservative members allied with the American Federation of Labor and more leftist members whose views were aligned with the Industrial Workers of the World (IWW or Wobblies) and Marxists.[12]

During World War I, Socialists across the ideological spectrum were persecuted for opposing U.S. involvement in the conflict, yet still party membership rolls increased. The Russian Revolution in 1917 and subsequent surge of worker uprisings in Europe inspired American radicals and seemed to portend the creation of workers' states around the globe. As Lizabeth Cohen has noted, 1919 saw "the greatest strike wave in American history" as steel workers, police officers, telephone operators, textile workers, coal miners, and other laborers across the nation sought to protect their jobs, wages, working conditions. According to Cohen, "one in five American workers eventually participated" in organized protests.[13]

The frustrating factionalism of the Socialist Party, though, limited its ability to tap into the rising tide of worker unrest, and in September 1919, Chicago hosted two separate conventions at which competing political parties were established: the Communist Party of America and the Communist Labor Party.[14] Two years later, the Communist Internationale (Comintern), based in Moscow, insisted that the two parties merge into what became known as the Communist Party, USA (CPUSA).

Throughout the 1920s, the CPUSA struggled to define its relationship to the global Communist movement while also trying to articulate an agenda that would appeal to the masses of American workers. The CPUSA's evershifting policies, internal political alliances, and organizing tactics were an attempt to respond to a continuous stream of Eurocentric dictates from the Comintern as various members of the Russian Communist Party sought to gain ascendancy in the international Communist movement.[15] The CPUSA's ability to gain widespread traction in the United States was further complicated by the large number of immigrants and non-English speakers who made up the CPUSA's membership. Citing the work of Nathan Glazer, Guenter Lewy notes that only one-third of CPUSA members were English-speaking at the end of the decade.[16]

With the onset of the Great Depression in the 1930s, the CPUSA shifted gears. Moving away from the sectarian politics and internal strife of the 1920s, the Party worked to address the needs of those hit hardest by widespread economic dislocations. Government officials, politicians, leaders of mainstream labor unions, and business owners all seemed incapable of responding effectively to the national crisis. The CPUSA stepped into the breach created by their inaction, and as Fraser M. Ottanelli notes, "The growing army of unemployed seemed ready for revolutionary organization; the inadequacy of public relief as well as the worsening of the depression generated a determination among many jobless not to suffer hardship passively but to adopt radical, if not political, solutions to their problems."[17] Party activists staged protests against evictions, foreclosures, and high rent; worked to lower the price of food staples and reduce housing costs; and demanded that government relief programs address the needs of families.[18]

The CPUSA's new focus on issues of immediate concern to impoverished families created opportunities for women to engage in the movement. In its early years the CPUSA had not been entirely friendly to women.[19] Traditionally, Marxism gave pride of place to the proletarian struggle, and women's issues would presumably be resolved by the creation of the worker-state. Feminism was a bourgeois project that would only distract working-class women from the proletarian movement that best served their interests. As the CPUSA shifted in 1930 from calling for the proletariat to mobilize around the slogan "Work or Wages" to urging families "Don't Starve! Fight!" the Party "began to evolve beyond the masculine, public spaces of street and factory."[20] When issues such as rent stabilization, food prices, and access to medical care were no longer subordinated to party in-fighting, women who had long labored on behalf of the CPUSA became more visible, and new women were attracted to the Party and its affiliated organizations. To be sure, the CPUSA's move to address the issues most directly affecting struggling families was motivated primarily by a desire to spread the Party's influence, not a newfound commitment to feminist principles. When Mary Inman called for greater attention to the productive value of women's domestic labor in a series of articles for the *People's World*, she was attacked by party leaders, and as Rosalyn Baxandall and Elsa Jane Dixler have noted in their fine studies of the CPUSA, women activists continued to be vexed by leaders in the party who viewed the class struggle from a masculine perspective.[21]

As the CPUSA's only publication that specifically addressed a female audience, the *Working Woman* was thus a crucial site where the relationship between the Party and America's working-class women was negotiated. Rather than merely addressing its readership, the *Working Woman* created a space in which women, whose voices had long been muted, could claim for themselves the power of authorship. I turn now to three specific pedagogical strategies the magazine used to encourage working-class women to take up the pen.

"A Club against the Bosses": Print as a Weapon against Poverty

An important first step in transforming an audience of working-class women into authors would be to provide them with reasons for writing, and the *Working Woman* sought to do so by explicitly positioning literacy as a weapon to be wielded by women working in factories, on farms, and in their own homes. With slogans like "Write as You Fight" and cartoons featuring inspiring images, the magazine sought to make its readers understand that the texts they produced could play a militant social function in their own daily lives. In the June 1930 issue the editors wrote: "The Working Woman is your mouthpiece. It speaks to you and for you. Write for it. Write about the wage slashing and the speed-up schemes of your bosses. The Working Woman . . . is a club against the bosses."[22] A subsequent issue featured an illustration of an attractive, well-muscled woman hitting a portly, expensively dressed man over the head with a copy of the *Working Woman*.[23] As a regularly appearing periodical, the *Working Woman* helped to establish a public identity for working-class women who could use print to engage in labor activism.

Rather than waging a solitary battle, the magazine suggested that working-class women could read and write their way into a community of women who were collectively confronting the effects of poverty and workplace exploitation. The *Working Woman* prevailed upon one of the most credible female voices in the labor movement to substantiate its message that the power of the printed word could be harnessed to create a sense of community among working-class women. Ella Reeve Bloor, popularly known as "Mother Bloor," contributed an essay titled "Prepare for the Future" in honor of her seventy-first birthday in 1933. In this article, Bloor encouraged working-class women to "read more about the workers and farmers' land [Soviet Union], and get the inspiration that must come to us, after every story of the new life that has come to the workers there." She went on to note that "Our magazine *The Working Woman* helps to break the ice of ignorance. With *The Working Woman* in our hands we can unlock the doors of many homes, homes of farmers as well as workers. We had the experience only last week which proved this. We took two copies, April and May numbers, to the wife of an isolated farmer, living quite a distance from town. She was deeply interested in the stories of the problems of working women; she drove with me to a meeting of unemployed workers and farmers in Fort Dodge and was deeply stirred by the alert, intelligent wives and daughters of the unemployed." Before leaving the no-longer-isolated farm wife, Bloor secured from her a promise that she would write to the *Working Woman* about the conditions of farm women, a task which "she can do well."[24]

Of course not all the magazine's readers and potential writers could expect a visit from Mother Bloor, but the *Working Woman* promised those who wrote to the magazine that it would help them connect with other activists in their communities. For example, in July 1931, the *Working Woman* featured an article that contrasted the suffering of the Porcellini family in New York City that had no money for food, shoes, or electricity with the affluence of a "Mrs. S. Etanwood Menken," who lived but a few blocks away and strolled the streets of Manhattan "bedecked . . . like a painted poster" in $200,000 worth of jewelry. Readers were encouraged to address this inequity by joining Unemployed Councils, the Trade Union Unity League, and the Communist Party. The article concluded, "If you want to join them in their struggles to put wages up and prices down, to gain social insurance for unemployed workers—write to the 'Working Woman' and we will let you know the people in your town or city who are carrying on the fight where you are."[25]

By positioning writing as a weapon women could use in the fight against poverty and workplace exploitation, the *Working Woman* encouraged its readers to recognize the power of the written word and to take up the pen themselves. Through textual activities, working-class women could unite with others and create their own activist communities as well as connect to Communist Party work across the nation and around the world. By writing, the readers of the *Working Woman* could help produce a militant working-class culture in which women were equal partners with men in the struggle against poverty and economic exploitation.

"No Pen around for Miles":
Alternative Visions of Authorship

While working-class women might be motivated by the written word and its ability to create a sense of community, the *Working Woman* also realized that it needed to offer alternative visions of writing so that working-class women could imagine themselves as authors. Some twenty years ago, Linda Brodkey documented how literary modernism in the early years of the twentieth century helped to create a pervasive of the image of the solitary writer isolated from the world in a garret.[26] For Brodkey, this image has powerfully served the interests of those already privileged by existing socioeconomic power relations, and women and members of other marginalized populations have had to challenge this conception of the writer with sufficient material resources to remove himself or herself from the work-a-day world to produce art. Brodkey points to Susan Sontag and Virginia Woolf as women writers who successfully disrupt this narrow vision of isolated authorial labor, and writers who were members of the CPUSA similarly attacked the notion of the author as genius who retreats from the world. In her essay "Formal Education in Writing," Meridel Le Sueur, an active Communist in the 1930s and one of only two women to address the American Writers Congress in 1935, attacked universities for teaching the literary arts in ways that preserve "with exquisite care the corpse of an old image whose spirit has long been dead," making it impossible for writers to come into contact with the "intervening confusion—the very substance of the life about [them]."[27] As Sontag, Woolf, and Le Sueur so powerfully articulate, if women and members of marginalized populations are to claim the power of print, alternative images of textual production need to supplant the vision of the singular genius isolated from the world.

The *Working Woman* thus offered its own competing image of the act of writing. To challenge the notion that authorship was a solitary endeavor, the editors published many different types of collaboratively written texts. Andrea Lunsford and Lisa Ede have pointed out that "[t]he meaning of the term *collaborative writing* is far from self-evident" and can include a range of authorial relationships and activities: multiple writers producing a single document; a writer who draws upon the expertise and talents of others to produce a single document; groups of writers who work together in planning and preparation but produce multiple individual documents.[28] The pages of the *Working Woman* contained many such varied forms of collaborative writing. For example, "Stockyard Stella," a serial love story composed by a group of workers, appeared in the magazine from January through April 1935, and the May 1935 issue included "A Poem" written by a group of twelve women from the Working Woman's Reading Club of Utah County, Utah. The August 1933 issue featured parallel articles written by Carrie Smith and Cora Lewis about their experiences as

African American women participating in a strike against the Funston Nut Company in St. Louis. Such parallel articles underscored the value of multiple perspectives while also pointing toward powerful possibilities for imagining new forms of collective action in both textual and nontextual arenas.

Collaborative writing also made it possible for workers who did not yet have great facility with the English language to make their voices heard. A "jobless girl worker" who signed her initials D.E.E. wrote to the *Working Woman* for a Spanish-speaking woman whose entire family worked in the beet fields of Colorado. Working as a translator, D.E.E. collaborated with the beet worker to produce three short paragraphs that chronicled the lives of agricultural laborers: working fourteen to sixteen hours a day in the scorching sun to weed and thin the beets in the summer and then finishing the harvest with cracked and bleeding hands when the weather turned cold. D.E.E. concluded "The fine militant spirit of these Spanish workers should be an inspiration to the American workers."[29] Facilitating such interaction between native speakers of English and English language learners was a crucial issue for a political organization like the CPUSA that could not claim that the majority of its members were American-born until 1936.[30]

In addition to collaboratively authored texts, the *Working Woman* published texts that challenged the traditional notion of authorship in other ways. For example, the June 1931 issue featured a collage of headlines and advertisements that contrasted the hardship of workers with the luxuries enjoyed by the wealthy members of society: "Eight girls found living on bananas" appeared above an ad for a flask of Renaud's Rare Amber Orchid perfume selling for nearly $2,000; a headline about the suicide attempt of an unemployed stenographer abutted an ad for mink coats at $1,200. Such assembled texts were particularly appealing to many activist writers in the 1930s because of the ways in which new textual meanings could emerge from the reverberation and refraction of words and ideas as they collided in new arrangements. Cary Nelson has noted that Mike Gold, Joe Freeman, and Tillie Olsen composed similar "found" poems; Gold "authored" a poem by selecting and arranging snippets from Bartolomeo Vanzetti's speeches and letters, and Olsen's "I Want You Women Up North to Know" was drawn from a letter that Felipe Ibarro sent to the *New Masses* in 1934. As Nelson cogently argues, such texts reflected a "shift away from an emphasis on self-expressive subjectivity" and a displacement of the tradition notions of authorship as readers and writers were simultaneously "hailed by other voices."[31] Featuring such nontraditional texts in the pages of the *Working Woman* helped to hail new worker-correspondents for the magazine and to encourage working-class women to partner with others—people and texts—to express their concerns.

Even the presentation of the editorial management of the *Working Woman* was handled in a way that de-emphasized individual achievement and cast textual activity as a shared responsibility. Though Anna Damon edited the magazine or served as head of its editorial committee for most of its six-year run, the magazine downplayed her role. Instead, appeals to working-class women to subscribe to the magazine or submit their texts for publication were issued by the *Working Woman* rather than the editor herself. Neither Damon nor the editorial committee directly addressed readers, cultivated a public editorial persona, or explicitly asserted ownership over the magazine and its message. By effacing their own editorial agency and personifying the magazine itself, Damon and the committee underscored what Jennifer Phegley has called "the collaborative nature of periodicals, in which no single author, originator, editor, or publisher can be identified as having sole responsibility for what emerges as its agenda."[32]

In addition to challenging the image of the writer as a singular genius, the *Working Woman* sought to disrupt the notion that writing could only be accomplished in quiet, secluded spaces. The magazine featured stories that described women writing in a variety of physical spaces and places. A woman who described herself only as a "Southern Textile Worker" wrote: "I am writing this in pencil because there is no pen around for several miles. I'm writing in a little wood shack with the wind blowing through all the corners. Making a little brush fire in the grate to take off the chill was a problem this morning because finances nowadays around here don't come up to the high point needed to keep the house in matches. Not a cent in this house and a heap of others like it. Two pounds of rusty fatback and six pounds of flour maximum rations—for four grown people—weekly. We can't even make regular bread because the oil stoves have no bakers. So we make primitive flat bread in an iron skillet on top of the stove."[33] Another article described the life of "Michaelovna," a thirty-nine-year-old woman in the Soviet Union, who learned to read and write by studying at the Red Banner textile factory where she worked.[34] Charles E. Clark has studied the history of Soviet literacy campaigns, and he notes that in 1923, the Soviet Union and its literacy commission had launched an ambitious campaign that targeted trade unions with the goal of having a fully literate industrial workforce within two years. Women like Michaelovna who were employed in urban factories were able to take advantage of a wide range of resources to support their efforts to become proficient readers and writers, including factory libraries, wall newspapers, clubs, and even nurseries that provided extended childcare so workers could attend classes. As funds for educational initiative were curtailed during the first Five-Year Plan in the late 1920s, the Soviet literacy campaign shifted its focus and began promoting group study in workers' and peasants' homes; women in particular seem to have been attracted to sewing circles that also served as sites for literacy instruction.[35] Recognizing that it was unlikely that most working-class women would ever have "a room of one's own," the *Working Woman* used accounts like the one from

Michaelovna and the Southern Textile Worker to foreground the idea that writing could be accomplished at a kitchen table with children noisily playing under one's feet, in a factory cafeteria when one was on a ten-minute work break, at a noisy gathering of neighborhood women, or while trying to keep warm in bus stations or waiting for food orders at relief offices.

Perhaps the most serious impediment to the *Working Woman*'s project of expanding the definition of writing so that it could become an activity in which working-class women would readily engage centered on issues of standard English grammar and usage. Many members of the magazine's target audience would not have had the opportunity to complete a full primary education, much less have access to secondary or college-level educational institutions. Though nearly 70 percent of school-age children were enrolled in school in 1930, the median number of years of school completed by adults was only 8.4, and these statistics were lower for African Americans and presumably members of the working class.[36] Mrs. George Montgomery may have been a typical subscriber to the magazine. She wrote to the *Working Woman* in June 1931 to describe her life growing up on a plantation in Marion, South Carolina: "I was eight years old when I first went to school. But that paradise lasted only one month and nine days. I had to go to work to support the family."[37] Given the limited experiences many working-class women had with formal education, it is not surprising that a reader like May Blake would express her anxiety about her literacy skills by ending the simple eloquence of her account of a series of a jobs with untenable working conditions this way: "Excuse this writing. It is not good. So good bye."[38]

To encourage women like Mrs. Montgomery and May Blake to continue writing, *The Working Woman* noted that texts submitted for publication did not need to conform to the rules of standard, edited English in order to be powerful. The magazine offered reassurance to women who might be deterred from acts of authorship by their preconceptions about the value of formal education. In December 1929, the *Working Woman* tackled the issue head on: "Working class women often do not have an elementary school education let alone college learning—but this is a working class women's paper read by working women who will understand what you are trying to say, even if it is not written in a literary fashion and perhaps just because it isn't. A new or rather a continuation of the last world war is looming. One of the first steps in fighting this war which the bosses will try to force upon us is to have a newspaper or magazine where we can talk things over so that we might organize our forces for a mighty blow against wars and their instigators, the bosses, the imperialists. WRITE! WRITE! WRITE!"[39] By privileging the content of written texts rather than their form, style, or compliance with the rules of standard, edited English, the *Working Woman* encouraged its readers to create a body of emotionally powerful texts that could function as testamentary evidence in the struggle to achieve social and economic justice.

To find writerly role models who were not dissuaded from taking up the pen by their lack of formal training in grammar and style, the *Working Woman* encouraged its readers to look to the Soviet Union. In a short letter addressed to "Dear Sisters," Pauline Clark pointed out that Soviet women were not deterred from picking up a pen or pencil due to a lack of formal education:

> The Working Woman must be controlled and conducted by working women. There is no need for talented writers to picture for us the future structure of society. We live now in an epoch of realism and we have realistic and practical examples of it in Soviet Russia.
>
> The working women of Soviet Russia participates [*sic*] in all the vital issues of the political and industrial developments, and as such, she is a spokesman for her own ranks. She shoulders all the burdens with all her heart and soul in the hard struggle of building socialism. She, in spite of her limited knowledge, can express the life and the problems confronting us in a more forceful way than a professional writer. Every working woman must participate and write for the Working Woman, sharing her experiences and voicing her opinions.[40]

More than just expostulating about Soviet women's abilities to chronicle their experiences, the magazine offered specific role models. In June 1931 readers of the *Working Women* were introduced to Shadiva, a miner's daughter from what is now Uzbekistan. Provided with no formal schooling, Shadiva was married at the age of ten to a middle-aged man, was forced to wear the black veil of the "paranja" that completely obscured her face, and was confined to the women's quarters of her husband's house. "When Russian women came [to Uzbekistan], bringing tidings of women's freedom," Shadiva was able to learn to read, and her Russian mentors helped her develop her "capacity for eloquence" so that she became "a spell-binding speaker before great audiences of men and women."[41] To be sure, the brief article fails to acknowledge the history of Russian colonialism in Central Asia and the ways in which the formation of Soviet Uzbekistan was based on land reform, collectivization, and the undermining of Muslim religious institutions. Drawing upon the work of Benedict Anderson, Marianne Kamp has documented the "circumscribed ascent" of Uzbek women like Shadiva, who found that their Soviet-sponsored education did not serve as a passport to the opportunities beyond their native region. In fact, Uzbek women who unveiled themselves and burned their paranji in ceremonies that marked their "transformation from housebound, unenlightened slave to modern, educated, politically active, liberated human being" were often subsequently the victims of physical violence and even murder at the hands of Uzbek nationalists.[42] By constructing Shadiva's experiences as a more simple narrative of oppression, communist liberation, education, and authorship, the *Working Woman* sought to inspire working-class women in the United States to generate textual productions about their own lives, regardless of the limits of their formal educational experiences.

"Write as You Wish":
The Dialogic Potential of the Periodical

A final pedagogical strategy I would like to highlight involves the *Working Woman*'s use of the dialogism inherent in the periodical format to acknowledge the complexity of women's lives and to recognize that even women devoted to the causes of the working class occupied diverse subject positions. Within magazines, newspapers, monthly journals, and other periodical forms, the meaning of any single item is always inflected by the surrounding material. For example, in the *Working Woman*, the appearance of an article on the Harlem Tenants League's efforts to combat exorbitant rent next to an account of a shoe workers' strike reinforced a common message about the importance of collective action. Similarly, when a photograph of a smiling young mother and her five children receiving food supplies after a CPUSA-led strike in the Pennsylvania coal fields appeared next to a headline proclaiming "Prostitution and Low Wages Go Hand in Hand," readers could draw inferences about the Communist Party's commitment to protecting traditional feminine virtue. Such dialogism was a pedagogical resource that could be used to reach a range of diversely circumstanced readers while also creating a discursive space in which the periodical's audience could become active and critically engaged with the periodical as a text of many parts.

The *Working Woman* magazine tapped into this dialogism by including material on the issues women faced on the job as well items on how economic deprivation affected women as mothers and homemakers. Articles and editorials thus addressed the organizing activities of women in a wide range of industries, the price of bread, the need for effective methods of birth control, the low wages of African American domestic workers, and the intrusiveness of social service and relief agencies into the housekeeping habits of families seeking aid. A wide range of working-class women were thus likely to find issues pertinent to their own lives addressed in the magazine's pages. Rather than lose potential readers/writers, the *Working Woman* attempted to make its pages a space in which the widest possible audience of working-class women could find their concerns represented. In fact, the magazine sought to reassure its readers that "traditional" female roles were absolutely compatible with the working-class cause.

Women who combined activism with motherhood were thus prominently featured in the magazine. The December 1929 issue featured a letter that Ella May Wiggins, the songstress and martyr of the 1929 Gastonia strike, wrote from Bessemer City, North Carolina, on August 23, just weeks before her tragic death on September 14. In the letter, Wiggins emphasized her role as a mother as much as her efforts as a nascent labor activist. She linked her low wages to her inability to provide her children with sufficient clothing to attend the local school, and she voiced her frustration with the inflexible shift schedule that

made it impossible for her to nurse her children when they were ill with in-
fluenza.[43] Several pictures of Wiggins's five children ran in the same issue.
Other "motherly" labor leaders and activists featured in the pages of the *Working Woman* included Ella Reeve "Mother" Bloor, Mary Harris "Mother" Jones,
and the mothers of the Scottsboro boys.

It should be noted that activist women in a variety of contexts have often
strategically blended discourses of the home and the workplace to create broad
alliances. Mary Frederickson has documented how Jones, Wiggins, and Lucy
Randolph Mason of the Congress of Industrial Organizations (CIO) all
adopted a "motherly guise" as a "shield against the oppressive dichotomy of
being seen as either a good or bad woman."[44] Kathleen A. Brown makes a similarly nuanced argument about the rhetorical efficacy of Elle Reeve Bloor's
designation as "Mother Bloor." By strategically embracing the idealized image
of the heroic "mother" within the labor movement, these women were able to
quiet questions about their personal lives as they spread their militant messages. Anne Goldman's work on the autobiographical writings of labor organizers Rose Pesotta, Rose Schneiderman, Elizabeth Hasanovitz, and others
further confirms that activist women often avoided inflammatory rhetoric and
instead used feminine tropes of motherhood and housekeeping to describe
their work for labor unions.[45] By couching their organizing work in such terms,
these women leaders avoided wasting energy in futile conflicts with male labor
leaders while simultaneously assuring other women who had not yet committed themselves to social action that working for the labor movement was compatible with traditional femininity. Likewise, the *Working Woman* sought to reassure its readership that writing for the magazine and taking an activist role
in the labor movement in no way required an outright rejection of traditional
gender roles.

The magazine even included columns solely devoted to homemaking
tips and fashion. A column titled "Household by Martha" offered recipes for a
"delicious macaroni salad" and "a very good fish pudding," as well as tips
on cleaning hairbrushes and combs, removing chewing gum from clothing,
smoothing rough hands, and keeping the drain in the kitchen sink fresh.[46]
Readers were invited to contribute to columns devoted to domestic concerns as
well as to write about their efforts to organize labor unions and to protest social
injustice. In fact, as the *Working Woman* worked to increase its circulation and
its influence, its pleas for texts shifted from calls for stories about workplace
exploitation to a more inclusive call for submissions: "We want you to . . . fill
the WORKING WOMAN with a constant interchange and flow of letters.
Here are a few suggestions about what to write. What kind of work are you
doing? What are the . . . difficulties on your job? What is your home life like?
What steps, if any, are being taken in your neighborhood to fight these conditions? These ideas are not intended to cover all points which you can write

about. Write as you wish."[47] Such open-ended calls for submissions signaled to readers that the *Working Woman* recognized the complexity of their lives and the wide-range of issues about which they might be concerned. The byline "worker-correspondent" thus appeared under articles about ways to alter hand-me-down clothes for children as well as efforts to organize walkouts over unfair labor practices in the garment industry and the need for adequate compensation for workplace injuries.

Some critics might charge that by tapping into powerful maternal images and publishing columns on homemaking, fashion, and cookery, the *Working Woman* was conceding to various traditional conceptions of femininity and a narrow understanding of what constitutes women's sphere of experience and influence. For Mary Templin, even though the magazine's more expansive focus on women as housewives and mothers points toward a productive politicization of traditionally female roles, the *Working Woman* still became mired in "the tensions that inevitably emerge from a project that works both with and against the mainstream culture."[48] Even as the magazine expressed outrage over the amount of money wealthy women spent on cosmetics, it offered readers tips on skin care. But rather than unacknowledged complicity with bourgeois culture in such gestures, I see instead a savvy rhetorical gesture that acknowledged the complex contingencies that impinge upon women's lives and that chooses to accommodate (and even strategically capitalize upon) their multiple interests in fair labor practices and tasty recipes, beauty tips and union organizing strategies, social justice and keeping a tidy home. By expanding the range of possible topics about which working-class women might write, the *Working Woman* gave its readers an opportunity to serve as representatives of worlds and experiences they knew well. Just as the CPUSA increased its influence in American life in the 1930s by moving away from a rigid script for workplace organization and addressing the myriad needs of working-class families impoverished by the Great Depression, so too did the *Working Woman* increase the likelihood of its impact as an educational agent for working-class women by acknowledging the range of their concerns and the complexities of working-class life.

Through the various pedagogical strategies I have highlighted here—motivating writers by making them see their texts as weapons to change their worlds and build community, expanding the definition of authorship, and acknowledging the complexity of women's lives—the *Working Woman* undermined the notion that authorship was the entitlement of a few gifted geniuses from economically elite social classes or that the worker-writer was necessarily gendered male. The magazine worked mightily to transform its working-class female readers into working-class female writers: It served as an authorizing institution that encouraged working-class women to participate more fully in a wider culture of print and education.

Readers' Responses to the *Working Woman*

It is difficult to precisely pinpoint the effects of the *Working Woman* on its read-ers. Its circulation numbers were certainly low when compared with other magazines that targeted women readers.[49] Circulation peaked at 11,000 in 1935. In his study of magazines in the twentieth century, Theodore Peterson documents that in the years between 1926 and 1955 "more women's magazines than any other type amassed circulations exceeding a million, and they were among the top leaders in circulation."[50] For example, *McCall's*, with its sections on news and fiction, homemaking, and fashion, had a circulation just under 2.5 million in 1935, and *True Story*, the leading "confession" magazine, sold at least 2 million copies annually between 1926 and 1955.[51]

Critiques of these more widely circulated magazines often appeared in the *Working Woman*. In March 1933 the editorial committee blasted the "thousands of women" who purchased magazines like the *Women's Home Companion* and *True Story*. The committee noted that such magazines taught a woman that "her chief desire should be to get a rich man and be a parasite, and that she should ape the rich and forget her class interests."[52] The *Working Woman* partic-ularly directed its ire toward *True Story* and its publisher, Bernarr McFadden, who opposed legislation mandating an eight-hour work day for women. In 1931 the magazine excoriated McFadden for not publishing the "true stories" of women who worked "long weary hours of back breaking toil."[53]

Even though the *Working Woman* could not compete with major players like *McCall's* or *True Story* in the wider print culture, the best evidence for the effec-tiveness of the magazine's pedagogical efforts can be found in its own pages. Many working-class women did take up the pen, and the pages of the *Working Woman* became a space within the wider print culture where they could repre-sent themselves and challenge the social and economic structures that left them impoverished. For some women, the magazine was an important outlet. De-nied the right to express themselves on the job or even in their homes, they turned to the *Working Woman*. "From morning to night we sit at the machine and are not permitted to utter a word. At times I feel I will forget how to speak," wrote a white goods worker from New York.[54] Another woman, who identified herself only as M. K., confronted both oppression on the job and her husband's resistance to her interest in the labor movement. Her struggle was apparent in the opening of the letter she wrote to the *Working Woman*: "Dear Editor: I really don't know how to start my letter. But this is the only place where I can write all this out." After describing frustrating conversations with her husband, M. K. concluded: "I try my best to make him understand the present system which forces us to fight against wage cuts and our very bread. I want him to be closer to his own class, to read and go to meetings to see that no woman is wrong by going to meeting. I think that you will do much good for me and my family by helping me out."[55] African American women in the South who were involved in the fight for social and economic justice also turned to the *Working Woman* and other CPUSA publications. Robin D. G. Kelley notes that black women who participated in "Sewing Clubs" affiliated with the Share Croppers Union "read the *Daily Worker*, the *Southern Worker*, and *Working Woman* when they could get it, and generated a stream of correspondence that linked their local struggles with the national and international movement. Union wives or girls with a modicum of formal education wrote brief descriptive letters to the Party's daily and regional tabloids. Usually the result of collective discussion within the union locals, the letters were 'often scribbled on a piece of sack or crumpled wrapping paper.'"[56] Economic exploitation and sexism often silenced working-class women in their daily lives, and their voices generally were not represented in the mainstream media. Yet, for women like M. K. and the African American women described by Kelley, the *Working Woman* provided an opportunity to make themselves heard.

The brevity of many articles attributed to such "worker-correspondents" pointed out not only the difficulty many working-class women faced in representing their lives in print but also to their commitment in attempting to act on the lessons provided by the *Working Woman*. A woman from Birmingham, Alabama, described her work life in just seventy-one poignant words: "I have one of those starving jobs. I go to work at seven a.m. in the morning, get coffee, water, and a slice of bread for breakfast. Work at breakneck speed until one p.m. then coffee, water, bread, soup; some times a small piece of left-over meat. All of this I refuse to eat. I work until two p.m. for four dollars a week. I have to buy groceries with that."[57] Similarly Mrs. E. from New Bedford, Massachusetts, composed a few paragraphs for the *Working Woman* but acknowledged that her brief text could not fully capture the complexities of her family's struggles in the face of her husband's unemployment and her numerous pregnancies. She noted, "This is only a half dozen words, but if it were to tell our life it would take at least four books."[58]

Though the articles appearing under the byline "worker-correspondent" were often short and the writers at times expressed some level of dissatisfaction with their own textual productions, these newly minted authors acknowledged the pedagogical role the *Working Woman* played in their lives. A member of a Women's Auxiliary of the Progressive Miners drew a sharp contrast between the educational potential of the *Working Woman* and the publications of the Progressive Miners. She noted that "Our Progressive Miner paper doesn't have hardly any educational articles for the womenfolk, but just announcements. What I think we need is some sort of educational activity in our branches, because that will also help to activize [sic] our members and teach them about the miners' fight."[59] Other women took to heart the *Working Woman's* lessons on writing as a powerful weapon that they could wield in the struggle to change

their daily lives and to connect with other like-minded women. An author identified only as J. C. wrote: "We women feel that spring is here. We also feel that
more worry is coming our way. So instead of sitting and weeping alone, we decided to organize and instead of crying we are to use our heads and our voices
and work out ways to better our position and our families by organizing a
neighborhood group. . . . We are also accepting the WORKING WOMAN
magazine as our official organ, for it is the only magazine that is published in
the interest of working class women. . . . Write to our magazine, women! *Organize! Fight!*"[60] Clearly, the *Working Woman* successfully motivated some of its
readers to become writers by positioning authorship as a potent role for those
engaged with others in the class struggle. Women were well aware, though, of
the risks that textual production could entail. A. Dupank wrote to describe the
exploitation she faced as a domestic worker, and she concluded this way: "Well,
I guess it's not only me that's treated like this. Some of the women are afraid to
write, so their mistress might find out and be fired. You're fired whether you
write or not, so what's the difference? We are their slaves. If all the workers
stick together, we would not need to be their slaves."[61] Dupank emphasized
the importance of workers sticking together, and the texts of other women who
were schooled by the *Working Woman* give evidence that they too recognized the
creation of a workers' community as one of the most compelling consequences
of authorship.

Many of the texts women published in the *Working Woman* explicitly called
for response from the wider community of readers. Henrietta Bonim's letter
about working conditions at the Moyer's Pants factory was representative.
After two paragraphs describing long work hours, low wages, speed ups, and
abusive bosses, Bonim concluded: "Some of us are beginning to understand
that the reason why the boss can take such advantage of us is because we are
unorganized and have no power to back us. . . . We are beginning to learn how
to stick together, but we need some help from workers who know more about
organization than we do. We hope that you comrades who are issuing the
"Working Woman" will give us some advice, we will be very thankful."[62] Similarly, Bessie Tierney, a side seamer at a clothing manufacturer in southern Illinois, chronicled a continual cycle of piece rate reductions, and she closed with
the query: "Working women, what does this mean?"[63] Though appearing ir-
regularly, the "Mail Box" feature in the *Working Woman* suggested that readers
adopted the magazine's view that textual production created an interactive
forum and combated the sense of isolation that working women faced. Women
wrote requesting advice on a variety of issues: how to sustain interest in the
tenants' league that had not yet been successful in garnering lower rent; how to
fashion clothes for children out of leftover feed bags; how to conquer one's fear
of workplace reprisals for being seen as a labor agitator.[64]

Conclusion

For some of its readers, then, the pedagogical agenda of the *Working Woman* was realized. Working-class women interacted with, internalized, and embodied the construction of authorship that emerged in its pages. The texts written by working-class women were often brief and sometimes expressed a sense of writerly inadequacy, but the *Working Woman* productively engaged its readers in a wider labor movement and print culture. The magazine's worker-correspondents aligned themselves with the proffered vision of writing as a weapon in the fight for social justice. They wrote against narrow conceptions of the writer as a solitary genius who retreated from the world, and they were not intimidated by their lack of mastery of standard English grammar. They gave voice to the complexities of their lives as women and as workers.

In sum, the *Working Woman* served as an authorizing institution for working-class women. Its pedagogical agenda consisted of giving them motivation to produce texts, helping them imagine themselves as authors, and acknowledging the complexity of their lives by expanding the range of topics and issues about which they might write. Positioned where print culture and education intersect, the *Working Woman* was a site where working-class women in the 1930s could explore writing as a creative act that would afford them a chance to grow individually and to work collectively to alter the world around them. To be sure, authorial identity does not necessarily translate into political power, but for members of disenfranchised groups, authorizing institutions such as the *Working Woman* are important. As Eli Goldblatt notes, "resistance without the authority of authorship is inevitably silent or silenced."[65] By encouraging readers to "write as you fight," the *Working Woman* was doing its part to ensure that working-class women had the educational opportunities they needed to begin to make their voices heard in authoritative ways.

Notes

1. Mike Gold, "Go Left, Young Writers," *New Masses* 4 (January 1929), 3–4.

2. Quoted in Barbara Foley, *Radical Representations: Politics and Form in U.S. Proletarian Fiction, 1929–1941* (Durham, NC: Duke University Press, 1993), 222.

3. Constance Coiner, *Better Red: The Writing and Resistance of Tillie Olsen and Meridel Le Sueur* (New York: Oxford University Press, 1995); Laura Hapke, *Daughters of the Great Depression: Women, Work, and Fiction in the American 1930s* (Athens: University of Georgia Press, 1995); Foley, *Radical Representations*; Paula Rabinowitz, *Labor and Desire: Women's Revolutionary Fiction in Depression America* (Chapel Hill: University of North Carolina Press, 1991).

4. As a novel, *The Girl* was not published until 1978 when John F. Crawford recovered the 1939 manuscript from Le Sueur's basement. Sections of the novel had been published, though, as short stories in the 1930s in periodicals like *The Anvil* and *New Masses*.

5. Karyn L. Hollis, *Liberating Voices: Writing at the Bryn Mawr Summer School for Women Workers* (Carbondale: Southern Illinois University Press, 2004), 6.

6. Mary Frederickson, "The Southern School for Women Workers," *Southern Exposure* 4 (1977), 72, 73.

7. For more on workers' education programs, see Joyce L. Kornbluh and Mary Frederickson, eds., *Sisterhood and Solidarity: Workers' Education for Women, 1914–1984* (Philadelphia: Temple University Press, 1984); and Richard J. Altenbaugh's *Education for Struggle: The American Labor Colleges of the 1920s and 1930s* (Philadelphia: Temple University Press, 1990).

8. Altenbaugh, *Education for Struggle*, 223.

9. The *Working Woman* can be viewed as part of the CPUSA's broader educational agenda. Like the Socialist organizations out of which it grew, the CPUSA recognized that mainstream educational institutions did not serve members of the working class. The Party sponsored its own schools to serve working adults, and comrades interested in studying at Comintern schools in Russia could avail themselves of stipends and scholarships. Less formally, educators who were members of or sympathetic to the Communist Party brought their Leftist perspectives to bear upon their work in mainstream classrooms and educational institutions.

Marvin E. Gettleman has undertaken the important work of recovering and writing about the pedagogical projects undertaken at CPUSA-sponsored schools, like the New York Workers School (1923–44), which offered day and evening classes on Marxism, economics, history, English, and public speaking. See Marvin E. Gettleman, "The New York Workers School, 1923–1944: Communist Education in America," in *New Studies in the Politics and Culture of U.S. Communism*, ed. Michael E. Brown, Randy Martin, Frank Rosengarten, and George Snedeker, 261–280 (New York: Monthly Review Press, 1993). For more on the Comintern schools in Russia and the experience of African American students, see Woodford McClellan, "Africans and Black Americans in the Comintern Schools, 1925–1934," *International Journal of African Historical Studies* 26 (1993), 371–390. Jonathan Hunt has charted Holland Roberts's long career in education as a professor at Stanford University, president of the National Council Teachers of English (NCTE), and teacher at the California Labor School.

10. Mary Templin, "Revolutionary Girl, Militant Housewife, Antifascist Mother, and More: The Representation of Women in American Communist Women's Journals of the 1930s," *Centennial Review* 41 (1997), 626.

11. Eli Goldblatt, *'Round My Way: Authority and Double-Consciousness in Three Urban High School Writers* (Pittsburgh: University of Pittsburgh Press, 1995), 42. Goldblatt is certainly not alone among educational researchers and literacy scholars in recognizing that "author-making" requires "sponsors" who both support and co-opt particular types of literacy performances. See Deborah Brandt, "Afterword: A Nation of Authors," in *Teaching Academic Literacy*, ed. Katherine L. Weese, Stephen L. Fox, and Stuart Greene (Mahwah, NJ: Lawrence Erlbaum, 1999), 197, as well as her groundbreaking *Literacy in American Lives* (Cambridge, UK: Cambridge University Press, 2001). See also Robert P. Yagelski's *Literacy Matters: Reading and Writing the Social Self* (New York: Teachers College Press, 1999). Literary scholars and researchers in the field of print culture who study periodicals have also documented the importance of "authorizing" agencies, particularly for members of marginalized populations. See, for example, Elizabeth McHenry's work

on the African American press in *Forgotten Readers: Recovering the Lost History of African-American Literary Societies* (Durham, NC: Duke University Press, 2002); and George L. Berlin's study of Jewish periodicals in "Solomon Jackson's *The Jew:* An Early American Jewish Response to the Missionaries," *American Jewish History* 71 (1981), 10–28.

12. Guenter Lewy, *The Cause That Failed: Communism in American Political Life* (New York: Oxford University Press, 1990); Fraser M. Ottanelli, *The Communist Party of the United States: From the Depression to World War II* (New Brunswick, NJ: Rutgers University Press, 1991); Van Gosse, "'To Organize in Every Neighborhood, in Every Home': The Gender Politics of American Communists between the Wars," *Radical History Review* 50 (1991), 109–141.

13. Lizabeth Cohen, *Making a New Deal: Industrial Workers in Chicago, 1919–1939* (Cambridge, UK: Cambridge University Press, 1990), 12.

14. Lewy, *The Cause That Failed*, 5.

15. Ibid., 7.

16. Citing the work of Nathan Glazer in ibid., 7.

17. Ottanelli, *The Communist Party of the United States*, 28.

18. Ibid., 28–36; Gosse, "'To Organize in Every Neighborhood, in Every Home,'" 112–113; Kathleen A. Brown, "The 'Savagely Fathered and Un-Mothered World' of the Communist Party, U.S.A.: Feminism, Maternalism, and 'Mother Bloor,'" *Feminist Studies* 25 (1999), 547. To be sure, some Party members regretted the loss of the CPUSA's sometimes fierce militancy and felt in adopting "a position only slightly to the left of Franklin Roosevelt," the Party sacrificed its radical potential in favor of increased membership. For a full exposition of this view of CPUSA activity in the 1930s and during WWII, see Elsa Dixler, "The American Communist Party and the Revolution," *American Behavioral Scientist* 20 (1977), 568.

19. For more on the place of women within the CPUSA, see Gosse, "'To Organize in Every Neighborhood, in Every Home'"; Brown, "The 'Savagely Fathered and Un-Mothered World' of the Communist Party, U.S.A."; Rosalyn Baxandall, "The Question Seldom Asked: Women and the CPUSA," in *New Studies in the Politics and Culture of U.S. Communism*, ed. Michael E. Brown, Randy Martin, Frank Rosengarten, and George Snedeker (New York: Monthly Review Press, 1993); and Elsa Jane Dixler, "The Woman Question: Women and the Communist Party, 1929–1941" (PhD diss., Yale University, 1974).

20. Gosse, "'To Organize in Every Neighborhood, in Every Home,'" 129.

21. For a concise recounting of Inman's struggle to obtain recognition of the value of women's domestic labor from the CPUSA, see Foley, *Radical Representations*, 227–228. See also Kate Weigand, *Red Feminism: American Communism and the Making of Women's Liberation* (Baltimore: Johns Hopkins University Press, 2000), for a reading of the Inman controversy that is more generous to the male leadership of the CPUSA.

22. "Read the Working Woman and The Daily Worker," *Working Woman* (June 1930), 5.

23. *Working Woman* (August 1931), 7.

24. Ella Reeve Bloor, "Prepare for the Future," *Working Woman* (June 1933), 17.

25. "Families in N.Y. City Verge on Real Starvation," *Working Woman* (July 1931), 7.

26. Linda Brodkey, "Modernism and the Scene(s) of Writing," *College English* 49 (1987), 396–418.

27. Meridel Le Sueur, "Formal 'Education' in Writing," *Harvest Song*, rev. ed. (Albuquerque, NM: West End Press, 1990), 208–209. For more on Le Sueur's work as a teacher of writing, see Jane Greer, "Refiguring Authorship, Ownership, and Textual Property: Meridel Le Sueur's Pedagogical Legacies," *College English* 65 (2003), 607–625.

28. Andrea Lunsford and Lisa Ede, *Singular Texts/Plural Authors: Perspectives on Collaborative Writing* (Carbondale: Southern Illinois University Press, 1990), 14–16.

29. "Work Side by Side with Men, Fight Side by Side with Them," *Working Woman* (March 1931), 6.

30. Lewy, *The Cause That Failed*, 7.

31. Cary Nelson, "Poetic Chorus: Dialogic Politics in 1930s Poetry," in *Radical Revisions: Reading 1930s Culture*, ed. Bill Mullen and Sherry Linkon (Urbana: University of Illinois Press, 1996), 41, 45.

32. Jennifer Phegley, *Educating the Proper Woman Reader: Victorian Family Literary Magazines and the Cultural Health of the Nation* (Columbus: Ohio State University Press, 2004), 35.

33. "No Pennies for Matches," *Working Woman* (June 1933), 13.

34. Vern Smith, "Woman of the New Order," *Working Woman* (April 1934), 3.

35. Charles E. Clark, "Literacy and Labour: The Russian Literacy Campaign within the Trade Unions, 1923–27," *Europe-Asia Studies* 47 (1995), 1335. See also Peter Kenez, *The Birth of the Propaganda State: Soviet Methods of Mass Mobilization, 1917–1929* (Cambridge, UK: Cambridge University Press, 1985).

36. Thomas D. Snyder, ed., *120 Years of American Education: A Statistical Report* (Washington, D.C.: National Center for Education Statistics, 1993), http://nces.ed.gov/pubs93/93443.pdf (accessed January 7, 2007), 14, 21.

37. "I Worked at 7," *Working Woman* (June 1931), 6.

38. May Blake, "Sharks Cheat Jobless," *Working Woman* (June 1930), 3.

39. "This Is Your Paper—Write to It," *Working Woman* (December 1929), 6.

40. Pauline Clark, "Dear Sisters," *Working Woman* (January 1930), 3.

41. "Flame-Like Shadiva," *Working Woman* (June 1931), 7. The article goes on relate that in addition to acquiring her new literacy skills, Shadiva's "new Russian friends" helped her secure a divorce and remarry a man closer to her own age who shared her modern communist outlook.

42. Marianne Kamp, "Pilgrimage and Performance: Uzbek Women and the Imagining of Uzbekistan in the 1920s," *International Journal of Middle East Studies* 34 (2002), 264, 272.

43. "Ella May Sent a Letter to the Working Woman," *Working Woman* (December 1929), 1.

44. Mary Frederickson, "Heroines and Girl Strikers: Gender Issues and Organized Labor in the Twentieth-Century American South," in *Organized Labor in the Twentieth Century South*, ed. Robert H. Zieger (Knoxville: University of Tennessee Press, 1991), 89.

45. Anne E. Goldman, *Take My Word: Autobiographical Innovations of Ethnic American Working Women* (Berkeley: University of California Press, 1996).

46. "Household by Martha," *Working Woman* (May 1933), 19.

47. "Readers," *Working Woman* (June 1933), 12.

48. Templin, "Revolutionary Girl, Militant Housewife, Antifascist Mother, and More," 630.

49. The business manager for *Working Woman* reported that the 11,000 copies of the magazine printed in April 1935 had sold out in just three days. Of course, each of these copies was likely read by multiple readers. In fact, the *Working Woman* encouraged the sharing of texts. Women were urged to pool their funds to purchase and share copies of proletarian novels by writers like Grace Lumpkins and to share issues of the *Working Woman* with as many other women as possible.

50. Theodore Peterson, *Magazines in the Twentieth Century* (Urbana: University of Illinois Press, 1956), 59.

51. Ibid., 56, 279.

52. "The Working Woman: Changes to a Magazine," *Working Woman* (September 1933), 2.

53. "Behind the 'True Stories,'" *Working Woman* (October 1931), 3.

54. "A Few Words about the Knit Form," *Working Woman* (September 1930), 3.

55. "How Can I Make My Husband Understand?," *Working Woman* (July 1933), 13.

56. Robin D. G. Kelley, *Hammer and Hoe: Alabama Communists during the Great Depression* (Chapel Hill: University of North Carolina Press, 1990), 46–47.

57. "Working Hard and Starving," *Working Woman* (April 1931), 3.

58. "Textile Workers and Wives in New Bedford Know Meaning of Joblessness," *Working Woman* (August 1931), 4.

59. "From a Coal Town," *Working Woman* (May 1935), 7.

60. "Seven Mothers Unite to Fight," *Working Woman* (June 1933), 8.

61. "Young Wives Forced Out to Work," *Working Woman* (February 1930), 3.

62. Henrietta Bonim, "Conditions Unbearable in Moyer's Pant Factory," *Working Woman* (September 1931), 3.

63. "From a Miner's Wife," *Working Woman* (September 1930), 5.

64. "The Mail Box," *Working Woman* (April 1931), 7.

65. Goldblatt, *'Round My Way*, 44.

"A Gentleman Is No Sissy"

Reading, Work, and Citizenship in the Civilian Conservation Corps

CATHERINE TURNER

AROUND 1937, the federal Office of Education, Division of Special Projects and Programs, began creating workbooks for the educational program of the Civilian Conservation Corps (CCC). Alongside materials for use in vocational training (including such titles as "Don't Monkey With Edge Tools"), the Office of Education created a series of six workbooks for literacy training. The workbooks, written for beginners, were called "Camp Life Readers."[1] The last chapter of the first book, "A Gentleman Is No Sissy," presented a lesson on the importance of courtesy:

> George Washington once said: "Be courteous to all."
>
> At other times he said: "Sleep not when others speak. Sit not when others stand. Speak not when you should hold your peace. Speak not louder than ordinary."
>
> Abraham Lincoln was called "a kind man and always a gentleman." Even his enemies liked him.
>
> We think of George Washington as a gentleman. We think of Abraham Lincoln as a gentleman. Being courteous was a part of the life of each man.
>
> Courtesy helps you get a job today. It is one of the first things men look for. Men who hire others today say: "Be courteous at all times."[2]

While the problems with this lesson were obvious—*courteous* was too hard a word for beginning readers, and Washington's and Lincoln's enemies shot at them—the "Camp Life Readers" shed a great deal of light on the way the leaders of the CCC education program used literacy training to promote a civically oriented, and decidedly masculine, reading public. Federal officials hoped to use the CCC literacy program to buttress and legitimize the growth of the federal welfare state, while at the same time encouraging CCC enrollees to see themselves as members of an active, reading, working-class America.

The key to understanding "A Gentleman Is No Sissy" was the link between masculinity, good behavior, reading, and work. Historian Jeffrey Ryan Suzik has shown how fears of "sissification" consumed Americans in the 1930s and explained how these fears led directly to the creation of the CCC. He cites observers who found Americans "deathly afraid" of the label *sissy*, which implied "dependence or fear or lack of initiative or passivity."[3] "A Gentleman is No Sissy" recognized those fears and, by linking American heroes to courteous behavior (and the ability to get a job), tried to diffuse them. As part of the "Camp Life Readers," this lesson illustrates the CCC's efforts to recast the meaning of reading from a leisure-time activity associated with a feminized public school system to an activity that could develop a vigorous, masculine reading public that, in turn, could create a dynamic, democratic, and productive society.

At the same time, however, the contradiction embedded in this lesson, which praised Washington and Lincoln for getting along with other people rather than leading the nation in war against unjust power, was hard to overlook. On the one hand, education in the CCC aimed at making enrollees independent citizens, capable of reasoned debate and thoughtful participation in the life of the nation. On the other hand, education in the CCC hoped to control young enrollees who, left unsupervised, might become wild and dangerous. Free discussion of every type of printed material was a cherished American value, yet, as Fascism and Communism spread across the globe, that freedom seemed to demand certain limits.[4] The CCC presents a case study of how government policy during the New Deal encouraged reading and, at the same time, placed limits on materials and discussion as the government became involved in what and how citizens could read. Searching for an appropriate balance, leaders in the Office of Education developed reading materials and programs they hoped would lead young men in the CCC to innovate and obey, to develop their individual abilities and connect to their communities. Most importantly, reading had to be turned into a rigorous type of work that would be appropriate for young men who previously associated reading only with leisurely study.

History of the CCC Education Program

President Roosevelt created the CCC to address the twin problems of unemployment and environmental degradation. The program, which came to be run jointly by the Department of Labor, Department of the Interior, the

Department of Agriculture, and the War Department, sent young, unmarried men between the ages of eighteen and twenty-four into rural areas, where they would work to "conserve the land" by building trails, bridges, and ranger stations in national and state parks; setting up phone lines; fighting forest fires; and other activities.[5] The government allocated thirty dollars a month to each man, allowing him to keep five dollars and send home the remaining twenty-five dollars. The idea of dispatching young men to work in the wilderness appealed to Americans' romantic associations between youth and labor. In addition, by focusing on manual labor, the CCC offered the type of rugged activity that Americans felt built character. As Roosevelt explained in his message to Congress on March 21, 1933, "We can take a vast army of these unemployed out into healthful surroundings. We can eliminate, to some extent at least, the threat that enforced idleness brings to spiritual and moral stability. It is not a panacea for all the unemployment but it is an essential step in this emergency."[6] Congress approved the bill forming the CCC at the end of March, and Roosevelt set a goal of enrolling a quarter of a million young men in over 1,000 camps by July.[7]

Roosevelt's plan addressed what many Americans in the 1930s had come to see as "the youth problem." While firm numbers on unemployment in the early 1930s are hard to come by, the National Education Association estimated that between 1933 and 1935 there were 3 to 6 million people below the age of 25 who were unemployed and not in school.[8] These young people became the focus of a number of different sociological exposés, including Thomas Minehand's *Boy and Girl Tramps of America* (1934). Alongside these works, American newspapers and popular magazines carried stories like Maxine Anderson's "200,000 Vagabond Children" in *Ladies Home Journal* (1932). Minehard, Anderson, and others presented a troubling image of the "All-American Boy" prematurely aged, unable to find work, hungry and exhausted, which confirmed for many Americans that the depression was indeed a catastrophe.[9] By sending these young men into the forests away from crowded urban centers or hobo jungles, Roosevelt could keep them safe from a life of poverty and crime.[10]

Not only were unemployed youth an economic and law enforcement problem, they also presented a moral challenge to the American system of democracy. Eleanor Roosevelt spoke to these concerns when she told women's clubs in 1934, "I have moments of real terror, when I think we may be losing this generation. We have got to bring these young people into the active life of the community and make them feel they are necessary."[11] Indeed, experts feared that without some experience of democracy and its benefits, many young people might be seduced by demagoguery. Not long after the Nazi's annexation of the Sudeten region in Czechoslovakia in May 1938, Charles Taussig, chair of the National Advisory Committee of the National Youth Administration (a federal program created in 1936 to address public concerns over the youth problem), explained that young people had begun to turn away from democracy and toward "vendors of gilt substitutes [who] find willing converts to political and social creeds that are destructive to much that this Nation stands for."[12] Ralph Flynt, one of the men behind the "Camp Life Readers," urged CCC enrollees to see democracy as a "struggle" and to see themselves "in the forefront of the fight to not only preserve but to perpetuate democracy."[13] Roosevelt may have created the CCC to conserve forests, but many believed the program would conserve democracy itself.

In this context, plans for reading programs that could improve the citizenship attitudes of unemployed youth began to surface in various federal departments. For example, William Biddle of Western Reserve University's School of Applied Social Science wrote to Secretary of Labor Francis Perkins suggesting that the problem of unoccupied youth could be addressed through "loafing centers" that would provide reading materials and comfortable places to sit. In these centers, young people could be organized into formal discussion groups where they would read about and discuss "economic and social events." Biddle hoped that some of the groups "might shortly begin to study and make recommendations concerning the community and the nation." Even if the groups did not get that far, he added, their reading and discussion would promote "a philosophy of creative activity and living, a philosophy of cooperative responsibility for the common good."[14] Along similar lines, Charles D. Daniel wrote to Roosevelt suggesting a plan that would provide one educational leader for every 1,000 enrollees in the CCC. These leaders, Daniel explained, would meet with 100 men for an hour a week and provide a list of readings for discussion. Then, once the enrollees had completed the reading, the leader would "umpire" the enrollees' discussions. These reading groups would give enrollees "a definite course of studies in the ordinary duties and privileges of citizenship," showing them that the depression was "only a disagreeable pause in the march of our country's progress." Once enrollees learned "the incalculable benefits of membership in our social order as compared with what other countries afford," Daniel predicted they would not expect further government help after leaving the camps.[15] As Daniel saw it, his plan was affordable—he estimated about five dollars per leader—and could save the government money in the long run.

Many of the letters that arrived in the Department of Labor were funneled to Frank Persons, director of the U.S. Employment Service. In May 1933, Persons drafted a plan for enrollee education that centered on reading. Because he was in the Labor Department, Persons's plan also focused on the role reading could play in making enrollees more employable. In his draft, he explained that the primary goal of CCC education programs should be to prepare enrollees for employment once they left camp. The first step in this program was "cultivating reading interests and habits." The other steps—"stimulating interests and hobbies," "systematic instruction," and "vocational guidance"—all required enrollees to read. Persons felt that for each camp, a local educator should create "reading plans for groups that desire to meet for discussion with him." The books in these plans would focus on preparing enrollees "to secure and hold permanent occupations in their life after the camp experience is over."[16] While some aspects of Persons's plan, such as recreational reading and reading discussion groups, did not appear to lead directly to employment, Persons believed that enrollees needed to read in order to find jobs and return the nation to economic health.

Persons sent his plan to state selection agents, whose responses were overwhelmingly positive. Only two agents felt the plan would not work. Most praised the "untold benefits" that Persons's plan would offer enrollees. The selection director in Delaware believed it would provide "proper guidance [to a] most important group of citizens during [a] period of economic social and spiritual instability." In New York state, the Temporary Emergency Relief Administrator offered to pay the camp educational leaders with state funds if Roosevelt did not approve the plan.[17] Another state agent wrote: "It is through education and right thinking that this present depression period can and will eventually be permanently defeated."[18] Like Persons, these state-level officials believed that reading would benefit both enrollees and the nation.

After receiving such positive responses from state selection agents, Persons presented his plan to a conference of University Adult Education and Extension Service directors. The response from the general secretary of the Colorado Prison Association, Robert G. H. Tallman, was typical. He believed the education program needed to encourage enrollees to "think through their problems as individuals and citizens." Tallman specifically focused on reading, asserting that books would provide "underprivileged groups" with a "vision of the world they are living in and their part in it." Arguing that reading would stimulate CCC enrollees to think "as straight as possible on the important matters of the day," Tallman insisted that a federally sponsored reading program would better equip enrollees "to take their place in the community as citizens with some fundamental ideas about their obligations as citizens."[19] Like many of his colleagues, Tallman believed that reading had the power to prepare enrollees not only for employment but also for life in a democracy.

Democracy, Reading, and Hard Work

Initially Roosevelt felt that food, shelter, and steady jobs would be enough to revitalize the young men in the CCC and prepare them for useful employment once they left the camps. He resisted the inclusion of an education program and staffed the CCC with leaders who were also inclined to resist. As late as August 1933, Colonel Duncan K. Major, the War Department's representative on the CCC advisory council, wrote to Roosevelt's secretary, Louis Howe, protesting the inclusion of an education program. "Instead of teaching the boys how to do an honest day's work we are going to be forced to accede to the wishes of the long-haired men and short-haired women and spend most of the time on some kind of an educational course."[20] As Major saw it, education was a distraction from job training—something only radicals would support. A reading program might turn CCC enrollees into sissies, the very fate the CCC ought to help them avoid. Many leaders agreed with Major, especially Robert Fechner, the conservative Southern labor leader Roosevelt appointed to head the CCC.

Unmoved by early calls for education to make the enrollees better citizens, CCC leaders responded instead to concerns about the enrollee's behavior. Throughout the nation, communities reported "riots" as a result of conflict between locals and off-duty enrollees. In Thomaston, Connecticut, high school students and CCC enrollees clashed when the enrollees "accosted" some local girls. The police chief claimed that he had had the "busiest night of my life," and, when questioned, leaders in charge of the camps claimed they had no responsibility for the men after they had finished the workday. Stories like this created demands for a program that would organize and control the enrollees after their working hours.[21] While Fechner resisted adding an education program, by November 1933 Roosevelt changed his mind. He made education an official part of CCC camp life and gave the Office of Education responsibility for administering a new reading program.[22]

As the reading program developed, advocates were careful to address the problem of sissified education. Aware that some forms of "progressive" education were associated with "feminized" learning, and that for the working class reading appeared a leisure activity compared with getting a job, program directors were careful to differentiate CCC reading programs from the type of reading enrollees had encountered in school. Ever since women became the majority of schoolteachers in the United States (sometime in the late nineteenth century), public schools had been accused of "infantilizing" American men.[23] In fact, studies of the CCC education program blamed women for that fact that many CCC enrollees did not like to read. Frank Hill, in his book *The School in the Camps* (1935), explained that the reason so many of the young men left school early was because of the "ministrations of nervous, unmarried women," which the future enrollee found "instinctively repugnant." Hill hoped that because CCC educational advisors were men who were "often physically as well as mentally [the enrollee's] superior," enrollees would be more likely to profit from CCC education.

Advice given to enrollees sought to reassure them that reading in the CCC would be a fully masculine activity. In his guide to the CCC, *Once in a Lifetime* (1935), Ned Dearborn explained that he was aware that enrollees had not enjoyed reading in "the old school you didn't like" where the teacher "didn't understand you" and forced boys to read flowery poetry by Tennyson when they wanted to be reading manly adventure stories like *Robinson Crusoe*.[24] Dearborn asserted that reading in the CCC camps would be different. He advised enrollees that they would get "the best results" from their CCC experience if they read whenever they got the chance. Dearborn, like Hall, made it clear that reading in the CCC would be a more masculine activity, independent of outside control.

Having shifted the meaning of reading away from the feminized school system, CCC leaders recast reading and education as a form of work, similar to the labor CCC enrollees performed during the day. Although some of the CCC's leaders, including Major and Fechner, felt the education program distracted from the focus on conservation work, others highlighted the connection between work, citizenship, and democracy. In his book about depression-era youth, *Millions Too Many?* (1940), Bruce Melvin wrote that "he who would enjoy the full benefits of [democracy] must work in the heat of the noon-day sun and burn brain and brawn between twilight and dawn."[25] Melvin's description echoed earlier CCC descriptions of the manual and intellectual labor expected of enrollees, as well as descriptions of the hard work required to maintain democracy. One plan for CCC education explained that enrollees hoping to profit from their experiences had to show a "disposition to do well the difficult tasks" of citizenship.[26] Dearborn's *Once in a Lifetime* claimed that it took "a good many people with good brains and fine ideals, working together day in and day out, to make a great nation."[27] Such ideas about citizenship allowed educational leaders in the CCC to promote education and reading as work, linking their program to the manual labor required of enrollees.

The link between work and citizenship included, of course, wage-earning work, but most of those engaged in planning the CCC reading program made it clear that a job could not fully address the "work" demands of citizenship. They saw the work program and the education program working together to develop young men into worker-citizens. Ralph Glass, a colonel with the 7th Infantry and commander of the Vancouver Barracks, described the CCC education program as having "a dual aim, *citizenship* and *employability*." For Glass, education and work together served to promote the "civic effectiveness of individual enrollees" by addressing the fact that "employability is a part of good citizenship"[28] but only a part. In the same way, C. T. Clifton, the Educational Advisor at Camp Yellow Springs in Ohio, explained to the "Town and Gown Club" of Yellow Springs that enrollees were not "beasts of burden, . . . but human beings who in a democracy have something to say about their lives." He went on to say that the CCC aimed to help enrollees find a place in "the nation's economy" while also developing "their understanding of political and social issues." For Clifton as for Glass, education for work and education for citizenship operated together; enrollees needed both to be real American men.[29]

Appropriate Materials

Many CCC camps developed libraries of their own and the selection of titles was a common problem. In a study sponsored by the American Youth Council, Kenneth Holland and Franklin Hill found that some exceptional camps had as many as 1,500 volumes. More typical camps had 150 to 250 books, of which many were "distinctly poor in character." In particular, those camps that relied on donated books had libraries full of "mere book rubbish." The reference sections, which the army provided, were "well chosen, except that some of the volumes were beyond the capacity of most enrollees to read and understand." The standard magazines and newspapers to which nearly every camp subscribed included *Life, Newsweek, American Forests, Farmer's Digest, Radio News,* and *The Saturday Evening Post.* Although Holland and Hill regretted that camp libraries lacked liberal journals such as *The New Republic* or *The Nation,* they felt that such journals were "over the heads of 75 percent of the enrollees." In fact, while *Life* magazine was popular, Holland and Hill found that enrollees often preferred to read illustrated catalogs like those from Sears, Roebuck and Montgomery Ward.[30]

Almost every leader in the CCC hoped that enrollees would advance from choosing to read the Sears Roebuck catalog, but they were not sure that the enrollees' next step should be *The Nation.* While leaders of the CCC may have censored materials because of their political and economic perspectives, they *claimed* that they censored these materials because they would have inculcated passivity. Reading and literacy training in the CCC hoped to avoid those "sissy" qualities and show enrollees the manly, working-class virtues demonstrated by reading the right materials. Unlike radio, theater, and movies, which seemed to be relatively passive activities, reading seemed to CCC officials to demand that enrollees work actively, not only to acquire the skills of literacy but also to understand the pressing social and political issues of the day.[31] Moreover, connecting the work of reading to the pursuit of masculine independence helped CCC educational leaders overcome enrollees' resistance to the education program. Yet the pursuit of masculine independence was more complicated than it first appeared. If reading was like work, then it seemed necessary to provide guidance about what—and how—enrollees read. Just as it was important for camp leaders to assign work tasks, so too was it important for leaders to assign reading tasks. Enrollees needed instruction to make sure they completed the right project safely.

Few of the reading plans that made their way to Frank Persons intended to give enrollees complete freedom to choose their own reading materials without guidance. Robert Tallman, the prison leader, understood that the reading groups he suggested could "stimulate thinking on the part of these young men" and could therefore seem "dangerous." He added, however, that any such danger could be avoided "if the choice of leaders was carefully made and they were supervised."[32] Charles Connelley of California echoed these sentiments. While he believed that creating a library for enrollees would be an excellent (and inexpensive) approach to education, he noted that CCC librarians must create a "proper" and "constructive" reading course.[33] State leaders expressed similar ideas. Selection agents in Alabama noted that Persons's plan only would work "with proper safeguards, particularly in selection of counselors."[34] Most agreed that proper reading could only be encouraged through careful surveillance of materials and ideas.

Local education advisors closely monitored CCC reading materials. One camp commander noted that "most of the literature recommended for use in the camps is of excellent character, but, scattered through its pages, one finds material of a subversive nature, material which tends to tear down our existing order of society and which is inimical to national defense."[35] Fechner, eager to appear supportive of enrollees' civil liberties, claimed that he did not prevent Communists from distributing literature in the camps. Nonetheless, historians have shown that Fechner and others *did* block the distribution of left-leaning materials, from *The New Republic* to publications of the Illinois Workers Alliance.[36] Fechner may not have been personally responsible for censoring reading material in the camps, but the CCC as a federal program actively discouraged the reading of leftist materials.

In two famous cases in which the CCC refused to distribute reading materials, leaders said the basis for doing so was the materials' "attitude" toward work. In 1934 Fechner prevented the distribution of *You and Machines*, a book written by University of Chicago professor William G. Ogburn expressly for the CCC and published by the federal Office of Education. In the book, Ogburn claimed that "the problem of the modern age is to adjust itself to a new monster, the Machine." The machine appeared to have "mastered" old institutions such as the family, the church, and the government. Conservatives might have wanted to "bring back the Good Old Days," Ogburn wrote, but a return to simpler times was impossible. Instead, the book suggested that young American workers needed to adjust to a society dominated by machines.[37] Fechner feared that *You and Machines* "might induce a desire to destroy our present economic and political structures." Even worse, Fechner claimed, *You and Machines* was "too gloomy" and could "inculcate a philosophy of despair, not a healthy questioning attitude."[38] Reading, Fechner concluded, should encourage action and work, not despair.

The Office of Education also decided not to purchase Secretary of Labor Henry Wallace's work, *America Must Choose*, for discussion in the CCC. This booklet ended with some fairly challenging questions for the enrollees to discuss: "How would a redistribution of the national income help to solve many of our problems?" "Why does Secretary Wallace say that weapons of economic warfare can be more deadly than artillery?" "Why do not more people see this truth?" and "In what sense is trade within the nation also a kind of warfare?"[39] Such questions may have inspired a "healthy, questioning attitude" on the part of enrollees, but the Office of Education chose not to distribute it. What really stood in the way of distribution was the fact that Wallace's publication was sponsored by the World Peace Foundation. As one of Frank Persons's correspondents noted, "while it does not seem that the War Department ought to try to censor the reading of the men in the Conservation Camps, and I have no doubt it makes no such effort, I still think that the Department will get itself into every kind of trouble if it participates in the distribution of literature bearing the World Peace Foundation label."[40] In this case, it was both the message and the associations of Wallace's text that made it unacceptable.

CCC education advisor C. T. Clifton in Yellow Springs, Ohio, was outraged by these acts of official censorship. Even as he celebrated the value of education to make enrollees good citizens, Clifton criticized the limits the army placed on enrollees' reading and discussion. "Lecturers, especially if they were patriotically 'hearty,' were always welcome," he noted, "but "debates and arguments of any kind, even bona fide discussions, were persona non grata" in CCC camps. According to Clifton, the army feared that real free discussion "could lead to criticism of camp administration and eventual mutiny." He described the texts the CCC censored and the guidelines the Office of Education gave for running any discussions. He was most angered by the advice for handling an undefined set of "dangerous issues" found in *A Manual for Instructors in CCC Camps.* This manual told advisors to try to lead discussion away from "dangerous" topics, or if the enrollees persisted, to promise to bring the issue up later and hope the enrollees would forget. If these evasions failed, the manual advised, the instructor should simply refuse to discuss the issue. Clifton lamented, "this, alas, was training for life in a democracy!"[41]

Official limits on reading may have controlled enrollees' access to reading material, but an even greater obstacle was the cost of books and the enrollees' own limited reading skills. Although they may have been less expensive than other forms of media, books were still costly. Books that Fechner might have found appropriate for enrollees, especially illustrated ones, were often out of reach. The fact that books represented one of the most expensive items of the camp education program meant that many commanders kept them locked up. Few if any camp libraries allowed browsing. Demand for material readily outstripped supply. According to Major Silas M. Ransopher, even the books of popular fiction traveling libraries made available in the camps "were thoroughly read out."[42]

Perhaps the most critical factor that limited enrollees' access to printed material was that many could not read or could not read well. Statistics on illiteracy in the camps varied, but most camp leaders estimated that 2.5 percent to

3 percent of enrollees could neither read nor write. However, certain corps areas, especially the South, had much lower rates of literacy than others. Contemporary historians have referred to the problem of illiteracy in these areas as "endemic" among both white and black enrollees.[43] Equally important was the rate of functional illiteracy, which leaders defined as the inability to read a newspaper or write a letter home. When Frank Hill and Kenneth Holland surveyed CCC camps in 1942, they estimated the number of functionally illiterate enrollees at about 22 percent.[44]

"Camp Life Readers," Citizenship, and Literacy Training

In the late 1930s Congress became more involved in CCC education. While initially Congress funded the CCC in a lump sum, allowing Roosevelt to spend as he saw fit, by 1938 Congress began to assert more oversight on CCC spending. In particular, Congress worked to formalize the camps' educational programs to focus somewhat more on vocational education and elementary skills such as reading and math. Despite its endorsement of the voluntary nature of CCC education, in 1938 Congress stipulated that illiterate enrollees would be required to attend basic literacy classes. At the same time, the Office of Education worked to define reading as a critical work skill that enrollees needed to fully be part of American life. Possibly having learned from its experience with *You and Machines*, the Office of Education designed a new set of basic workbooks to promote reading and citizenship as active and engaged activities, closely linked to work and masculine vigor. In July 1938, the Office of Education asked Ralph Flynt to organize and improve instructional materials in elementary and vocational subjects. He worked with several area educational advisors to create the "Camp Life Readers," a series of six workbooks intended to provide enrollees with "functional use of the English Language" as well as to "increase employability" and offer lessons in "good citizenship."[45] In addition, Flynt created these readers to provide CCC enrollees the "materials and techniques suited to grown men" that critics of traditional school-type literacy programs had been calling for since 1933.[46]

These lessons often cast citizenship in terms of obedience to authority. For example, in "Camp Life Reader #3," the lesson entitled "Learning to Be a Citizen" told enrollees that "most persons are good citizens . . . most persons would rather obey laws than disobey them. They do not care to trouble themselves with being bad citizens." Enrollees could be good citizens by learning "to respect the property that is furnished them by the government" and by giving "the government a day's work for a day's pay and all that it stands for."[47] Many of the lessons in the "Camp Life Readers" sought to prepare enrollees for lives of manual labor. "My First Day of Work" in "Camp Life Reader #1" told the following story:

> Some one gave me a shovel.
> I was told to dig.
> My hands became sore.
> My back hurt.
> It was a change for me.[48]

Later lessons also emphasized the value of manual labor. "Painting Screens," in "Camp Life Reader #2," described the care with which enrollees followed directions. When a leader found "we were doing our work well," their reward was another job described in the next lesson "Building a Coal Bin."[49]

When Holland and Hill studied citizenship training in the CCC, they complained that most CCC camps prepared enrollees for what they called "conforming" rather than "contributing" citizenship.[50] "Camp Life Reader #3," for example, contained the series' most doctrinaire lesson, "The Flag." This lesson included the following excerpt from the Flag Code of the American Legion: "When you see the Stars and Stripes displayed, son, stand up and take off your hat. Somebody may titter. It is in the blood of some to deride all expression of noble sentiment. . . . Your flag stands for humanity, for an equal opportunity to all the sons of men. Of course, we haven't arrived yet at that goal; there are many injustices yet among us, many senseless and cruel customs of the past still clinging to us, but the only hope of righting the wrongs of men lies in the feeling produced in our bosoms by the sight of that flag."[51] "The Flag" encouraged a symbolic patriotism that had little to do with thoughtful or engaged discourse. Although it noted that American democracy was less than perfect, it did not encourage enrollees to question American shortcomings or take an active stand against the "senseless and cruel customs of the past." Instead, it implied that enrollees should simply *feel* patriotic rather than act.

In other cases, however, citizenship lessons in the "Camp Life Readers" linked reading and work in ways that allowed enrollees to imagine themselves as engaged citizens and to see reading as a form of democratic participation. For example, "People Ask Questions," a lesson in the first workbook, encouraged enrollees to answer the question "What are you doing in the CCC?" by saying "I am learning to read."[52] Rather than emphasizing the work project, this lesson linked reading to the CCC's work. In "Camp Life Reader #3" several lessons made the connection between reading and wise participation in a democracy. In "Money" and "A Voter," enrollees were encouraged to read and think about how they spend their money and how they "spend" their vote. "A Voter" depicted enrollees engaged in rational and critical debate. As a result of reading the newspapers and listening to speeches on the radio, the story explained, men had "been discussing the fitness of each candidate." In the end, the lesson asserted, citizens needed to read and study and listen to arguments because they had a "duty to elect only the highest type citizens to public office."[53]

The linkage of reading, citizenship, and hard work surfaced throughout the "Camp Life Readers." In a lesson called "Membership in the American Society," the link between citizenship and work was explicit. The freedom Americans had to "publicly discuss matters of government" and "express their opinions as freely as they like" was not some "miracle." Public discussion of politics represented "deep thought, hard work, and untiring efforts on the part of our early leaders."[54] The "Camp Life Readers" stressed the idea that citizenship was a form of work and the effort required to participate in democratic politics was a duty, very much like the "day's work for a day's pay" that CCC enrollees owed their government.

The "Camp Life Readers" connected self-improvement and community improvement to manual labor and masculinity. Perhaps the most interesting example of this connection appeared in "Camp Life Reader #2." "Building Walks," like many other lessons, combined the idea of work, gender, and citizenship into one. On the way to a date, the narrator of this lesson got mud on his clothes. Noting that "my girl does not like muddy clothes," the narrator found that he could not enjoy the date because he was so self-conscious about the mud. He returned to camp and found his friends also suffering from muddy clothes. As a result, they "talked about the mud," and together decided to build a network of boardwalks so they could keep their clothes clean. They discussed the matter with the camp commander, who was pleased with their initiative and hoped that as a result of their effort their camp might get "the flag for being the best camp." They did not get the flag, but as the narrator explained, "we did get the walks" and by extension the clean clothes that could help them get dates.[55] This lesson was obviously about being a good worker and a man, but it was also about individual initiative within a community. Instead of suggesting blind obedience, the lesson valued community improvement over the mark of distinction that might be granted by external authority.

How successful was the CCC education program—particularly in its attempt to link reading, citizenship, and work? Holland and Hill "recognized that CCC enrollees were relatively poor candidates for discussion activity," because they had so little education and many misconceptions about current issues.[56] In fact Holland and Hill found that participation in classes labeled "current affairs" or "citizenship" made little difference in enrollees' attitudes toward American democracy. On entering the camps, only 57 percent of enrollees agreed with the statement "Democracy is the best form of government." After participation in the CCC and a course that might address this issue, only 1 percent more (58 percent) agreed that democracy was the best form of government. Responses to statements such as "a dictator helps a country" and "the government should allow newspapers and speakers to say what they believe" showed similarly small changes. Support for dictators only dropped 4 percent and support for free speech increased only 1 percent.[57] As a way to impart information about democracy, the CCC education program evidently did little to change enrollees' attitudes. On the other hand, Holland and Hill's survey of enrollees' letters showed that many felt that their time in the CCC made them better people and better Americans.[58]

Conclusion: War, Education, and Eliminating Illiteracy in the CCC

In 1938 the federal Office of Education carried out a series of conferences on education in each corps area. These conferences began with an address by the corps area commander who invariably praised the CCC's efforts to end illiteracy. The 4th Corps Area Commander, Lt. Colonel Stanley D. Embick, expressed this attitude most clearly. Embick noted that "the removal of illiteracy from all CCC companies is expected as a basic accomplishment." Ending illiteracy was the first step toward the ultimate goal of "fitting young men for the self supporting, useful and self respecting life after leaving camp."[59] At the Educational Advisors' conference in 1940, held at the Presidio in San Francisco, Lt. General Albert J. Bowley complained that the vocational aspects of CCC education were distracting from basic academic training. He believed the army should work to make sure every enrollee read at the eighth-grade level—the level at which they could be inducted into the army.[60]

Indeed, by 1940, ending illiteracy became an element of military preparedness. In press releases in 1941, John Studebaker, director of the federal Office of Education, connected reading and national defense. He demanded that Americans "must once and for all eliminate illiteracy" as the first step in a series of "practical measures of defense." Pointing to the rise of fascism abroad as well as fears of communism at home (the House Committee on Un-American Activities had been established three years earlier in 1938), Studebaker added that "civic illiteracy is an open invitation to a Fifth Column of American propaganda." He therefore encouraged "systematic study and discussion" of citizenship, democracy, and American history because "the only protection against an effective invasion by propaganda is a state of enlightenment and understanding among the people generally."[61] In September 1941, as the school year began, he called on educators to "Act Now!" insisting that Europeans had fallen to dictators because they had responded "too late and too little." Appealing for a vigorous citizenship education program, Studebaker wrote that "eradication of illiteracy is our job—this year!"[62]

The United States' entry into World War II ended the CCC but not the values the federal government associated with reading. In fact, the sense that reading and literacy was an instrument that could create better workers and citizens was strengthened.[63] Historian Christopher Loss has shown how the federal Council on Books in Wartime used similar rhetoric to give printed materials, particularly paperback Armed Services Editions, both ideological and strategic importance to the war effort. While Loss shows how this rhetoric emerged in response to concerns about propaganda in World War I, the discourse surrounding reading during the Great Depression also played a key role in the popularity of the Armed Services Editions.[64] Loss's work shows that the links New Deal leaders made between reading, work, and citizenship had solidified in the 1940s. Loss's work also demonstrates that, in the Armed Services Editions, as in the "Camp Life Readers" federal officials used reading to encourage citizens to conform and cooperate. Educational leaders stressed that reading was an activity on which enrollees could "work," maintaining their sense of rugged individualism. At the same time, leaders retained the right to control materials and through the "Camp Life Readers" series created materials that would lead to "proper" attitudes toward reading and citizenship. As Studebaker's comments on reading and national defense show, reading appeared to have the power to direct enrollees' individualism toward larger organizations and connect intellectual development and personal initiative to community and government.

Notes

I completed the research for this chapter with a summer stipend from the National Endowment for the Humanities using the New Deal records found at the National Archives and Records Administration (NARA) II in College Park, Maryland. Records from there are abbreviated NARA II and then list the location of materials by Record Group (RG), Entry number (E), box and folder if applicable. The most important Record Groups I used for this study were RG 12 archives of the Office of Education and RG 35 archives of the CCC. I want to thank Gene Morris at NARA II for his invaluable aid in finding materials on reading and literacy in the CCC. His knowledge of the New Deal archives provided more leads than I could possibly follow up on. I also want to thank Gordon Witty, Lisa Gitelman, Francesca Bavuso, and Paul Erickson for reading and commenting on drafts of this chapter.

    1. The title "Camp Life Readers" echoed the title of adult literacy readers, the "Country Life Reader" created by Cora Wilson Stewart at her "Moonlight Schools" in Kentucky. Stewart was an energetic promoter of literacy programs for adults, but her books were deemed too moralistic for the CCC. Willie Nelms, *Cora Wilson Stewart: Crusader against Illiteracy* (Jefferson, NC: McFarland, 1997), 60–68.

    2. "Camp Life Reader #1," 50. All Camp Life Readers can be found at NARA II: RG 12, E 134, Box 2, "Ralph Flynt's File on Instructional Materials Projects."

    3. Jeffrey Ryan Suzik, "'Building Better Men': The CCC Boy and the Changing Social Ideal of Manliness," *Men and Masculinities* 2, no. 2 (October 1999), 156.

    4. For two important models of the relationship between print democracy and nationhood see Jurgen Habermas, *The Structural Transformation of the Public Sphere: An Inquiry into a Category of Bourgeois Society*, trans. Thomas Burger and Frederick Lawrence (Cambridge, MA: MIT Press, 1991); and Benedict Anderson, *Imagined Communities: Reflections on the Origin and Spread of Nationalism* (London: Verso, 1983).

5. For the history of how Roosevelt pulled together these departments, and particularly the necessity and controversy surrounding the involvement of the army, see John A. Salmond, *The Civilian Conservation Corps, 1933–1942: A New Deal Case Study* (Durham, NC: Duke University Press, 1967), 10–32.

6. Ibid., 13.

7. Ibid., 8–54. For a comparison of the development of the CCC with the similar German labor service the Reichsarbeitsdienst (RAD) see Kiran Klaus Patel, *Soldiers of Labor: Labor Service in Nazi Germany and New Deal America, 1933–1945*, trans. Thomas Dunlap (Washington, D.C.: German Historical Institute; New York: Cambridge University Press, 2005). For an additional sense of the romance of the CCC at the time see Kenneth Holland and Frank Ernest Hill, *Youth in the CCC* (Washington, D.C.: American Council on Education, 1942), 8–10. And for a sense of how lasting that impression has been see Arthur M. Schlesinger, Jr., *The Age of Roosevelt: The Coming of the New Deal* (Boston: Houghton Mifflin, 1958), 335–340.

8. Educational Policies Commission, *The Civilian Conservation Corps, the National Youth Administration, and the Public Schools* (Washington, D.C.: National Education Association of the U.S. and the American Association of School Administrators, 1941), 9.

9. Jon Savage, *Teenage: The Creation of Youth Culture* (New York: Viking Penguin, 2007), 277–283. For more on the "youth problem" of the 1930s see Richard Reiman, *The New Deal and American Youth* (Athens: University of Georgia Press, 1992).

10. John A. Pandriani, "The Crime Control Corps: An Invisible New Deal Program," *The British Journal of Sociology* 33, no 3 (September 1982), 348–358. It is worth noting that Roosevelt also saw the CCC as a way to placate veterans of World War I, who were still in Washington, D.C., after the "Bonus March" of 1932.

11. "'Blind Voting' Hit by Mrs. Roosevelt," *New York Times*, May 8, 1934, 25.

12. Charles W. Taussig, "Introduction," in *A New Deal for Youth: The Story of the National Youth Administration*, ed. Betty Lindley and Ernest K. Lindley (New York: Viking Press, 1938), viii.

13. Ralph Flynt, "Why Teach: The Objectives of Good Teaching," speech delivered December 12, 1938, at the Office of Education (NARA II: RG 12, E 134, Box 3, Folder "Ralph Flynt's File on Instructional Materials"), 5.

14. William W. Biddle, letter to Francis Perkins, May 10, 1933 (NARA II: RG 35, E 45, Box 6, Folder "Correspondence with Universities").

15. Charles D. Daniel, letter to Franklin Delano Roosevelt, April 10, 1933 (NARA II: RG 35, E 45, Box 6, Folder "Correspondence with Universities").

16. W. Frank Persons, "Suggestions for Educational and Vocational Counselors for Forest Camps," May 22, 1933 (NARA II: RG 35, E 45, Box 1, Folder 1 "Advisory Committee Minutes").

17. The two negative selection agents were C. R. Burnett (May 23, 1933) in New Jersey and Raymond B. Wilcox (May 23, 1933) in Oregon. The untold benefits comment came in a telegram from Harper Gatton of Kentucky, May 20, 1933, and the proper guidance idea from E. G. Ackart in Delaware, May 20, 1933. The director in New York state, Frederick I. Daniels, wrote on October 25, 1933. Telegrams from all the state selection agents can be found at NARA II: RG 35, E 45, Box 6, Folder 2.

18. Walter C. Chapman, letter to W. Frank Persons, "Suggested Educational Program for Forest Camps," October 23, 1933 (NARA II: RG 35, E 45, Box 5, Folder 1 "Education General Correspondence A–E").

19. Robert G. H. Tallman, letter to W. Frank Persons, May 22, 1932 (NARA II: RG 35, E 45, Box 5, Folder 2 "Education General Correspondence F–Q").

20. Quoted in Salmond, *The Civilian Conservation Corps*, 47.

21. "Three Forest Workers Get Jail Terms," *Hartford Courant*, June 2, 1933. Reports of other CCC related disturbances include Arthur Williams, letter to W. Frank Persons, May 31, 1933 (NARA II: RG 35, E 45, Box 5, Folder 2 "Education General Correspondence F–Q"). Williams, director of the National Recreation Association, enclosed two articles on disturbances in Bethlehem and Littleton, New Hampshire, and encouraged Persons to consider these events as he developed the after-work education program. Events in Sackets Harbor, New York, and Accotink, Virginia, made the *Washington Post*, "15 Veterans Lose Forestry Jobs as Mob Invades Town," June 8, 1933, 1; and "Forest Corps Row Terrorizes Village," June 11, 1933, 3.

22. For a more detailed examination of the history of the education program in the CCC, including the contributions of George F. Zook, Clarence Marsh, and Howard Oxley to the evolution of the education program for the CCC, see Calvin Gower, "The Civilian Conservation Corps and American Education: Threat to Local Control?" *History of Education Quarterly* 7, no. 1 (1967), 59–62; Salmund, *The Civilian Conservation Corps*, 47–53; and Charles Frederick Ralston, "Adult Education as a Welfare Measure during the Great Depression: A Historical Case Study of the Educational Program of the Civilian Conservation Corps, 1933–1942" (PhD diss., Penn State University, 2000), 248–282.

23. Dominic W. Moreo, *Schools in the Great Depression* (New York: Garland Publishing, 1996), 114.

24. Frank Hill, *The School in the Camps: The Educational Program of the CCC* (New York: American Association for Adult Education, 1935), 70; Ned Dearborn, *Once in a Lifetime* (Chicago: Charles E. Merrill, 1935), 16.

25. Bruce L. Melvin, *Youth—Millions too Many?* (New York: Association Press, 1940), 180.

26. J. B. Edmunson, "An Educational Program for the Civilian Conservation Corps," August 9, 1933 (NARA II: RG 12, E 134, Box 3, Folder "Emergency Conservation Work: Materials Relating to Educational Program in Work Camps").

27. Dearborn, *Once in a Lifetime*, 21–22.

28. Ralph R. Glass, "An Introduction to the CCC Educational Program of Vancouver Barracks CCC District," November 15, 1938 (NARA II: RG 35, E 45, Box 2, Folder 1 "Committee on CCC Instructional Material").

29. C. T. Clifton, "Education in the CCC," paper delivered before the Town and Gown Club of Yellow Springs, Ohio, May 15, 1938 (NARA II: RG 35, E 45, Box 6, Folder "Correspondence with C. T. Clifton), 16.

30. Holland and Hill, *Youth in the CCC*, 156.

31. Sue Currell has explained in her book *The March of Spare Time: The Problem and Promise of Leisure in the Great Depression* (Philadelphia: University of Pennsylvania Press, 2005) that the Great Depression exacerbated concerns about the apparently passive responses new media like radio and movies seemed to demand from their audiences. Critics accused Americans of suffering from "spectatoritis." Reading, Currell says, "was made to combat the lazy-minded habits of the public" (84–85).

32. Robert G. H. Tallman, letter to W. Frank Persons, May 22, 1932 (NARA II: RG 35, E 45, Box 5, Folder 2 "Education General Correspondence F–Q").

33. Charles F. Connelley, letter to James Rolph, Jr., May 15, 1933 (NARA II: RG 35, E 45, Box 5, Folder 2 "Education General Correspondence F-Q").

34. Alabama State Selection Agency, telegram to W. Frank Persons, May 21, 1933 (NARA II: RG 35, E 45, Box 6, Folder 2 "Correspondence with State Selecting Agencies").

35. Major General A. J. Bowley, letter to W. Frank Persons, August 9, 1934 (NARA II: RG 35, E 45, Box 6, Folder 1 "Correspondence with Secretary of Labor; Mr. Fechner; Cooperating Departments").

36. Salmond, *The Civilian Conservation Corps*, 115.

37. Clifton, "Education in the CCC," 24.

38. Fechner quoted in Salmond, *The Civilian Conservation Corps*, 80–81; and Calvin Gower, "The Civilian Conservation Corps and American Education: Threat to Local Control?" *History of Education Quarterly* 7, no. 1 (1967), 63–64.

39. John Elliott, letter to C. S. Marsh, May 10, 1934 (NARA II: RG 12, E 122, Records of Special Projects and Programs, CCC Camp Education, "Correspondence of the Director, 1934").

40. Newton D. Baker, letter to Raymond T. Rich, August 3, 1934 (NARA II: RG 12, E 122, Records of Special Projects and Programs, CCC Camp Education, "Correspondence of the Director, 1933–1936").

41. Clifton, "Education in the CCC," 16.

42. "Transcript of CCC Education Conference Held December 7, 1938" (NARA II: RG 35, E 45, Box 7, Folder "Conferences 1938 1–3 Divisions").

43. Robert A. Waller, "Happy Days and the CCC in South Carolina, 1933–1942," *The Historian* 64, no. 1 (Fall 2001), 46.

44. Holland and Hill, *Youth in the CCC*, 173–174.

45. Ralph Flynt, "Suggestive Themes—Workbooks and Readers" (NARA II: RG 12, E 134, Box 1, Folder "Camp Life Reader General Correspondence").

46. J. B. Edmunson, "An Educational Program for the Civilian Conservation Corps," August 9, 1933 (NARA II: RG 12, E 134, Folder "Emergency Conservation Work: Materials Relating to Educational Program in Work Camps").

47. "Camp Life Reader #3" (NARA II: RG 12, E 134, Box 2, "Ralph Flynt's File on Instructional Materials Projects"), 82–83.

48. "Camp Life Reader #1" (NARA II: RG 12, E 134, Box 2, "Ralph Flynt's File on Instructional Materials Projects"), 10.

49. "Camp Life Reader #2" (NARA II: RG 12, E 134, Box 2, "Ralph Flynt's File on Instructional Materials Projects"), 6–10.

50. Holland and Hill, *Youth in the CCC*, 221–234. For further details about Depression-era fears about militarization in the camps, see Suzik, "'Building Better Men.'" Recent historians, following Michel Foucault, have become increasingly concerned about the totalizing nature of the CCC camps. These studies include Kiran Klaus Patel, *Soldiers of Labor*; Olaf Stieglitz, "New Deal Programmes for Youth: Recent Historiography and Future Research," in *The Roosevelt Years: New Perspectives on American History, 1933–1945*, ed. Robert A. Garson and Stuart S. Kidd (Edinburgh, UK: Edinburgh University Press, 1999); Eric Gorham, "The Ambiguous Practices of the Civilian Conservation Corps: The Position of the Civilian Conservation Corps in the Struggle over the New Deal," *Social History* 17, no. 2 (May 1992).

51. "Camp Life Reader #3" (NARA II: RG 12, E 134, Box 2, "Ralph Flynt's File on Instructional Materials Projects"), 106–107.

52. "Camp Life Reader #1" (NARA II: RG 12, E 134, Box 2, "Ralph Flynt's File on Instructional Materials Projects"), 12.

53. "Camp Life Reader #3" (NARA II: RG 12, E 134, Box 2, "Ralph Flynt's File on Instructional Materials Projects"), 86–87.

54. "Camp Life Reader #3" (NARA II: RG 12, E 134, Box 2, "Ralph Flynt's File on Instructional Materials Projects"), 52–53.

55. "Camp Life Reader #2" (NARA II: RG 12, E 134, Box 2, "Ralph Flynt's File on Instructional Materials Projects"), 14–15.

56. Holland and Hill, *Youth in the CCC*, 255.

57. Ibid., 230–231.

58. Ibid., 130–132.

59. Lieutenant Colonel Stanley D. Embick, letter to all District Commanders, Company Commanders, and Educational Advisors (NARA II: RG 35, E 45, Box 8, Folder, "Corps Area Educational Conferences").

60. "Minutes of District Adviser's Training Institute, October 30, 31, and November 4, 1939" (NARA II: RG 35, E 45, Box 8).

61. John Studebaker, "Citizenship Education to Meet Propaganda Threat Urged by Studebaker," FSA Press Release, August 22, 1940 (NARA II: RG 35 E 45, Box 6, Folder "Publicity").

62. John Studebaker, "Act Now!" FSA Press Release, September 11, 1940 (NARA II: RG 35, E 45, Box 6, Folder "Publicity").

63. It is possible to see this focus on the utilitarian nature of reading as part of a long anti-intellectual tradition in America. Nonetheless, these divisions are not clear. A number of different historical studies have shown the difficulty of trying to pin down "intellectuals" in the 1930s on the value of reading. The attitudes of "middlebrow" literary figures described by Joan Shelley Rubin in *The Making of Middlebrow Culture* (Chapel Hill: University of North Carolina Press, 1992) would have been shared by many of Roosevelt's advisors and cabinet members who we would now categorize as intellectuals. Both groups believed that wide, popular reading would uplift the reader and improve the nation. My own work, Catherine Turner, *Marketing Modernism between the Two Wars* (Amherst: University of Massachusetts Press, 2003), reveals that this was not just a middlebrow faith; in the 1930s, highbrow readers were encouraged to use books like James Joyce's *Ulysses* as guides to modern life. On the other hand, Brett Gary's book, *The Nervous Liberals* (New York: Columbia University Press, 1999), details the fears that some intellectuals had about allowing "the masses" to read. Despite their intellectual leanings, they would have controlled reading in the CCC in the same way the army did. It is also worth noting that the army was not consistently anti-intellectual. While the Council on Books in Wartime's Armed Services Editions might have seemed the most utilitarian project possible, it created a list, which the War Department's morale branch printed and distributed, that included both Bob Hope's *I Never Left Home* and I. A. Richards's translation of *The Republic of Plato*, Mark Twain's *A Connecticut Yankee in King Arthur's Court* and Jack Godman's *The Fireside Book of Dog Stories*. Finally, as Trysh Travis has shown, the drive to make reading a masculine pursuit by linking it to the war effort was also tied to efforts to make literature more abstract and intellectual. See Trysh Travis, "Books as

Weapons and 'The Smart Man's Peace': The Work of the Council on Books in Wartime," *Princeton University Library Chronicle* 60 (Spring 1999), 353–99. While it is true that the ideology of reading found in the CCC developed out of a sense that intellectual pursuits, such as reading, had very utilitarian results both for the individual and for the nation, that sense was not *always* anti-intellectual nor were intellectuals always proreading.

64. Christopher P. Loss, "Reading between Enemy Lines: Armed Services Editions and World War II," *Journal of Military History* 67 (July 2003), 811–834.

4

Print, Education, and the State

State Regulation
of the Textbook Industry

ADAM R. SHAPIRO

THE ADOPTION AND REGULATION OF TEXTBOOKS in America today is largely focused on the control of textbook content. As has been well documented, the relationships between publishers, state boards of education, and outside political pressure groups have combined to turn the production and adoption of textbooks into a process in which every word and image of a textbook is deeply scrutinized.[1] Given this current state of affairs, it is ironic if not outright surprising that the rise of statewide regulation of textbooks was rooted almost entirely in causes *other* than the desire to control textbook content. This is not to say that statewide regulation did not *affect* the content of textbooks. It did—almost as soon as state-level regulation became a reality. But in today's politicized environment, textbook regulation seems to be focused exclusively on content. Recognition of the context in which the political structures of textbook adoption came to pass sheds important light on how the state's role in education has evolved and how the relationship between publishers and states in shaping textbook content has also changed over time.

Throughout most of the nineteenth century, the largest textbook markets were in locales that did not have statewide adoption, and many publishers worked hard to oppose legislation for statewide adoption instead of developing marketing strategies to work within it. Rather than producing textbooks that would appeal to statewide constituencies, publishers sought to influence text-book choices of local school boards.

It was not until the late nineteenth and early twentieth centuries that more and more states took over the control of textbook adoption from local districts. By the time Mississippi Governor Theodore Bilbo devoted over one-third of his 1928 address to the legislature to the topic of textbook reform, such efforts had been underway for about half a century.[2] There were two principal reasons for this shift to state textbook adoption. The first was economic. Although competition among publishers was fierce, there was a feeling among state officials that the industry as a whole kept prices artificially high. By soliciting bids for a statewide adoption, states hoped to secure lower prices for textbooks. Also, the potential for the resale or reuse of books over a multiyear adoption period provided an economic incentive for the states.

The second reason for the shift to statewide adoption was more telling. The public was fed up with the competitive practices of textbook publishers. These companies fought ruthlessly, slandering rival publishers, insinuating sales agents onto local school boards, and bribing or arranging kickbacks with local board members. Textbook sales agents were ubiquitous and battled one another relentlessly at both an individual and corporate level. Regulation of textbooks, state leaders hoped, would reduce the number of agents and restrict their methods.

Politicians frequently discussed these problems when advocating textbook regulation. Corruption among book companies and local school officials not only limited competition and allowed publishers to maintain high prices, but also resulted in constant pressure to buy new textbooks and little opportunity to reuse them. Corruption also let publishers establish local monopolies, cornering the market for all books within a district or county and enabling certain companies to set prices higher and higher.

Of course, textbook controversies and competition were nothing new in the late nineteenth century. As publishers began to print books specifically for use in schools, the profusion of textbooks and textbook marketing concerned early leaders in the common school movement. The best-selling *McGuffey's Eclectic Readers*, first published in 1835, helped usher in the publication of books specifically for use in schools.[3] This marketing of books for school use caused concerns almost as soon as it began. Horace Mann wrote in 1837 (the year he became superintendent of the Massachusetts Board of Education): "Publishers often employ agents to hawk their books about the country; and I have known several instances where such a peddler,   or picaroon;—has taken all the old books of a whole class in school, in exchange for his new ones, book for book,—looking of course, to his chance of making sales after the book has been established in the school, for reimbursement and profits; so that at last, the children have to pay for what they supposed was given them. On this subject, too, cannot the mature views of competent and disinterested men, residing, respectively in all parts of the state, be the means of effecting a much needed reform?"[4] While Mann offered one of the clearest antebellum articulations of concerns over textbooks, textbook controversies became more pressing after the Civil War.

When it came to controversies over textbook *content*, the Civil War was itself cause for much debate and conflict. Frances Fitzgerald's *America Revised* and Joseph Moreau's *Schoolbook Nation*, focus on history textbooks and their portrayals of slavery, race, and interpretations of the war.[5] Several publishers, they show, issued separate lines of history textbooks for northern and southern constituencies.[6] It was in response to these controversies that history books began to be written specifically for school use. As the number of readers multiplied and the amount spent on textbooks increased, publishers began employing strategies to assure themselves sales in a competitive environment.

In the post–Civil War period, textbook controversies were not only about the content of particular textbooks but also about the newly emergent structures for printing, distributing, and selling books. New printing and transportation technologies expanded the potential market for individual publishers. New companies arose, as partners or employees of older publishing houses set off on their own, and a new culture of salesmanship emerged throughout American industry. This new commercial environment placed greater emphasis on a salesman's innate qualities and personal relationships with clients than in touting the features of a particular item being sold. As textbooks publishers began to compete within a newly industrialized and ideologically transformed environment, Horace Mann's early call for state-level reform gained new resonance; it seemed unlikely that local regulation could contain the fast-growing textbook industry.

The changing face of the textbook industry in the late nineteenth century came at a time when other industries were also experiencing rapid growth and consolidation. Antitrust feeling built among critics of the textbook industry, perhaps even earlier than such sentiments emerged against other industries. In the 1870s a succession of trade associations between major publishers formed and collapsed.[7] Finally in 1880 an alliance was created among the three largest U.S. educational publishers. This was supposed to have represented, according to an industry executive's reflection, "a new concept, the textbook publisher's *syndicate*, a term which later became one of approbation [*sic*] and was promptly changed to *alliance*."[8] In 1885, this new alliance grew into the School Book Publishers' Association, an arrangement signed onto by sixteen publishers.

Not surprisingly, the creation of this alliance prompted worry within the rest of the schoolbook publishing industry. An article in *Publishers Weekly* in 1889 addressed the critics concerns:

> Some time ago some of the leading school-book publishers formed themselves into an association with the purpose of working in harmony rather than in

opposition, that is to say, of restraining their rivalry within specific limits. . . . It is not, in any sense a Trust, nor will it destroy competition of the right sort. Any business arrangement which undertakes to diminish competition in quality or price is against the public interest and ought not to succeed. This combination, as we understand it, has the contrary purpose of serving the public by saving labor and cost. If it should go farther than this, and bring the trade into the stagnation which comes from the destruction of competition, the results would not be good, and the arrangement, we believe, would not last. There is not the slightest thought, however, of any such scheme.[9]

In 1890, after the passage of the Sherman Antitrust Act, the School Book Publishers' Association dissolved, but the worries articulated the previous year did not go away. Instead, they came closer to fruition. That year, the four largest textbook publishers agreed to consolidate and incorporate, forming a new entity, the American Book Company (ABC). According to the ABC's internal history: "There is some evidence that an attempt was made to draw other houses into the group, in particular Harper & Brothers, Ginn & Co., and D. C. Heath & Co," but these others refused.[10]

A few weeks later, the ABC stunned the industry by purchasing Harper and Brothers' textbook line. The transaction was completed at a cost of $400,000 plus another $150,000 to cover existing stock materials.[11] This was not the only surprise. *Publishers Weekly* reported that "The American Book Company, by some magical means, has succeeded in accomplishing what few would have believed possible three weeks ago—the control of the public school books of Harper & Brothers, and of the plant of The Standard Publishing Co. and D. D. Merrill & Co." The acquisition of such large houses was a major corporate coup. As *Publishers Weekly* wrote, "Their surrender and the purchase of the Harper books now practically puts all the public school business in the hands of the American Book Company, and places it in a position of grave responsibility."[12]

The "magical means" by which Harpers' textbook division was sold was the unexpected death, on May 22, 1890, of Fletcher Harper, Jr. He was the largest stakeholder in the company and had designated no heir. Faced with amortizing his equity, a board meeting the day after his death revealed concern over the company's available capital. Accepting the ABC's offer seemed both reasonable and necessary.[13] However, the result of this transaction was a major boost in the publishing power of the new, but already formidable, ABC conglomerate. Though *Publisher's Weekly* was undoubtedly aware of Harper's death, it did not seem to connect this event to the growing influence of the ABC. While the growth of the ABC was in large part due to a long-developed corporate strategy, its exploitation of the unexpected was also key to its rapid ascent.

The consolidation of many of the leading schoolbook publishers into a single corporation did not bring an end to corrupt practices in the textbook industry. The first test of the ABC's power came in June 1890 with the textbook adoption debate in the State of Washington. When the ABC lost the initial vote on math books to Ginn and Company, the ABC's sales agents tried some old methods to ensure the success of the new company. Later court records told the story. "According to the prosecuting attorney, the American Book Company agents, S. W. Womack and R. L. Edwards (already famous for Montana scandals), 'did then and there, unlawfully, wickedly, and corruptly' pay one of the [members of the Washington state textbook] adopting board, L. H. Leach, $5000 *by check* to reopen the adoption. An indictment was handed down."[14] Needless to say, the ABC did not win Washington's state textbook contract.

The formation of the ABC and its purchase of Harper and Brothers' textbook division set it into direct, often personally acrimonious competition with its largest competitor, Ginn and Company, and its president, Edwin Ginn. Ginn wrote and distributed a series of pamphlets denouncing the ABC as anticompetitive and dangerous to education. These circulars came with ominous titles such as "Are Our Schools in Danger?"[15] The ABC responded in turn with counter-accusations and its own pamphlets.[16] These pamphlets became a primary weapon in the competition between rival sales agents, who canvassed local territories to secure adoptions. In perhaps the most notorious of these pamphlet battles, the ABC sued the Kingdom Publishing Company for libel, alleging that its pamphlet, entitled "A Foe to American Schools," by Grinnell College President George A. Gates, accused the ABC "of being a trust and monopoly."[17] The ABC won its suit and Kingdom went out of business.[18]

Throughout the 1890s, Ginn accused ABC of anticompetitive practices, and ABC accused Ginn of hypercompetitive practices, and both accusations played into the debate over state-level regulation of the textbook industry. Both Ginn and ABC wanted to *avoid* state-level regulation in this period. In "Are our Schools in Danger?" Edwin Ginn claimed that he had "tried very hard to persuade [the companies consolidating] not to form this company, for I feared that it would tend to stir up fresh legislation in regard to the book business, which has generally been an injury to both publishers and the public."[19] The "new era" of statewide adoption may have taken the ABC by surprise, but it should not have surprised anyone that attempts to regulate the textbook industry by state governments gained momentum shortly after the consolidation of the Company in 1890. Local governments were ill-equipped to control large corporations, and the federal government never considered the textbook industry among the other great trusts of the period. Perhaps textbook regulation was perceived as an education issue for the states, rather than a trusts issue for the federal government. In either case, the rhetoric that grounded textbook regulation was less about textbook content and more about sales practices. Perhaps nowhere else was this concern about sales practices more apparent than in California, where some of the most radical approaches to textbook reform were first introduced.

State Printing of Textbooks in California

In 1894 California passed a constitutional amendment requiring the state printing of textbooks. Twenty years earlier in 1874, the State Board of Education
had been given the authority to adopt textbooks for the state as a whole.[20] This
authority itself marked a continuation of past trends. California's original
constitution had been ratified in 1849, the year after the conclusion of the
Mexican-American War (and the discovery of gold) and the year before state-
hood. Though at that time Californians were distrustful of centralized govern-
mental control, they made an exception for education. The state constitution
included a provision declaring that all revenue from the sale of land granted
by the United States would go to meet the costs of education in the state.
Education's attraction to would-be settlers with families was a rationale advanced in favor of a large fund for education.[21] "We can create no fund too
large for the purpose of education," argued John McDougal, a delegate from
Sacramento. "I call upon my old bachelor friends to support this if they want
wives, for it will introduce families into this country."[22]

The 1849 Constitution had made no direct reference to textbooks, but it
had invested in the state legislature the authority to "provide for a system of
common schools."[23] In the words of one delegate, "the Legislature cannot encroach upon the fund thus set apart for educational purposes."[24] Three years
later, in 1852, the legislature established a State Board of Education.[25] This
board had the power to select textbooks for local districts; although until 1874,
local districts were also free to choose their own books.[26] California's state
system of education boosted school attendance tremendously. According to
census statistics, California had only 993 students enrolled in schools in 1850,
but the state had 25,916 enrolled in 1860, and 91,176 enrolled in 1870.[27]

A mistrust of government (reflected in the concern that the legislature
might "encroach" upon federal land grants) carried over into the constitutional
convention of 1879, which took up the question of statewide textbook adoption.
At this convention, the delegates voted to do away with the state board of education and leave all educational decisions up to the counties.[28] After eliminating
the state board of education, the convention turned to the issue of textbooks.
The delegates voted to place responsibility for textbook adoption upon local
school boards, but seeking to mitigate some of the effects of the cost of books,
they required that "the text-books so adopted shall continue in use for not less
than four years."[29] An amendment to the proposed section was offered, which
would have added the caveat "subject to general legislative enactments." But
one delegate reacted negatively to this proposal, stating, "It seems to me that
will open the door to bring back the old system. We have got rid of the Board of
Education, but that thrusts us back to the old system, whenever the Legislature
desires to have it so."[30] Amid concerns that the progress of the constitutional

convention could be undone by a legislature sufficiently enabled, the amendment was rejected, and textbook adoption remained in local hands.

Not everyone was happy with these votes. San Francisco delegate James O'Sullivan (who was not present for the votes concerning county-level adoption of school books), proposed an additional section to the article on education, suggesting that the state should print a series of textbooks for use throughout the state. In his words: "The Legislature, at the first session after the adoption of this Constitution, shall provide for the appointment of a Commission to compile a series of school text-books, which, after preparation, shall be printed in the State Printing Office. The text-books thus compiled and printed shall constitute a uniform series of text-books, to be used in the public schools of this State on and after the first day of January, eighteen hundred and eighty-two, and shall be furnished to pupils at cost price."[31] O'Sullivan offered two reasons in support of his proposal. "First, the adoption of the system which I propose will completely destroy all motive or inducement to a lobby on the school book question. Once the State prepares and publishes its own school books, the corrupting influence attached to the private competition and speculation of the present system will be effectually prevented in the future."[32] On the effects of the textbook lobby, O'Sullivan continued, "These lobbies were here in force about the last Legislature, and if it were not for their influence, it is not improbable that this school book question would have been settled at that session."[33]

O'Sullivan's proposal to allow the State Printing Office, which published the legislative record, to print schoolbooks in the off-season when the legislature was in recess and the printing presses idle, had much support in certain areas of the state. O'Sullivan claimed, based upon estimated costs from the Superintendent of State Printing, that such a measure would save the state $50,000 and would be a way of "encouraging home industry in a most practical manner. The money now goes to eastern gentlemen, McGuffey & Co., who pay their journeymen printers Chinese wages."[34] Whether O'Sullivan knew that the publisher of the *McGuffey Readers* was one of the companies soon to join the School Book Publishers Association (the "alliance" created just a few months after California's constitutional convention), his argument was rooted in social and economic concerns related to the book trade.

O'Sullivan's argument for "home" production was a variation on an argument made earlier by California publishers themselves. In California, San Francisco publisher A. L. Bancroft and Company went head-to-head with McGuffey and Company and tried to enlist local support by offering even exchange of *McGuffey Readers* for its own *Pacific Coast Readers*. In an 1875 advertising pamphlet, Bancroft offered itself as an alternative to "Eastern" publishers marked by corruption. A local, more altruistic, monopoly, it portrayed itself as a California "home" industry—and therefore preferable to the invasion of foreign sales agents: "We stand as the pioneers in this department of industry.

If our hands are properly held up—as we have full confidence they will be—
other houses will be encouraged to embark on the same line of investment, and
all the text books for our schools will eventually be made at home. If, on the
other hand, the people suffer the Eastern monopoly, through its paid agents in
California, to array themselves in hostility to the enterprise now, after all the
liberal sacrifices that have been made to facilitate the introduction (vastly more
liberal than were ever made in California by any Eastern House) you may
be equally certain that no California House will ever again embark in such a
losing investment."[35] As it happened, similar arguments for "home" production
circulated in this period in the South, where Reconstruction-era legislators
vehemently denounced Northern textbooks for their "anti-Southern" content.
In California, though, advocates for state adoption—or state printing—did not
appeal for state control on grounds of controlling textbook content.

O'Sullivan's proposal for state textbook printing was defeated by a vote
of 73 to 42. Many who voted against it voted instead for county-level textbook
adoption. Most delegates did not want the state to control the choice of textbooks. While everyone agreed that textbook companies were a corrupting influence, the proposal that carried the day pushed for local control in the hope
that local boards would be less susceptible to corruption. Far from disagreeing
with O'Sullivan that textbook agents were an unwanted and malicious lobby,
the proponents of local control felt that hundreds of local school boards would
be harder for textbook agents to infiltrate than one state board of education.
"This amendment will lodge the power in the local Boards, where it should re-
side," one delegate noted. "This matter of State uniformity has done great evil
to the State and mischief to the people." Another delegate, supporting the four-
year adoption rule, continued to list the crimes of the status quo. "Wherever it
has been tried the same thing has almost invariably resulted. It induces these
men who publish books in other States to come here and purchase their en-
trance into our schools by the use of bribes. We are ashamed to contemplate it,
and yet every man knows it is true."[36]

O'Sullivan joined his colleagues in castigating the sources of corruption. He
pointed in particular to the lobbying activities of Bancroft and Company, located in his own district in San Francisco: "At the last session of the Legislature,
bills were introduced, . . . proposing to take this vexed question away from the
Legislature, and away forever from the corrupt lobby influence. But Bancroft
had his agents, attorneys and lobbyists upon the floors of your halls, and the bills
never became laws. MacGuffey and Bancroft are powerful in this building. I
understand that both firms have their legions hovering around this Convention.
Some of our teachers are simply agents and lobbyists for Bancroft & Co."[37] The
defeat of state printing of textbooks in 1879 illustrated that, while the corruption
of textbook publishers and the cost of books were indeed concerns, the concern
over state control was even greater. Specifying a minimum adoption period

addressed the problems of high costs and constant pressures to buy new books without giving the state control over the process of adoption itself.

Five years later, however, the legislature changed its mind. Problems with textbook publishers had grown to such an extent that state printing was established in 1884 with an amendment to the constitution.[38] The 1884 amendment had the support of all major political parties and was endorsed in their state platforms.[39] It read as follows: "The Governor, Superintendent of Public Instruction, and the principals of the State normal schools shall constitute the State Board of Education, and shall compile, or cause to be compiled and adopt a uniform series of textbooks for use in the common schools throughout the State. The State board may cause such textbooks, when adopted, to be printed and published by the Superintendent of State Printing at the State Printing Office, and when so printed and published, to the distributed and sold at the cost price of printing, publishing, and distributing the same."[40] On the face of it, the California publishing plan seemed like a utopian one. The state would save a tremendous expense by printing its own textbooks. Meddlesome textbook agents would disappear from the state. Local authorship of texts could be encouraged, and the public school system would thrive. In practice, this ideal quickly fell apart. In 1885 the Legislature appropriated $150,000 for the expense of equipment and manufacturing, and an additional $20,000 for the printing of textbooks.[41] After the initial startup, state printing was supposed to pay for itself, funded by the sale of books "at cost." But this plan proved optimistic; between 1887 and 1911, an addition $507,104.57 had to be allocated to the printing office.[42]

When James O'Sullivan proposed his original textbook printing amendment in 1879, one of the arguments he advanced was that it would encourage home industry. Local authors could be hired. This was attempted with mixed success; the State Board of Education hired teachers and faculty of state universities to write educational materials.[43] But the effort to procure sufficient and qualified writing talent failed. The best California authors were offered greater royalties by commercial publishers, and the books written in California were perceived to be inferior.[44] In 1890, a convention of California school superintendents adopted a resolution stating that "while certain of the state text-books . . . have met with the approbation of the public school teachers of the state, we desire to record our severe criticism and disapproval of others of the state series."[45]

Consequently, in 1903, the state changed tack. It began leasing plates from commercial publishers and paying royalties for their use, a standard practice in novel publishing in this era.[46] These plates, already made, could be used to print books. By this point, much of the original purposes of the constitutional amendment had already been lost. By seeking plates from commercial publishers, the potential for the corrupting influence of the textbook industry was reintroduced. The state became a customer of commercially produced textbook plates. Leasing the plates from such publishers also negated much of the planned savings in cost. Moreover, many publishers simply refused to cooperate. Nearly half of the textbooks available in the United States were unavailable in California because their publishers, including most of the largest, declined to lease plates for statewide adoption.[47] The companies that opted to provide plates frequently did so only for books that were already several years old and were no longer being produced. A primer published by Ginn and Company in 1891 was thus published by California in 1905.[48] The pages were identical; only the cover and title pages were new.

Because texts were hard to come by, and once adopted, frequently took over a year to distribute to schools, new adoptions were rare. Books stayed in circulation as many as a dozen years, and in a few cases as many as sixteen.[49] Most textbook publishers sought to introduce new books after a few years on the market, but in California, the length of adoption was almost always more than a decade. It was possible some children in California used textbooks originally written a quarter-century earlier. This was far from the ideal that James O'Sullivan had had in mind.

California's state monopoly on textbook printing also demonstrated that private commercial publishers had no monopoly on corruption. In January 1913 the state printer was condemned for his handling of his duties. A Senate committee reported "the manner in which the State Printing Office was being and had for years been conducted . . . was as deplorable as it was astounding, and . . . tolerated a system reeking with fraud and dishonesty."[50] Graft and corruption as well as basic inefficiency cost the state far more than it likely could have saved by "home" printing.

Independent of debates over its economic viability and whether it successfully shut the door on corrupt textbook agents, the California amendment to the constitution was also roundly criticized because of its effect on textbook content. California printed obsolete books, and some worried that the best educational materials were unavailable to California students. This was a perception cultivated by publishers, who frequently invoked novelty as a measure of a book's quality.

Thus while state regulation of textbooks in California was not explicitly about content, content was nonetheless affected. As concern about quality grew, the issue of textbook content began to be invoked against the California plan. California was the first state to regulate textbooks at the state level; it was also the first to suffer from the unintended consequences of that regulation.

State-Level Textbook Regulation across the United States

While California was the first, it was not the only state to regulate textbooks. State regulation spread quickly across the country as states worried about corruption and pricing in the textbook industry. Some of the earlier (though unsuccessful) efforts at state adoption arose in the South, where "as early as 1856, the New Orleans PICAYUNE put forward a scheme by C. K. Marshall of Mississippi for a combination of states to produce educational books and to promote production of home-made school and text books."[51] Though Southern states did not adopt legislation governing textbook adoption in this period, a number of Northern states did so later in the century.

In 1889 Indiana passed a uniform textbook law. The impetus for this law, according to one contemporary account, came from "the instrumentality of a man who felt that he had in past years been wronged by the agents of a prominent publishing firm." The movement for state adoption in Indiana began in frustration with the corrupt actions of sales agents and culminated in a populist denunciation of monopoly. "The potent and at times not wholly unselfish interest of school-book agents in our teachers and school officers is no secret," one report stated.[52] "Patriotism and revenge worked side by side in raising in the ready press the war-cries: 'Smash the book trust!'; 'Cheap books for the children!'"[53] Textbook corruption and political manipulation was supported by the existence of local de facto monopolies in which a single publisher forced out competition. This in turn kept the price of textbooks high. These motivations culminated in textbook adoption becoming a political issue in Indiana and the passage of statewide adoption.

In 1892 *Publishers Weekly* noted that "an unprecedented number of bills" regarding the provision and adoption of textbooks had been introduced in state legislatures "within the last three years."[54] The rush of new legislation coincided with the alliance of the largest publishers and the formation of the ABC in 1890. By 1892 thirteen states besides California adopted textbooks at the state level and there were more to come.[55] In 1897 the Kansas state legislature passed legislation creating a textbook commission and requiring statewide uniform adoption.[56] In 1913 it became the only state besides California to require the state printing of textbooks.[57] That same year, Georgia, which already adopted textbooks at the state level, appointed a commission to investigate the possibility of printing textbooks, but the lessons of California's plan had begun to spread. The commission's report concluded that "the cost in Georgia is not only reasonable but actually considerably less than the average" noting that the "California plan, which involves the purchase and equipment of a printing plant, managed by State officials, for the purpose of printing school books, does not appear to be desirable."[58]

Another form of regulation consisted of state boards of education fixing maximum prices for all books to be sold in the state, while allowing local boards to choose among many books. Ohio enacted such a plan in 1905, requiring local boards to adopt books for five years.[59] The fixed duration of adoption was supposed to safeguard against corruption and encourage book reuse.

Another reform consisted of plans for "free" textbooks, in which books were purchased by the state and then loaned to students in local schools.

Tennessee passed its first uniform textbook law in 1899. Under this law, a state textbook commission solicited sealed bids and entered into five-year contracts with publishers. Textbooks were then distributed to authorized regional depositories, which in turn were expected to provide an adequate supply of books to local retailers.[60] Alabama had already instituted statewide adoption in 1915 when it appointed a commission to investigate more cost-effective ways to procure books, such as state publication.[61] Nevada created a similar commission the same year.[62]

While such a system could potentially benefit publishers, ensured of having a market for five years and a local monopoly on particular textbooks, publishers themselves largely resisted statewide adoption and lobbied against it. Reflecting on the ways in which statewide adoption had cost the ABC any hope for business in Texas for decades, the company's internal history described the shift toward statewide adoption: "The single-basal state adoption was a decidedly mixed blessing. More than anything else it turned the thoughts of a number of our key executives backward nostalgically to our great days and prevented them from planning adequately for the new era rapidly developing."[63] The reasons for ABC's slow response to statewide adoption pertained mostly to the structure of the industry's marketing practices. The big firms relied on local sales agents to secure contracts. With fewer (albeit bigger) adoptions, fewer agents would be needed. Even if agents' tactics worked as effectively on state boards as local boards, companies could still get by with fewer agents. But these companies' armies of agents had an interest in preserving their own jobs, and, because they were responsible for reporting on local conditions to the publishers' main offices, they had little incentive to encourage a shift in corporate strategy. The industry's sluggish reaction to state adoption was therefore unsurprising. The population of textbook salesmen played an important role in shaping the relationship between the industry and the public.

Publishers and editors might have taken greater notice of statewide adoption had it occurred in New York, Illinois, Pennsylvania, or Massachusetts, where the majority of publishing houses were located. But this was not the case. Of the fifty-five publishers mentioned in a 1925 report, all but one (from Nebraska) were located in those four states. Therefore, the vast majority of textbook publishers continued to use marketing strategies that fit the context of their own (very populous) states. The map below depicts the "Extent of Textbook Uniformity in Each of the Forty-Eight States in 1925–27" based upon a similar map published in 1928.[64] From this map, a clear regionalism is apparent. States in the West and South, such as California and Tennessee, adopted textbooks at the state level, while those of the Northeast did not. Indiana adopted

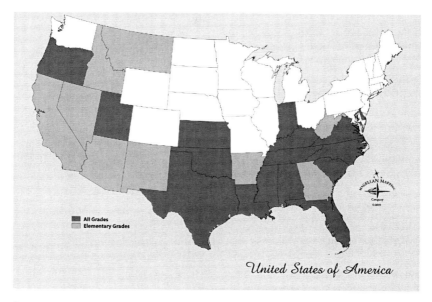

State textbook adoptions in the United States, 1928.

statewide, while the rest of the Midwest did not. Ohio, Illinois, Michigan, Minnesota, North Dakota, and Wyoming negotiated price limits with publishers but left adoption decisions at the local or county level. Almost the entire South adopted statewide for high schools as well as elementary schools.

Given that so many states were moving to regulate textbook adoption, it would seem that publishers ought to have changed their publication strategies accordingly—creating textbooks that could be used across an entire state. Yet publishers largely failed to do this, which may be accounted for by the distribution of those states that embraced statewide adoption. Because many of the largest states left textbook adoption to local decision makers, they could sell different books to localities across different states. In 1870, only four states had school enrollments over 500,000: New York, Pennsylvania, Ohio, and Illinois. None of these had statewide adoption. Of the nine states with more than 100,000 students in 1870, only three, Kentucky, Indiana, and Tennessee, had statewide adoption.[65] By 1920 the overall number of students enrolled in schools was much higher, yet the four largest states with school populations over a million were still in New York, Pennsylvania, Illinois, and Ohio, and all of these states had resisted statewide adoptions. Texas ranked fifth with 992,900 students, followed by Massachusetts and Michigan, but of these three, only Texas had statewide adoption. Nationwide, about 68 percent of students attended school in states *without* statewide adoption.[66]

The states without statewide adoption included those most affected by mid-nineteenth century battles over the use of the King James Bible in compulsory public schools. The so-called "Bible Wars," which led to riots in Philadelphia, Cincinnati, and many northeastern states, had led in part to the rise of separate Catholic school systems. The history of violence over schools may not have been responsible for preventing statewide textbook adoption, but debates over Bible reading in schools powerfully shaped the debates over local, county, and state control of education and may have influenced the spread of textbook regulation. While many states regulated the use of the Bible as a textbook, this regulation was not seen as part of a larger state authority to regulate textbook content altogether.

One notable exception to state regulation of textbooks was Colorado. In its constitution written in 1876, the state specified that "neither the General Assembly nor the State Board of Education shall have the power to prescribe text books to be used in public schools."[67] The wording of this section illustrated the intent of the Colorado delegates. It read: "The General Assembly shall have no power to encourage a monopoly in the sale of text books to be used in the public schools of this State by prescribing a uniform system thereof."[68] This desire to prevent a "state monopoly" coincided with the thought of the California state constitutional convention three years later in 1879.

Textbook Content and Unintended Consequences of Statewide Adoption

The history of state regulation of textbooks, through policies of uniform adoption and state publication, was deeply rooted in the competitive and political machinations of textbook publishers. Corruption and high prices were the rallying banner under which states, particularly those in the West, implemented statewide uniformity. The ABC throughout this period was the largest publisher, and, as a result of its size and strategies, probably the most significant catalyst of statewide adoption. This is not to suggest that other companies did not undertake the same tactics, but that the size of the ABC enabled it to implement those tactics to greater effect.

The origins of statewide adoption of textbooks had less to do with the content of textbooks and more to do with the perceived corruption of textbook publishers and the high prices they charged. Arguments for and against statewide adoption did not focus on textbook content, and textbook publishers did not alter their books' content in response to statewide adoption. If anything, the reaction of most publishers was to refuse to embrace statewide adoption. As two-thirds of the textbook market was still not affected by statewide adoption in 1920, publishers continued to focus on writing books for audiences adopted at more local levels, even as those same books were sold in other states. The largest markets for textbooks were not in jurisdictions where textbooks were adopted statewide. Until public education became more widespread in those states and more students needed books, it made more sense for publishers to plan and publish books with an eye toward the large markets in American cities. Because the publishers themselves were also located in New York, Chicago, Philadelphia, and Boston, the Northern and urban focus of many textbooks was often pronounced.

By the 1920s some publishers began to offer two lines of books, one intended for rural schools and another for urban schools. This happened not only in history textbooks, but also in the sciences, especially biology and general science. The idea that urban and rural communities had different needs was apparent not only in the content of textbooks, but also in a hostility felt in both environments toward state control. This hostility was felt particularly in rural environments in the South, where state-mandated education was seen as a threat to local culture and values.[69] Given that the majority of textbook publishers and authors—and consequently the subject matter produced by them—came from the North, urban-rural tensions overlapped with North-South tensions. Thus the content-oriented controversies regarding American history textbooks, which led to separate books for Northern and Southern audiences after the Civil War, overlapped geographically with the textbook controversies arising from the regulation and distribution of textbooks. That these newly enacted structures for textbook control and regulation would impact content became a foregone conclusion once state decisions about textbook adoptions became, in effect, decisions about the economic and cultural identity of a state as a whole, that is to say, as soon as these newly created state agencies began to make adoptions.

In principle, state regulators might have based their adoption choices largely on factors such as paper and binding quality, price, and availability. As seen in California, where perhaps the strongest form of regulation was attempted, the process dissolved into accusations that the state was providing books of inferior content. This rhetoric became exacerbated in places where corporate publishers presented two lines of textbooks for the same subjects (for urban and rural schools, for example). Even if a state agency chose a book based upon price and durability, opponents of the adoption would claim that it had chosen books with unsatisfactory content for their local population. Ultimately, state-level textbook regulation became contested for a new set of reasons, unrelated to publishers' marketing practices and more centered on their publishing practices. This has led to a continuing evolution of the relationship between states and the material and print cultures they employ in regulating education.

Notes

1. Diane L. Ravitch, *Language Police: How Pressure Groups Restrict What Students Learn* (New York: Vintage, 2004).

2. Clyde L. King, "Legislative Notes and Reviews: Governors' Messages, 1928," *The American Political Science Review* 22, no. 3 (August 1928), 638.

3. John Tebbel, *A History of Book Publishing in the United States*, vol. 1 (New York: R. R. Bowker, 1972), 551–552.

4. Horace Mann quoted in Tebbel, *A History of Book Publishing in the United States*, 550.

5. Frances Fitzgerald, *America Revised: History Schoolbooks in the Twentieth Century* (Boston: Little Brown, 1979).

6. Joseph Moreau, *School Book Nation* (Ann Arbor: University of Michigan Press, 2003), 84–85.

7. Mauck Brammer, "Our Heritage and History" (unpublished), American Book Company Archives, Syracuse University Library, 255–256. Brammer observes that Barnes called this the School Book Publisher's Board of Trade. The words "School Book" seem to be a conflation with the name of the School Book Publishers Association.

8. Ibid., 264.

9. "American School-Book Publishing," *Publishers Weekly* 912 (July 20, 1889), 46a.

10. Brammer, "Our Heritage and History," 276. Moreau, *School Book Nation*, 68–69, mistakenly identifies Harper and Brothers as a fifth partner in the initial merger forming the ABC.

11. John Tebbel, *Between Covers: The Rise and Transformation of Book Publishing in America* (New York: Oxford University Press, 1987), 94.

12. *Publishers Weekly* 957 (May 31, 1890), 717.

13. Eugene Exman, *The House of Harper* (New York: Harper and Row, 1967), 171–172.

14. Brammer, "Our Heritage and History," 303.

15. Edwin Ginn, *Are Our Schools in Danger?* [pamphlet] (1895), 2. This essay had been previously published as "Educational vs. Political Interests in the School-Book Business," *Publishers Weekly*, 1012 (June 20, 1891), 864–868; and in the *Saturday Evening Post* on June 6, 1891.

16. American Book Company, *Who Is Edwin Ginn?* (New York: American Book Company, 1895), 1–2.

17. George A. Gates, *A Foe of American Schools* (Minneapolis, MN: Kingdom Publishing, 1897); *American Book Company v. Kingdom Publishing* and others, 71 Minn 363 (1989). In a pamphlet of their own released after Kingdom was found guilty of libel, the ABC asserted "1000 copies, comprising one-half of the first edition of this pamphlet, were furnished by the Kingdom Company to Ginn Company, Chicago, by order of President Gates."

18. American Book Company Letter, California Department of Public Instruction, Pamphlets on Education [microfilm], 1861–1896.

19. Ginn, *Are Our Schools in Danger?*, 3.

20. A. L. Bancroft and Company, *The Adoption of the Pacific Coast Readers* [pamphlet] (1875), 2.

21. Amanda Meeker, "Overview of the History of Constitutional Provisions Dealing with K-12 Education," http://www.worldcat.org/arcviewer/1/CAX/2006/06/05/0000020402/viewer/file181.html (accessed October 4, 2009).

22. McDougal quoted in J. Ross Browne, *The Debates in the Convention of California, on the Formation of the State Constitution* (Washington: John T. Towers, 1850), 353.

23. *Constitution of the State of California* (San Francisco: Office of the Alta California, 1849), 12. Facsimile reprinted in *Constitution of the State of California, 1849* (San Marino, CA: Friends of the Huntington Library, 1949).

24. Francis J. Lippitt quoted in Browne, *The Debates in the Convention of California*, 353.

25. John Aubrey Douglass, "Creating a Fourth Branch of State Government: The University of California and the Constitutional Convention of 1879," *History of Education Quarterly* 32, no. 1 (Spring 1992), 45.

26. E. B. Willis and P. K. Stockton, stenog. *Debates and Proceedings of the Constitutional Convention of the State of California*, vol. 2 (Sacramento: State Printing Office, 1881).

27. Bureau of the Census, *Ninth Census of the United States*, vol. 1 (Washington, D.C.: Government Printing Office, 1872), 394–395.

28. E. B. Willis and P. K. Stockton, stenog. *Debates and Proceedings of the Constitutional Convention of the State of California*, vol. 3 (Washington, D.C.: Government Printing Office, 1872), 1400.

29. Ibid.

30. Thomas H. Laine quoted in ibid.

31. Ibid., 1401.

32. O'Sullivan quoted in ibid.

33. Ibid.

34. O'Sullivan quoted in ibid., 1402.

35. A. L. Bancroft and Company, *The Adoption of the Pacific Coast Readers*, 32.

36. Joseph W. Winans quoted in Willis and Stockton, *Debates and Proceedings of the Constitutional Convention of the State of California*, vol. 3, 1108.

37. O'Sullivan quoted in ibid.

38. Percy Roland Davis, *State Publication of Textbooks in California* (dissertation, University of California, Berkeley, 1930).

39. Winfield J. Davis, *History of Political Conventions in California 1849–1892* (Sacramento: California State Library, 1893).

40. "1879 California State Constitution Article IX (including amendments)," http://content.cdlib.org/view?docId=hb409nb2hr&chunk.id=div00001 (accessed October 4, 2009).

41. Browne, *The Debates in the Convention of California*, 5.

42. Ibid.

43. Lewis B. Avery, "State-Printed Textbooks in California," *Elementary School Journal* 19, no. 8 (April 1919), 628.

44. Ibid., 631.

45. Quoted from *San Francisco Examiner*, December 4, 1890, in Jeremiah W. Jenks, "School-Book Legislation," *Political Science Quarterly* 6, no. 1 (March 1891), 105–106.

46. Avery, "State-Printed Textbooks in California," 628.

47. Percy Roland Davis, *State Publication of Textbooks in California*, 38–39.

48. Ellen M. Cyr, *The Children's Primer* (Boston: Ginn, 1891); Ellen M. Cyr, *The Children's Primer*, State Text-Book Committee and approved by the State Board of Education, comp. (Sacramento: State Printing Office, 1905).

49. Percy Roland Davis, *State Publication of Textbooks in California*, 33.

50. Senate Daily Journal quoted in Browne, *The Debates in the Convention of California*, 44–45.

51. William E. Pulsifer to George A. Plimption, November 11, 1913, George A. Plimpton Papers, Rare Book and Manuscript Library, Columbia University, New York. Pulsifer was President of D.C. Heath and Company.

52. Jenks, "School-Book Legislation," 90–91.

53. Ibid., 91.

54. "State Text-Book Laws and Systems," *Publishers Weekly* 1068 (July 16, 1892), 108.

55. Ibid., 109–110. These were: Indiana, Kentucky, Louisiana, Minnesota, Missouri, Montana, Nevada, North Carolina, Oregon, South Carolina, Virginia, Washington, and West Virginia.

56. *Kansas v. American Book Company*, 69 Kan. 1 (1904).

57. John Franklin Brown, *State Publication of Schoolbooks* (New York: Macmillan, 1931), 24.

58. M. L. Brittain, *Report of the School Book Investigating Committee to the General Assembly of Georgia* (1914), 22.

59. Ohio School Book Commission, *Report of the State School Book Commission for the Year 1905* (Columbus: State of Ohio, 1905), 1.

60. P. L. Harned, *Textbook Law of Tennessee* (Nashville: State of Tennessee, 1927), 5.

61. John A. Lapp, "Legislative Notes and Reviews," *The American Political Science Review* 10, no. 3 (August 1916), 546.

62. Ibid., 552.

63. Brammer, "Our Heritage and History," 439.

64. Clyde J. Tidwell, *State Control of Textbooks* (New York: Teachers College, Columbia, 1928).

65. *Ninth Census of the United States*, 394.

66. Bureau of the Census, *Fourteenth Census of the United States*, vol. 2 (Washington, D.C.: Government Printing Office, 1922), 1047.

67. *Proceedings of the Constitutional Convention* (Denver: Smith-Brooks Press, 1907), 688.

68. Ibid., 359.

69. Jeanette Keith, *Country People in the New South* (Chapel Hill: University of North Carolina Press, 1995).

Teaching Reading with Television

Constructing Closed Captioning
Using the Rhetoric of Literacy

GREG DOWNEY

THE DEAF JOURNAL *Silent Worker* proclaimed in 1910 that "every one who knows the deaf child knows how dear the moving picture is to its heart, and, if properly selected, how full of educational value it is."[1] Through the 1910s and 1920s, film—silent, but with printed dialogue intertitles—was a unique and special tool for deaf education, on par with musical education for the blind.[2] And although deaf educators sometimes feared the negative effects of film on their students—worrying that "the motion pictures become to [them] teachers whose attraction and potency are in direct proportion to [their] isolation"[3]— most agreed that taking control of the new medium in residential schools was the best strategy for deaf education, especially if one could find films that were both "educational in character and yet attractive-fairy stories."[4]

Calls for "visual education" of the deaf continued through the 1930s and 1940s, but as silent, intertitled films became increasingly scarce, educators grew increasingly aware that film was "the most expensive of all visual aids."[5] Moreover, without printed translations, the use of commercial films in the deaf classroom was frustrating. In one case from 1935, instructors resorted to starting and stopping the film so that students could lip-read what their teachers might have to say about a particular scene. These same deaf educators noted that if one or another film production center could "be designated as a distributor for a group of the outstanding industrial films and have them retitled, if possible at the expense of the industries which they represent, a great service would be rendered."[6]

In the immediate postwar period, many educators of the deaf shared this idea. Shunned by Hollywood ever since the end of the silents fifteen years earlier, deaf educators began to subtitle their own films—a process they referred to as "captioning." Their experimentation with captioned film in the 1940s and 1950s later translated into advocacy for a state-sanctioned system of captioned television in the 1960s and 1970s. These efforts paid off in the 1980s, when a public-private partnership under the oversight of the federal government brought captioned television into the living room of any deaf household willing to buy a $300 set-top "decoder." But supply and demand under this partnership had trouble connecting, and it took new regulations in the 1990s to make the text-on-television system universal and sustainable. In the end, constructing closed captioning relied on the same early educational framework—teaching literacy through the association of sound, image, and text—but in a way that broadened the audience for captioning beyond the deaf and hard-of-hearing community.

This chapter considers the historical connection between print culture and visual culture in the decades-long effort to provide a form of "media justice" to deaf and hard-of-hearing film and television viewers through synchronized text captioning. This was a project pitting the activists and educators of a minority language community—those who communicate with eyes, hands, and signs rather than ears, voices, and utterances—against a mainstream film and television industry intent on minimizing its risks and costs by selling news and entertainment only to its most profitable audience of hearing consumers. Thus it became a familiar question of the role of state subsidy and regulation versus the actions of private capital in serving a minority interest over the public airwaves. Yet the construction of closed captioning was also an example of the way that a new feature of an old media system, provided through a combination of digital technology and information labor, was carefully framed as a standard service for the majority of consumers rather than a remedial benefit for only a minority. What tied both of these processes together was an evolving notion of multimedia literacy that, though applied to different audiences at different points in the story, remained firmly tied to the notion that the ability to read was a crucially important skill for society to provide to all its members, minority and majority alike, in a multicultural, media-saturated society.[7]

Deaf Education and Captioned Films

The decades-long collective captioning effort began around 1947 when Edmund Boatner, superintendent of the American School for the Deaf in West

Hartford, Connecticut, charged his vocational education teacher, J. Pierre Rakow, with the task of "studying and learning the techniques of film captioning."[8] Rakow, who was deaf himself, first "approached one of the major motion picture companies" to do the subtitling, but was "told that the cost of such an operation would be prohibitive."[9] Undeterred, Rakow contacted Titra Film Laboratories in New York and secured an affordable production process for his subtitles.[10] Despite the fact that "film producers were plagued by widespread film piracy" and were thus "unwilling to sell or lease prints of any of their better films," Rakow convinced one producer to lease the Abbott and Costello film *The Noose Hangs High* (1948) to him, for which he wrote all the subtitles himself.[11]

Encouraged by Rakow's success, in 1949 Boatner and fellow educator Clarence O'Connor, director of the Lexington School for the Deaf in New York City, incorporated Captioned Films for the Deaf (CFD) and began to seek financial backing.[12] Over the next decade, this group purchased and captioned nearly 30 feature-length films, some of them entertainment features purchased from studios (at up to $500 each) and others educational films donated by corporations. Although the target audience was children in residential schools for the deaf, Boatner maintained that the intent was to caption not just educational films, but "wholesome feature films, which the deaf child can understand."[13]

By the mid-1950s the CFD experiment had become so successful that the wider deaf and hard-of-hearing community—a diverse set of interests often at odds over whether deaf education should focus on signed languages or speech training—lobbied the federal government to fund the program so it could scale up to serve the entire nation.[14] As a later president of CFD put it, "Not only did the NAD [National Association for the Deaf], the NFSD [National Federation of Schools for the Deaf], state associations, and local clubs work together, but [they] were joined by the Office of Vocational Rehabilitation, the Conference of School Executives, the Convention of Instructors, the A. G. Bell Association, parent groups—in fact everyone who has an interest in the deaf joined hands to promote this film legislation."[15] President Eisenhower authorized the national Captioned Films for the Deaf agency in 1958—part of the post-Sputnik, cold war education boom—and an educator at Gallaudet College for the deaf and hard-of-hearing, John Gough, was hired as its first national director.[16]

The fact that Gough was not deaf himself caused some worry, but by the following year he had hired CFD's first deaf manager, Malcolm "Mac" Norwood.[17] Educated at both the American School and at Gallaudet, Norwood had "established a budget to encourage his teachers to rent old-time silent films with captions for use in their classes" at his previous job at the West Virginia School for the Deaf.[18] To secure a labor force of captioners, in December 1959 J. P. Rakow traveled to Washington, D.C., to train three deaf Gallaudet instructors in his captioning technique.[19] Rakow continued to consult for CFD through the early 1960s, captioning at least a dozen films himself through his new private company "Superior Films," while the Gallaudet captioners learned their craft.[20] "Thus to a considerable extent," commented the *Silent Worker*, "the program is not only for, but also by the deaf."[21]

Although the program had been started by educators from residential deaf schools for children, it also served an estimated 260,000 people in the adult deaf community through screenings at a nationwide network of deaf clubs.[22] In 1960 at 259 screenings of captioned films across the United States, over a third of the audience was made up of adults.[23] But as further legislation appropriated larger budgets for CFD, the mission of the agency shifted more to education, not entertainment—stressing, in Gough's words, "the educational and language retardation of the deaf and the promise of captioned films to help improve this situation."[24] The definition of "film" was expanded to include the more school-friendly media of filmstrips, slides, and transparencies, all of which were expected "to promote the academic, cultural, and vocational advancement of deaf persons."[25] A larger staff of eleven was authorized, including "a writer who . . . specialize[d] in captioning and teaching guides."[26] And the agency made use of teachers in deaf schools as far away as New York and California to write captions for its first round of thirteen educational science films.[27] Not only a tool to teach English language skills to deaf students, captioned films were now seen as ways to teach everything else as well.

By the mid-1960s, a balance of sorts had been reached. The program listed 125 educational films in circulation, compared to 212 entertainment features.[28] However, CFD was now captioning more educational films (51) than features (44) per year, and although children still outnumbered adults in the audience by a margin of 2 to 1, the *Deaf American* reported that "Many of the educational titles originally captioned for use in schools for the deaf [were] now being made available to the adult deaf through normal distribution channels."[29] CFD purchased some 1,000 overhead projectors, 1,000 filmstrip projectors, 2,000 screens, and 50 Technicolor projectors "for release on loan" to deaf groups and schools.[30] Over the next decade, with the help of federal funds, "four thousand classrooms and training centers were provided with basic media equipment."[31]

In this way, the federal CFD program inspired and supported local film captioning efforts in deaf education around the country. Recalled educator Robert Stepp, Jr., "As a greater variety of new materials became available, teachers became actively involved in the adoption process—selecting, adapting, designing, and producing materials tailored to the particular needs of their students and to their own teaching methods."[32] A 1962 survey in the *American Annals of the Deaf* reported that "almost every [deaf] school and class owns at least one movie projector."[33] But while captioned film was firmly rooted in the institution of childhood education, captioning for the deaf would soon branch out into the world of adult entertainment and information—on television.

Finding a Way to Caption Television

In a nation still reeling from both the rapid diffusion of television and the birth of the modern civil rights movement, it was clear to almost everyone in the late 1960s that the next challenge for captioning was broadcast television. All through the 1950s, instructors of the deaf had experimented with lip-reading, signing, and various forms of captioning on locally broadcast educational television (ETV) stations—a myriad of local efforts that came together at the "Symposium on Instructional Media for the Deaf," held at the University of Nebraska in 1964.[34] Two years after this conference, deaf educators organized four Regional Media Centers for the Deaf (RMCDs) at the University of Massachusetts–Amherst, the University of Tennessee–Knoxville, New Mexico State University in Las Cruces, and the University of Nebraska–Lincoln.[35] Each center specialized in a particular form of media: transparencies at Amherst, films at Lincoln, "programmed instructional materials" at Las Cruces, and educational television at the Southern RMCD in Knoxville.[36] The Southern RMCD trained a generation of media-savvy educators who "developed production and utilization skills which undoubtedly led to hundreds and hundreds of items of teacher-produced materials," from the do-it-yourself classroom project at the Clarke School for the Deaf for captioning documentaries, to the $100,000 closed-circuit television production and distribution installations of the Kansas School for the Deaf.[37]

Yet by 1970, the year of the first conference on "Communicative Television and the Deaf Student," overall use of television at deaf schools was still estimated at only about 25 percent.[38] Given this limited average, deaf educators began to discuss ways of creating a system for distributing captioned television analogous to the system for distributing captioned film. One advocate imagined a world where "a simple, relatively inexpensive captioning process [was] devised whereby televised programs from the educational channel could be videotaped and suitable captions added by students and teachers in the school setting," eventually scaling up to a "Regional Captioning Center."[39] Education was always the focus of these initial ideas, as when the Southern RMCD experimented with storing captions on punched paper tape, or when the American School for the Deaf experimented with captioning videotaped episodes of *Sesame Street*.[40] But increasingly in the 1970s, educational goals were tied to the more general pursuit of broadcast justice and universal access to television viewership.

The shift from "visual education" to "media equality" in the captioning community mirrored a wider shift beginning at about the same time in the deaf community as a whole. Long seen by outsiders as a "disability" or a "handicap," the fact that deaf persons could not hear was beginning to be reimagined not as medical deficiency, but as a form of cultural diversity.[41] One catalyst for this shift had been the publication of William Stokoe's *Sign Language Structure* (1960), which argued that American Sign Language (ASL) was "a full (though not written) language, with a logical internal grammar and the capacity to express anything."[42] This finding came as little surprise to generations of deaf persons who had grown up "speaking" in sign and, in the process, seeking out the company of others who did so as well; however, it was a dramatic shift from earlier "oralist" presumptions that signed languages such as ASL were inherently inferior to spoken and written English. As one deaf culture activist later explained, "Although signed language has been suppressed in education for over a century in many lands, it could not be banished from the lives of Deaf people; most of them continued to take Deaf spouses and to use their manual language at home, with their children, and at social gatherings."[43]

Not all deaf and hard-of-hearing individuals or advocates shared this cultural view of deafness, but as with captioned films a few decades earlier, television captioning gradually became a shared goal. On the one hand, captioning was embraced as the ultimate "mainstreaming" tool, helping to teach deaf individuals better English skills and lip-reading techniques. On the other hand, captioning was seen as the epitome of broadcast justice, a subtitling tool analogous to cinematic language translation for a cultural minority shut out of television participation simply because they communicated with their hands and not their mouths. In either case, universal captioned television promised to address what author Tom Humphries later called "audism"—"paternalism and institutional discrimination toward Deaf people."[44]

The growing demand for accessible television came at a politically opportune moment, just as the Corporate for Public Broadcasting (CPB) was created in 1967 in the wake of a Carnegie Commission report on educational television.[45] A year later, Captioned Films for the Deaf was renamed "Media Services and Captioned Films" (MSCF) with Mac Norwood as its new director and a modified mission "to cover all handicapped individuals," not just the deaf.[46] The two organizations, CPB and MSCF, soon connected. Shortly after the new Public Broadcasting System (PBS) began broadcasting in 1970, Norwood contacted Phil Collyer at the PBS station WGBH in Boston "to produce a demonstration captioned program for use by PBS."[47] By October of the next year, Norwood had secured $274,000 from the recently reorganized Bureau of Education for the Handicapped (BEH) for a pilot project to caption the popular cooking program *French Chef* with Julia Child.[48] For PBS, captioned programming was a great example of a "market failure" that only publicly supported (that is, federally funded) television could remedy.

Yet the technology of "open captions," visible to all on the television screen without added equipment, was soon eclipsed by that of "closed captions," developed as part of a wider effort by the National Bureau of Standards to hide digital time-and-frequency signals inside the analog television signal. The hiding spot they chose for their "TvTime" system was known as the "Vertical Blanking Interval" (VBI), "that 21-line portion of the 525-line NTSC television signal which does not contain picture information."[49] At an early demonstration of the system, ABC television executive Julius Barnathan and his staff "determined that in addition to presenting the time of day, they could insert captions on the television screen."[50] In December 1971 the technology was showcased at the first National Conference on Television for the Hearing Impaired, held at the Southern RMCD at the University of Tennessee–Knoxville.[51] Conference participants had already been scheduled to view a prerelease screening of the first WGBH-captioned *French Chef* episode; now they would be treated to a demonstration of TvTime captions as well. Norwood declared that "This demonstration proved the feasibility of a 'closed caption' system which permits captions to be seen only by a viewer who has a specially equipped television set."[52] The long campaign to institutionalize affordable closed captioning systems had begun.

Captioning for Reading Improvement versus Captioning for Content Comprehension

With government support from the Bureau of Education for the Handicapped, a broadcast infrastructure in PBS, and a vast network of interested and active deaf educators, the Line 21 closed captioning project gradually built an uneasy coalition of industry support through the 1970s. But while this new sociotechnological system was being constructed, a vigorous argument emerged over whether captioned television programming should be edited for the lower reading level expected of deaf viewers or presented verbatim for equality with hearing audiences. The fact that deaf and hard-of-hearing students scored statistically lower on reading tests across a wide variety of grade levels had long been acknowledged by deaf educators. As one author later put it, "The average deaf sixteen-year-old reads at the level of a hearing eight-year-old. When deaf students eventually leave school, three in four are unable to read a newspaper. Only two deaf children in a hundred (compared with forty in a hundred among the general population) go on to college."[53] But what to do about this statistical difference was a point of debate, with real implications for both captioning accessibility and captioning labor costs, especially in what was widely considered the single most important type of television programming to caption: nightly news.

Even before the closed-captioning system was fully developed, the Caption Center at WGBH-Boston had taken the lead in providing open-captioned nightly news to a national deaf audience. ABC allowed WGBH to tape its 6 p.m. national news feed each night, quickly caption it, and then rebroadcast it at

11 p.m. over participating PBS affiliate stations.[54] From its earlier *French Chef*
work, the Caption Center had already assembled the equipment and the staff
to do the captioning. However, the tight turnaround time of five hours demanded a precise division of labor, and the complex syntax and vocabulary of
the evening news demanded a strict policy on editing.[55] Citing a Gallaudet
finding that "the average graduate from an educational program for deaf and
hard of hearing students read at about a third-grade level," WGBH extensively
trimmed the original ABC news script:[56]

ORIGINAL AUDIO TRACK

Now credit card companies testifying before the Federal Privacy Protection
Commission have disclosed they also give out the details of what their clients
buy and pay for, or don't pay for, to government agencies and private attorneys
on presentation of subpoenas. American Express says it does not even tell its
clients when this happens.

EDITED CAPTIONS

Now credit card companies have testified that they also give out the details of
what their clients buy and pay for to government agencies and private attorneys
when subpoenas are presented. American Express does not tell its clients when
this happens.

Captioning researcher Carl Jensema later recalled that "the word count was
cut by about a third and the reading level was cut from roughly a sixth-grade
level to a third-grade level. All passive-voice sentence construction was removed, nearly all idioms were removed, contractions were eliminated, clauses
were converted into short declarative sentences, and even jokes and puns were
changed if it was felt the deaf and hard of hearing audience would not understand them."[57]

Viewers were not deterred by the editing; on the contrary, the *Captioned
ABC Evening News* was a hit. After its debut on a handful of East Coast stations
in December 1973, local affiliates signed on rapidly.[58] A year later, when PBS
went national with the program, over fifty stations were airing the program.[59]
This success was not only due to deaf and hard-of-hearing viewers. In some
areas, the local ABC affiliate demanded that the captioned program air not at
11 p.m., but at 11:30 or 12 p.m. to avoid competition with the affiliate's local
news program.[60] The *New York Times* noted that "many of the ABC stations are
reluctant to have their local late-evening news compete with Howard K.
Smith, Harry Reasoner, and the rest of the network's Evening News team."[61]
Local affiliates feared that even hearing viewers would prefer watching the
open-captioned network news rather than the uncaptioned local news, an
assumption that ran directly counter to the conventional wisdom that hearing
viewers would never willingly choose to view open captions. Thus when

WGBH attempted to promote its own captioning standards of heavy editing, it spoke from a position of both intensive daily experience and unquestioned national success with both hearing and nonhearing audiences.

But not all captioners in the mid-1970s agreed with the WGBH editing philosophy. At the other end of the spectrum from the Caption Center was Gallaudet College, home of the original CFD captioners, where a new group led by professor Donald Torr had been open-captioning videotaped material for in-house educational use since 1970. Saying "it would never be practical to caption at different reading levels," Torr "asked that every word be captioned, including those in the commercials."[62] Explained Torr, "students might not comprehend certain structures or words, but neither do hearing infants and children, who gradually master the language through continual exposure to it."[63] Preserving the integrity of the original text affected the time and cost of all captioning at Gallaudet: "The captioners strive for accuracy and must research technical terms, names of people and places, and foreign terminology."[64] Here the goals of improving the reading skills of the deaf took priority over imparting any particular content information—and there was of course no consideration made for a hearing audience at all.

However, there were intermediate positions between the editing and verbatim philosophies. The WGBH caption editing strategy was less controversial when applied to children's programming, where the caption presentation rate was further reduced to sixty words per minute.[65] In fact when the Caption Center was charged with captioning thirty-nine episodes of the PBS kids' show *ZOOM* in the summer of 1975, it let its captioners' creativity run wild: "When the Zoomers [kids] jump up and down, the words jump up and down. They grow BIGGER, smaller, and if the Zoomers tear across the stage during a musical number, the words race across the screen as if they had personalities of their own."[66] *ZOOM* illustrated one compromise position on the captioning debate: verbatim for adults, edited for children.

Another compromise was illustrated by the captioning policy of the National Technical Institute for the Deaf (NTID), where 97 percent of the school's 900 college students had lost some or all of their hearing either at birth or prior to age four.[67] Like Gallaudet, NTID captioned video in-house to screen for its students. But their captioning producer, Linda Carson, instructed that while "programs captioned for entertainment purposes will not be edited, . . . programs captioned for instructional purposes will be edited when necessary to conform to the reading and language level requirements of the intended audience," usually 140 words per minute.[68] Here was a second captioning compromise, based not on audience age but on program content: verbatim for entertainment, edited for instruction.

Besides WGBH, the major producer of open-captioned material for broadcast during the 1970s was PBS, through its "Interim Captioning Service" (so named because its open-captioned programming was to be seen as an interim step on the way to the more desirable goal of a closed-captioning system). PBS captioner Doris Caldwell instructed her staff to put audience age and program content compromises together. She agreed that in teaching deaf children to read, "graded [edited for reading level] captions permit the use of language controls and the application of developmental reading principles."[69] But she also argued for "keeping the script as verbatim as possible while condensing to a grade readability level and reading speed appropriate for the target audience (adults or children)."[70] Thus Caldwell took the Gallaudet verbatim position for adult entertainment programming and the WGBH editing position for children's educational programming.

While WGBH was largely captioning news and PBS was largely captioning entertainment, in the late 1970s a rift developed between these two public captioning organizations. WGBH's Phil Collyer began a correspondence with PBS's Doris Caldwell on the nature of "good captioning." Collyer argued, "I don't believe precision is that important. . . . You state that oversimplification of the content abuses the integrity of the producers of the program. I do not believe this is necessarily so." Collyer added that "our objective is to serve as great a number of the audience as possible by seeking a more common denominator: a lower reading level and reading speed."[71] Caldwell disagreed, asking Collyer, "Does this mean you are opting to serve only that relatively small segment commonly referred to as the 'low-verbal deaf?'" She argued, "the low-verbal group (largely, the prelingually deaf with inadequate schooling) is continuing to lessen due to improved educational strategies."[72] For Caldwell, the purpose of broadcast captioning was not to advance deaf reading education.

In the end, the two captioners—and the captioning agencies they represented—had to agree to disagree. WGBH's Collyer ended his letter saying "I hope you will agree that you and I, both as hearing people and caption producers, are not the ones who should determine that approach. The decision should be made by the deaf themselves. I hope that somehow this will be done."[73] PBS's Caldwell expressed a similar sentiment, saying that "open availability of PBS-designed encoding units and expanding developments such as real-time captioning [which was assumed to be verbatim] will make many of our present concerns obsolete."[74] Both seemed to hope that the verbatim versus editing question would fade away when closed captioning finally scaled up to a national system. But the question of whether words on television were best used to teach reading or to impart content did not go away.

Defending the National Captioning Institute through Literacy

Though the debate over open-captioning standards was left unresolved, the development of a production caption-editing console and a consumer set-top decoder for the closed-captioning system moved forward. Despite network reservations over costs, in March 1979, a deal was announced by federal Health, Education, and Welfare (HEW) secretary Joseph Califano. Proclaiming that "we celebrate the immense good that can come about when government, private industry and the voluntary agencies join hands and cooperate in the public interest," he explained that PBS, ABC, and NBC would participate in a new Line 21 closed-captioning system.[75] The plan seemed simple: the federal government would create a new, private, nonprofit corporation called the National Captioning Institute (NCI), which would produce the actual captions, manage the development and marketing of decoders, and research future possibilities in captioning.[76] Networks would pay to have their own programming captioned, and consumers would pay to purchase their own set-top caption decoders.

Yet this public-private partnership, headed by John Ball of PBS, rested on a set of production and consumption goals that proved elusive. NCI charged the networks $2,000 per broadcast-hour for captioning services; if each network paid to caption an expected 5 hours per week of programming, the total cost to each network would be roughly $500,000 per year.[77] These labor costs were not the only form of income for NCI, though. Each time a home decoder was sold, now at an expected price of $250 each, NCI would reap an $8 royalty fee.[78] With this dual revenue stream, one from the producer side and one from the consumer side, NCI was expected to be commercially self-sufficient after four years.

Unfortunately, the pace of decoder sales would soon begin to haunt NCI. PBS publicly estimated that some 13 million deaf and hard-of-hearing persons would be interested in purchasing caption decoders. But about six months after the September 1980 debut of closed captioning, Doris Caldwell (who had moved to NCI along with Ball) asked Donald Torr back at Gallaudet to help her estimate how many decoders might truly be sold each year. Estimating the size of the relevant deaf and hard-of-hearing community at only 4 million, Torr came up with a ballpark figure of 200,000 deaf households willing to purchase a caption decoder and reasoned that those purchases might be stretched out over 4 or 5 years, yielding an expectation of 40,000–50,000 sales per year.[79] Unfortunately, NCI proclaimed that it would manufacture and sell 100,000 decoders per year, for "a total of about 400,000 sales over the next three or four years."[80] Thus when closed-captioning hit its one-year mark in March 1981, NCI was in trouble: only about 35,000 homes were estimated to have captioning decoders (a figure below even Torr's estimate). Similarly, the total amount of captioned programming was lower than expected at only 25 hours per week—or an average of a little over one hour of captioned fare on each network per day. NCI president Ball admitted that captioning suffered a "chicken and egg problem:" people would not buy caption decoders without more captioned programming, but programmers would not caption more content without a larger audience of decoder-owning viewers.[81]

By the late 1980s it became clear that the wider the audience activists could claim for captioning, the more likely captioning would be to find continued government funding. This was especially important after 1989 when a Department of Education study recomputed the market for closed captioning downward from Torr's previous estimate of around 4 million to only one million people, "eliminating people under five who may be too young to read the captions and people with low levels of educational attainment who may not read well enough to benefit from captioning."[82] Finding a wider audience for broadcast television captioning meant drawing upon the long history of film captioning in deaf education to make the claim that a *universal* closed-captioning system—with decoders in every household and captions on every program—would serve not only the cause of broadcast justice, but also the causes of childhood literacy education and adult immigrant Americanization. In other words, through its ability to help people learn to read, captioning was to be recast as a tool for the hearing as well as for the deaf.

First, however, the deaf and hard-of-hearing community had to show that captioned media actually contributed to learning in the deaf classroom. Research performed at schools for the deaf in the early 1970s comparing both captioned and uncaptioned video had concluded that words on the screen helped to convey information to students.[83] In the late 1970s, the WGBH Caption Center had spent three years researching "multi-level captioning" for children, "a system which generates captions at three reading levels" corresponding to grades 2, 3, and 4.[84] And in 1980 NCI itself had captioned "23 hours of educational programming" for use in schools, part of a three-year contract (which incidentally brought in much-needed revenue).[85]

At a time when research on the effectiveness of federally funded literacy programs was attracting interest—and controversy—in fields ranging from special education to bilingual education, NCI returned to its own literacy research with new vigor. A 1985 study in a Chicago school argued that even though "deaf students do not have the opportunity to hear the sounds and patterns of English," making learning to read "a difficult task," in general "deaf students are highly motivated to read print when it is in the form of captions on television."[86] Such research recalled the claims that television was, in Newton Minnow's words, a "vast wasteland" (fears that had led to the creation of PBS itself), but turned these fears around: "Television, which is sometimes charged with contributing to reading problems, may now be used as one of the solutions to these problems."[87] By 1987 John Ball had rewritten history in his own public statements, claiming that NCI had been created not to bring broadcast justice to deaf viewers but "to open new educational horizons for all hearing-impaired Americans through access to television."[88]

Calling attention to the literacy benefits of captioning, NCI began to widen the target audience for this technology. As part of NCI's budget request for the

1984 fiscal year (FY), Doris Caldwell had claimed that "retarded children in Florida are learning to speak through use of captions, normal hearing students in Fairfax County, Virginia public schools, who are slow readers, have markedly improved their reading and comprehension skills through use of captions, and Harvard University is experimenting with English language captions with their students who are non-native speakers of English."[89] In its FY 1985 appropriation request, NCI specifically asked for $200,000 for research on "the potential educational benefits of closed-captioned television for prospective beneficiaries beyond the deaf population."[90] NCI-funded researchers studied captioned video with "normal" hearing children, ESL students, and learning disabled students, finding encouraging results each time.[91] Outside researchers sometimes reached more skeptical or limited findings, especially when studying the effects of captions on learning for hearing college students but, for the most part, NCI was buoyed by the increased focus on captioning's educational value.[92] By the time John Ball made his FY 1987 budget request to Congress, he was citing "at least 1,500,000 learning disabled children" as part of the audience for captioning (and the market for decoder purchases).[93]

NCI did not restrict its educational arguments to the plight of children, however. In 1988 NCI deflected attention away from its still-weak decoder sales by bragging that "over 10,000 [captioning] units last year [out of a total of 45,000] were sold to folks with no hearing impairment whatsoever."[94] In the marketing materials produced for its TeleCaption 4000 decoder in 1989, NCI claimed "people who speak English as a second language . . . accounted for over 40 percent of all TeleCaption decoders sold in 1988!" The sales pitch reported that this market of 20 million "and growing daily" had a "combined disposable income" of $169 billion.[95] According to June 1990 Senate testimony by Ball, *most* of the 1989 decoder sales "were to people learning English as a second language."[96] And as a 1990 NCI report by Susan B. Neuman put it, "35 million of our nation's children come from homes where English is not spoken."[97] Counting up all of these literacy students—native-born and immigrant, adult and child—gave a combined captioning audience with both the numbers and the wealth to attract government attention (or so NCI hoped).

The effort to recast captioning as a general force for literacy education had two main results. First, in terms of deaf and hard-of-hearing education, mandatory captioning was now cast as an essential ingredient in deaf educational reform, receiving prominent attention in the *Toward Equality* report commissioned under the federal Education of the Deaf Act of 1986 and published in 1988. Declaring the state of deaf education in the United States "unsatisfactory," this report proposed that "Congress should require the Federal Communications Commission to issue regulations as it deems necessary to require that broadcasters and cable-TV programmers caption their programming" and "to make new TV sets capable of decoding closed captions." For the deaf, the report asserted that "the attainment of literacy and a wider acquaintance with the world at large" were processes that could be "most effectively enhanced by the accelerated use of captioned TV."[98] Second, in mainstream education, a long-standing assumption about captioning going all the way back to the early 1970s was finally questioned: the idea that hearing viewers could gain no benefit from, and thus would not stand for, text on their screens. Education specialists who looked at the record realized "there was no research that substantiated this belief." The notion that hearing viewers could benefit from captioning opened the door to a new set of arguments that captioning was not only a broadcast right for the few, but a broadcast enhancement for the many.[99]

Captioning Reregulated, but at a Price

These new arguments, plus the long-awaited appearance of a "decoder on a chip" that could be inexpensively included in all new television sets, motivated Senators Tom Harkin (D-IA), John McCain (R-AZ), Daniel Inouye (D-HI), and Paul Simon (D-IL) to introduce the "Television Decoder Circuitry Act" (S.1974) in November 1989. The law required that "any television with at least a thirteen-inch screen which is manufactured, or imported for use, in the United States be equipped with built-in decoder circuitry designed to display closed-captioned TV transmissions."[100] As in previous debates over captioning, the size of the deaf and hard-of-hearing audience (this time estimated at "more than 15 million Americans [with] some degree of hearing loss") figured prominently in the discussion.[101] But this debate also saw the new rhetorical construction of a captioning audience made up of more than just deaf and hard-of-hearing viewers. The House report on the hearings cited 24 million "deaf or hearing impaired" people in the United States, and claimed that 38 percent of "older Americans" who had "some loss of hearing" would benefit from the Act. The House report also cited "23–27 million functionally illiterate adults, 3–4 million immigrants learning English as a second language, and 18 million children in grades kindergarten through three, learning to read" as potential beneficiaries of the legislation. Finally the report claimed that, according to the Department of Education, "13 percent of the adult population is unable to read."[102] Captioning no longer pitted a profitable television audience against a minority viewing community; instead, it offered a low-cost technology that would end up in every single American household, reminding each citizen that Congress was watching out for the interests of many different groups.

The Television Decoder Circuitry Act, signed by President George H. W. Bush in October 1990, was cast as a triumph for minority rights during the same year that the landmark Americans with Disabilities Act was passed.[103] But NCI saw the legislation as a triumph for the majority as well, predicting that soon "virtually every home in the country" would have a caption-capable

TV.[104] Not even a shift in the control of Congress with the 1994 "Republican revolution" could derail the momentum of captioning reregulation now. The 1996 Telecommunications Act called for virtually all television content, old and new, to be captioned by the turn of the millennium, again drawing on general education and literacy arguments.

The legislative captioning successes of the 1990s had one negative side effect: they exposed this new "educational" captioning to public scrutiny like never before. In March 1998 Senators Daniel Coats (R-IN) and Joseph Lieberman (D-CT) publicly attacked *The Jerry Springer Show* as "the closest thing to pornography on broadcast television" and called upon Secretary of Education Richard Riley to end federal funding for closed-captioning of the show—some $50,000 in subsidies per year.[105] "We are confident," the senators wrote, "you will share in our outrage that the federal government is not only using taxpayer funds to subsidize their degrading and prurient program at all, but it is also judging it to be of some educational and cultural value."[106] The Department of Education responded that the total of $7 million or so it spent on captioning that year was the only way to provide deaf and hard-of-hearing viewers "access to the shared cultural experiences of television" and that not only taxpayers, but also the television industry and private charitable donations, funded captioning costs.[107] Two peer-review panels drawn from the deaf and hard-of-hearing community, one at NCI and one at the Department of Education, selected the TV shows to be captioned, to ensure that the selections reflected the needs and desires of deaf and hard-of-hearing viewers.[108] At issue was the question of whether captioning was for literacy education or cultural participation. Secretary Riley argued that "As distasteful as *The Jerry Springer Show* may be to you and me, I do not believe it should be the role of this Department in administering the captioning program to single out particular television programs and make a cultural judgment that individuals who are deaf or hard of hearing will be denied the same access to those programs that are watched by America's hearing community."[109] Senator Lieberman responded, "I think the least that *The Jerry Springer Show* could do, based on the enormous amounts of money it appears to be making from the garbage it's putting on the air, is to pay for the closed captioning itself."[110]

The attack on closed captions for *The Jerry Springer Show* quickly became a symbol for other causes against government "waste" and "abuse." In April 1998 representatives Joseph Pitts and Roy Blunt used the flap to promote their "Dollars to Classroom Act"—which would have affected many more education programs than just captioning—arguing that "while American school children lag behind the rest of the developed world in basic academic skills, our federal education dollars are paying for children to learn about prostitution, racism, polygamy, and other values which are completely contrary to traditional family values."[111] Similarly, Representative Pete Hoekstra (R-MI) argued against increasing funding to the Department of Education, saying "we're struggling with reading, writing and math—where do some of these dollars go? Federal dollars pay for closed-captioning of *Baywatch* and *Jerry Springer*—is that going to help us teach our kids how to read, write and do math?"[112]

The irony in these accusations was that a law had been passed in 1997 to phase out funding for captioning of noneducational programming by 2001.[113] In the Individuals with Disabilities Education Act amendments of 1997, the Department of Education was instructed that captioning funds could be used only for "educational, news, and informational television, videos, or materials." But after the *Springer* debate, the Department found itself in the odd position of soliciting "comments and recommendations from the public on what the term 'educational, news, and informational' encompasses in reference to the description and captioning of television, videos, and materials."[114] In future years, recipients of government captioning funds would be expected to "identify and support a consumer advisory group, including parents and educators, that would meet at least annually" to "certify that each program captioned or described with project funds is educational, news, or informational programming."[115]

Today captioning remains an easy target for those eager to score "family values" points against the perceived excesses of "big government." Despite its own previous rules, the Department of Education under the administration of George W. Bush "cut off its closed captioning for nearly 200 TV shows" in late 2003.[116] Bypassing the deaf and hard-of-hearing parent committees and professional educator recommendations, the Department based its decision to cut certain shows on "an external panel of five unnamed individuals."[117] A federal spokesperson "declined to name the five experts who volunteered their time . . . or to offer the parameters, indicating that *Andy Hardy* and *Inside Edition* are educational and informational but *Discovery Jones* and Lifetime's *Biographies of Women* are not."[118] The National Association of the Deaf argued that the department's actions amounted to "censorship," excluding deaf and hard-of-hearing children from "shows that help them learn about the trends, culture, and society around them."[119] Broadcast justice was not the central purpose of federal funding for closed-captioning, the NAD argued: cultural education was. Yet the same rhetoric that had helped universalize the captioning infrastructure—the rhetoric of cultural education—had also helped to minimize the power of captioning's core audience of deaf and hard-of-hearing Americans.

Debates over the proper relationship of text to sound and image—and over who pays to produce and maintain that relationship—will no doubt continue as television receivers transition from analog to digital, as media corporations increasingly deliver audiovisual content over mobile wireless electronics, and as media consumers become more accustomed to seeking and experiencing video content over the Web. The same captioning standards and norms that were finally achieved in analog television must be continually rearticulated and defended within each of these new media contexts. Similarly, debates over the place of print in an electronic society continue to unfold as Google attempts to digitize and index the world's library collections over the Internet, as Amazon attempts to sell and deliver the publishing industry's latest products over its Kindle appliance, and as public schools struggle with punitive laws demanding that "no child be left behind" in standardized reading scores. If the history of closed captioning is any guide, activists' efforts to make sure that the benefits of each new articulation between print culture and audiovisual culture are brought to the widest possible audience will continue. Rather than the narrow minority interests that such efforts may be said to serve by their detractors, television captioning reminds us that both the widespread circulation of text and the universal literacy that circulation demands remain crucial preconditions for the success of the information society—serving not just special interests, but the public interest.

Notes

1. "A Night in Arcady," *Silent Worker* 23 (November 1910).

2. "Moving Pictures," *American Annals of the Deaf* 65 (1920), 138.

3. Lucile M. Moore, "The Deaf Child and the Motion Picture," *American Annals of the Deaf* 63 (1918), 472.

4. "Moving Pictures," 137. For more on the D/HOH experience with silent film, see John S. Schuchman, *Hollywood Speaks: Deafness and the Film Entertainment Industry* (Urbana: University of Illinois Press, 1988).

5. Nettie McDaniel, "Visual Education: Introduction," *Volta Review* 34 (1932), 61; William J. McClure, "Visual Education and the Deaf," *American Annals of the Deaf* 86 (1941), 175; Sylvia Wudel Sanders, *The Use of Visual Aids in Teaching the Deaf* (MA thesis, Gallaudet College, 1946), 18.

6. Grace Heider and Fritz Heider, "Motion Pictures in Classroom Work," *Volta Review* 37 (1935), 72–76.

7. For a fuller treatment of this story, see Gregory J. Downey, *Closed Captioning: Subtitling, Stenography, and the Digital Convergence of Text with Television* (Baltimore: Johns Hopkins University Press, 2008).

8. George Propp, "The History of Learning Technology in the Education of Deaf Children," in *Learning Technology for the Deaf*, ed. C. R. Vest (Proceedings from the Second International Learning Technology Congress and Exposition on Applied Learning Technology, February 1978) (Warrenton, VA: Society for Applied Learning Technology, 1978), 5; "Destry Rides Again (For the Deaf)," *Silent Worker* (December 1961), 3.

9. Frederick Rukdeshal, "J. Pierre Rakow: Pioneer in Captioned Films," *Silent Worker* (May 1962), 3.

10. Ibid.; Edmund B. Boatner, "Captioned Films for the Deaf," *American Annals of the Deaf* 126 (1981), 521; "Motion Picture Subtitling Corporation Violated 'No Solicitation' Provision of Final Judgment," *New York Law Journal* (November 14, 2001).

11. Boatner, "Captioned Films for the Deaf," 522; "Destry Rides Again," 3; Rukdeshal, "J. Pierre Rakow," 3; *The Noose Hangs High*, http://www.imdb.com/title/
tt0040652/ (accessed March 26, 2004).

12. Boatner, "Captioned Films for the Deaf," 521; Patricia Cory, *Report of [the 4th]
Conference on the Utilization of Captioned Films for the Deaf*, Lexington School for the Deaf,
New York, New York, June 8–10, 1960 (Washington, D.C.: U.S. Department of Health,
Education, and Welfare, 1960), 1–2.

13. Edmund B. Boatner, "Captioned Films for the Deaf," *American Annals of the Deaf*
96 (1951), 346–350.

14. "Minutes of the 65th Annual Meeting, Alexander Graham Bell Association for
the Deaf," *Volta Review* 57 (1955), 313.

15. John Gough, "Captioned Films for the Deaf," *Silent Worker* (August 1960), 18.

16. Michael P. du Monceau, "A Descriptive Study of Television Utilization in
Communication and Instruction for the Deaf and Hearing Impaired, 1947–1976" (PhD
diss., University of Maryland, 1978), 40; Mark G. Borchert, "The Development of
Closed-Captioned Television: Technology, Policy, and Cultural Form" (PhD diss.,
University of Colorado, Boulder, 1998), 151; "The Editor's Page," *Silent Worker* (March
1959), 2; "The Editor's Page," *Silent Worker* (October 1959), 2; "Captioned Films for the
Deaf," *American Annals of the Deaf* 104 (1959), 398–399; Robert Panara and John Panara,
"Malcolm Norwood: Captioned Media Specialist," *Great Deaf Americans* (Silver Spring,
MD: T. J. Publishers, 1989), 101.

17. Gough, "Captioned Films for the Deaf," 19; "Film Fare," *Silent Worker* (January
1961), 13.

18. Panara and Panara, "Malcolm Norwood: Captioned Media Specialist,"
100–101.

19. "Trainees Start Films Captioning at Gallaudet," *Silent Worker* (January 1960), 32.

20. Rukdeshal, "J. Pierre Rakow: Pioneer in Captioned Films," 3; Gough, "Captioned Films for the Deaf," 19; "Film Fare," *Silent Worker* (November 1960), 24.

21. "Destry Rides Again," 4.

22. Cory, *Report of [the 4th] Conference on the Utilization of Captioned Films for the Deaf*, 3.

23. "Film Fare," *Silent Worker* (January 1961), 13.

24. "Film Fare," *Silent Worker* (October–November 1962), 10; Gough, "Captioned
Films for the Deaf," 19; John A. Gough, "Captioned Films for the Deaf: The New
Program," *Volta Review* 65 (1963), 24–25.

25. "Production and Distribution of Captioned Films for the Deaf," *Federal Register*
(December 1, 1964), 15955–15956.

26. Gough, "Captioned Films for the Deaf: The New Program," 24.

27. "Film Fare," *Silent Worker* (May 1962), 5; "Film Fare," *Silent Worker* (April
1963), 12.

28. John A. Gough, "Captioned Films for the Deaf," *American Annals of the Deaf* 111
(1966), 407 410.

29. "Film Fare," *Deaf American* (May 1966), 9; "Captioned Films, an Up-to-Date
Report," *Deaf American* (June 1965), 13–14.

30. "Film Fare," *Deaf American* (May 1966), 9.

31. Propp, "The History of Learning Technology in the Education of Deaf Children," 5.

32. Robert E. Stepp, Jr., "A Technological Metamorphosis in the Deaf Students," *American Annals of the Deaf* 139 (1994), 15.

33. Jerome D. Schein and John J. Kubis, *A Survey of Visual Aids in Schools and Classes for the Deaf in the United States* (Washington, D.C.: Gallaudet College, 1962), 3, 10.

34. Lucile Cypreansen and Jack McBride, "Lipreading Lessons on Television," *Volta Review* 58 (1956), 346; "Television for Deaf Children in Chicago," *Volta Review* 64 (1962), 30; B. G. Cross, "At Work and Play: Television in the Lives of the Deaf and the Hard of Hearing," *Volta Review* 69 (March 1967), 203; Gallaudet College, *Now See This: A List of TV Stations Presenting Broadcasts Captioned or Interpreted for the Deaf Television Audience* (Washington, D.C.: Gallaudet College, 1972); William Jackson and Roger Perkins, "Television for Deaf Learners: A Utilization Quandary," *American Annals of the Deaf* 119 (1974), 538.

35. Robert E. Stepp, Jr., "Educational Media and Technology for the Hearing-Impaired Learner: An Historical Overview," *Volta Review* 83 (1981), 267; James J. Kundert, "Media Services and Captioned Films," *American Annals of the Deaf* 114 (1969), 692.

36. John A. Gough, "Report from Captioned Films for the Deaf," *American Annals of the Deaf* 112 (1967), 644.

37. Propp, "The History of Learning Technology in the Education of Deaf Children," 6; "A Campus Wide Closed Circuit Television System," *Volta Review* 72 (1970), 60; Michael Z. Waugh, "Captioned Television for Hearing Impaired Viewers at the Kansas School for the Deaf: Method and Applications," in *Captioning: Shared Perspectives*, ed. Barbara Braverman and Barry Jay Cronin (Proceedings of the National Captioning conference, National Technical Institute for the Deaf, Rochester, New York, June 1–3, 1978) (Rochester, NY: National Technical Institute for the Deaf, 1979), 46–53, 46–47.

38. "Symposium on Research and Utilization of Educational Media for Teaching the Deaf: Communicative Television and the Deaf Student," *American Annals of the Deaf* 115 (1970), 543–545; George Propp, "Introduction," *American Annals of the Deaf* 115 (1970), 549; William Jackson, "1970 Survey of Instructional Television in Programs for the Deaf," *American Annals of the Deaf* 115 (1970), 615.

39. E. Jack Goforth, *Suggestions and Guidelines for Development of Television Facilities in Schools for the Deaf* (Knoxville, TN: Southern RMCD, 1968), 5, 22.

40. William Jackson, "Designing a Prototype Television Studio-Laboratory," *American Annals of the Deaf* 115 (1970), 560; Joel Ziev, "Sesame Street Captioned for the Deaf," *American Annals of the Deaf* 115 (1970), 630–631.

41. Gary L. Albrecht, *The Disability Business: Rehabilitation in America* (Newbury Park, CA: SAGE, 1992), 19.

42. Andrew Solomon, "Away from language," *New York Times* (August 28, 1994); William C. Stokoe, *Sign Language Structure: The First Linguistic Analysis of American Sign Language*, revised edition (Silver Spring, MD: Linstok Press, 1978).

43. Harlan Lane, Robert Hoffmeister, and Ben Bahan, *A Journey into the Deaf-World* (San Diego: DawnSign Press, 1996), 63.

44. Katherine A. Jankowski, *Deaf Empowerment: Emergence, Struggle, and Rhetoric* (Washington, D.C.: Gallaudet Univ. Press, 1997), 80.

45. Carnegie Commission on Educational Television, *Public Television: A Program for Action* (New York: Bantam, 1967).

46. U.S. Congress, House Committee on Education and Labor, *Handicapped Individuals Services and Training Act*, House Report 97–950 (December 9, 1982), 8; James J. Kundert, "Media Services and Captioned Films," *American Annals of the Deaf* 114 (1969), 680; Robert Root, "A Survey of the Reaction of Hearing Individuals to Captioned Television to Benefit the Hearing Impaired," *American Annals of the Deaf* 115 (1970), 566.

47. "The Caption Center Turns 20," *Deaf Life* (March 1992), 26; Mardi Loeterman, "The Caption Center at Nineteen," *Deaf American* (Spring 1989), 9.

48. Sharon Earley, "Captioning at WGBH-TV," *American Annals of the Deaf* 123 (1978), 657; Malcolm J. Norwood, "Media Services and Captioned Films," *American Annals of the Deaf* 117 (1972), 554.

49. Normal Felsenthal, "Closed Captioning," in *Museum of Broadcast Communication Encyclopedia of Television*, ed. Horace Newcomb, vol. 1 (Chicago: Fitzroy Dearborn, 1997), 384–385.

50. "ABC Inc. Cited by HEW Secretary Califano for Eight-Year Effort to Develop Industry-Wide Closed-Captioning Program to Serve Deaf," *Deaf American* (April 1979), 5.

51. R. Perkins, ed., *Proceedings of the First National Conference on Television for the Hearing-Impaired* (conducted by the at the University of Tennessee, Knoxville, December 14–16, 1971) (Knoxville, TN: Southern Regional Media Center for the Deaf, College of Education, the University of Tennessee, 1972), ii–iii.

52. Norwood, "Media Services and Captioned Films," 554.

53. Edward Dolnick, "Deafness as Culture," *Atlantic Monthly* (September 1993), 40.

54. "Television News with Subtitles Planned in Boston for the Deaf," *New York Times* (December 1, 1973); "Harry and Howard for the Hearing-Impaired: PBS Stations Set to Start Carrying Captioned 'ABC Evening News,'" *Broadcasting* (December 3, 1973), 28.

55. Jeff Hutchins and Carole Osterer, "Captioning Process at the Caption Center, WGBH," in Braverman and Cronin, *Captioning: Shared Perspectives*, 38–42.

56. du Monceau, "A Descriptive Study of Television Utilization in Communication and Instruction for the Deaf and Hearing Impaired 1947–1976," 90.

57. Carl Jensema, Ralph McCann, and Scott Ramsey, "Closed Captioned Television Presentation Speed and Vocabulary," *American Annals of the Deaf* 141 (1996), 285.

58. Earley, "Captioning at WGBH-TV," 656.

59. "The Caption Center Turns 20," *Deaf Life* (March 1992), 27.

60. "The Captioned ABC Evening News: Common Questions and Accurate Answers," *Deaf American* (March 1975), 3–4.

61. "ABC Evening News with Captions for Deaf on PBS," *New York Times* (October 1, 1974), 83.

62. Donald Torr, "Gallaudet Update," in *Update 74: A Decade of Progress; Symposium on Research and Utilization of Educational Media for Teaching the Deaf*, ed. Robert E. Stepp (conference proceedings, University of Nebraska, Lincoln, April 2–4, 1974).

63. Donald V. Torr, "Captioning Philosophy: Verbatim Captions," in Braverman and Cronin, *Captioning: Shared Perspectives*, 16–17.

64. Sandra L. White and Bill Pugin, "The Captioning Process: Production Techniques [Gallaudet College]," in Braverman and Cronin, *Captioning: Shared Perspectives*, 66.

65. Hutchins and Osterer, "Captioning Process at the Caption Center, WGBH," 44.

66. Leonard Bickman, Thomas Roth, Ron Szoc, Janice Normoyle, H. B. Shutterly, and W. D. Wallace, *An Evaluation of Captioned Television for the Deaf: Final Report*, 4

vols. (Evanston, IL: Westinghouse Evaluation Institute, 1979), 1–5; "The Caption Center Completes 5 Years of Programming for Hearing Impaired," *Deaf American* 31, no. 4 (1978), 5–6.

67. Janice H. VanGorden, "Audience Consideration and Its Impact on Captioning at the National Technical Institute for the Deaf," in Braverman and Cronin, *Captioning: Shared Perspectives*, 73.

68. Linda Carson, "The Captioning Process: Production Techniques at the National Technical Institute for the Deaf," in Braverman and Cronin, *Captioning: Shared Perspectives*, 27–29.

69. Doris C. Caldwell, "Use of Graded Captions with Instructional Television for Deaf Learners," *American Annals of the Deaf* 118 (1973), 501.

70. Doris C. Caldwell, "The Caption-Production Process at PBS [Public Broadcasting Service]," in Braverman and Cronin, *Captioning: Shared Perspectives*, 55.

71. Letter from Philip W. Collyer to Doris C. Caldwell (April 23, 1976), National Public Broadcasting Archives, University of Maryland, College Park, Donald R. Quayle papers, s. 1, b. 1, f. 21.

72. Letter from Doris C. Caldwell to Philip W. Collyer (May 4, 1976), National Public Broadcasting Archives, Donald R. Quayle papers, s. 1, b. 1, f. 21.

73. Letter from Philip W. Collyer to Doris C. Caldwell (April 23, 1976).

74. Letter from Doris C. Caldwell to Philip W. Collyer (May 4, 1976).

75. "Captioned TV for Deaf Soon to be Announced," *Broadcasting* (March 12, 1979), 42.

76. Press release from Joseph A. Califano, Jr., on new closed captioning project (March 23, 1979), Gallaudet University Archives, Donald V. Torr papers (MSS 28), b. 1, f. 4; John E. D. Ball, "National Captioning Institute," in *Gallaudet Encyclopedia of Deaf People and Deafness*, ed. John V. Van Cleve, vol. 2 (New York: McGraw-Hill, 1987), 221; "The Caption Race: Who's Ahead and What's Ahead," *Deaf Life* (February 1990), 10; Carl Jensema and Molly Fitzgerald, "Background and Initial Audience Characteristics of the Closed-Captioned Television System," *American Annals of the Deaf* 126 (1981), 32; "John E. D. Ball Named President of National Captioning Institute, Inc.," *Deaf American* (December 1979), 21; "Door Is Opened on Closed Captioning," *Broadcasting* (March 26, 1979), 32–33; "National Captioning Institute Names Hearing Impaired Advisory Boards," *Deaf American* (April 1980), 4; "John Ball: TV's Wordsmith," *Broadcasting* (August 27, 1990), 87.

77. Press release from Joseph A. Califano, Jr., on new closed captioning project (March 23, 1979); "Captioned TV for Deaf Soon to be Announced," 42; "Door Is opened on Closed Captioning," 32; "Closed-Captioning Set to Start up in the Spring," *Broadcasting* (January 28, 1980), 99.

78. "NBC and Its TV Affiliates to Participate in Industry Effort to Provide Captioned Programs for Hearing-Impaired Viewers," *Deaf American* (April 1979), 10; "Door Is Opened on Closed Captioning," 32.

79. Memo from Donald V. Torr to Edward C. Merrill, "Estimate of Number of Persons Who Would Be Interested in Purchasing a Line 21 Decoder" (September 10, 1980), Gallaudet University Archives, Donald V. Torr papers (MSS 28), b. 2, f. 3.

80. "Door Is Opened on Closed Captioning," 33; Norman Black, "Deaf Will Soon Be Able to Follow Prime Time Television," Associated Press (January 6, 1980).

81. "NCI's Non-Growing Pains with Captioning," 202; Norman Black, "One Year Later, Some Successes, Some Setbacks," Associated Press (March 16, 1981).

82. Renee Z. Sherman and Joel D. Sherman, *Analysis of Demand for Decoders of Television Captioning for Deaf and Hearing-Impaired Children and Adults* (Washington, D.C.: Pelavin Associates, U.S. Dept. of Education, Office of Educational Research and Improvement, Educational Resources Information Center, 1989), v.

83. Lawrence O. Reiner and Dale L. Rockwell, *A Study of Instructional Film Captioning for Deaf Students* (Rochester: National Technical Institute for the Deaf, Division of Research and Training, 1971), 12; Robert R. Davila, "Effect of Changes in Visual Information Patterns on Student Achievement Using a Captioned Film and Specially Adapted Still Pictures" (PhD diss., Syracuse University, 1972), 75; George Propp, "An Experimental Study on the Encoding of Verbal Information for Visual Transmission to the Hearing Impaired Learner" (PhD diss., University of Nebraska, 1972), 89; E. Ross Stuckless, *A Review of Research at NTID, 1967–1976* (Rochester: National Technical Institute for the Deaf, 1978), 16–17.

84. Jill Shulman and Kirk Wilson, "A Multi-Level Linguistic Approach to Captioning Television for Hearing-Impaired Children," in *Learning Technology for the Deaf*, ed. C. R. Vest (Proceedings from the Second International Learning Technology Congress and Exposition on Applied Learning Technology, February 1978) (Warrenton, VA: Society for Applied Learning Technology, 1978), 73–80, 75; Jill Shulman and Nan Decker, "Multi-Level Captioning: A System for Preparing Reading Materials for the Hearing Impaired," *American Annals of the Deaf* 124, no. 5 (1979), 565.

85. John E. D. Ball, "Reaching Millions of Viewers through Closed Captioning," *Public Telecommunications Review* (November/December 1980), 30–32, 38, 31; *Caption* [National Captioning Institute newsletter] (Fall 1980).

86. National Captioning Institute, *Using Closed-Captioned Television in the Teaching of Reading to Deaf Students*, report 85-2 (Falls Church, VA: National Captioning Institute, 1985).

87. Patricia S. Koskinen and Robert M. Wilson, *Have You Read any Good TV Lately? A Guide for Using Captioned Television in the Teaching of Reading* (Falls Church, VA: National Captioning Institute, 1987), 3.

88. Ball, "National Captioning Institute," 221.

89. United States Congress, House of Representatives, Committee on Appropriations, "Departments of Labor, Health and Human Services, Education, and Related Agencies Appropriations for 1984, Part 8: Testimony of Members of Congress and Interested Individuals and Organizations," CIS-NO: 83-H181-75 (May 5, 9–12, 16, 1983), 363.

90. United States Congress, House of Representatives, Committee on Appropriations, "Departments of Labor, Health and Human Services, Education, and Related Agencies Appropriations for 1985, Part 9: Testimony of Members of Congress and Interested Individuals and Organizations," CIS-NO: 84-H181-87 (May 1–3, 7, 1984), 807.

91. National Captioning Institute, *A Report on Two Pilot Projects Which Used Captioned Television in Schoolrooms to Teach Reading to Hearing Children*, report 83-6 (Falls Church, VA: National Captioning Institute, 1983); "Captions for Deaf Help Some Kids Too," Associated Press (September 23, 1983); National Captioning Institute, *Closed-Captioned Television: A New Technology for Enhancing Reading Skills of Learning Disabled Students*, report 86-1 (Falls Church, VA: National Captioning Institute, 1986).

92. Stephen Dee Reese, "Multi-Channel Redundancy Effects on Television News Learning" (PhD thesis, University of Wisconsin–Madison, 1982); Richard M. Ruggerio, "Impact of Television Captioning on Hearing Audiences" (EdD thesis, University of California, Los Angeles, 1987).

93. United States Congress, House of Representatives, Committee on Appropriations, "Departments of Labor, Health and Human Services, Education, and Related Agencies Appropriations for 1987, Part 10: Testimony of Members of Congress and Other Interested Individuals and Organizations," CIS-NO: 86-H181–57 (May 6, 7, 1986), 96.

94. Jeffrey A. Tannenbaum, "TV Decoders Find a Wider Audience," *Wall Street Journal* (October 19, 1988), 1.

95. Eileen R. Smith, "National Captioning Institute, Inc. Telecaption Decoders: Expanding the Horizons of Television, 1989 [press release]" (National Captioning Institute, 1989), National Public Broadcasting Archives, Bill Reed papers, b. 32, f. 9, citing *American Demographics* (March 1989).

96. U.S. Congress, Senate Committee on Commerce, Science, and Transportation, *Television Decoder Circuitry Act of 1990*, S. Rpt. 101–393 (Washington, D.C.: Government Printing Office, 1990), 2.

97. Susan B. Neuman, "Using Captioned Television to Improve the Reading Proficiency of Language Minority Students" (1990), National Public Broadcasting Archives, Bill Reed papers, b. 32, f. 10.

98. Commission on Education of the Deaf, *Toward Equality: Education of the Deaf* (Washington, D.C.: Government Printing Office, 1988), viii, xxi, 111.

99. Ruggerio, "Impact of Television Captioning on Hearing Audiences."

100. "The Caption Center Turns 20," 29; U.S. Congress, Senate, *Television Decoder Circuitry Act of 1990*, 6; 101st Congress, S. 1974 (http://thomas.loc.gov).

101. Rodney Ferguson, "Media: Law May Soon Ease Access to Captioned TV for Deaf," *Wall Street Journal* (August 22, 1990); "New Law Will Expand TV Captions for the Deaf," *New York Times* (October 16, 1990), A22; U.S. Congress, Senate, *Television Decoder Circuitry Act of 1990*, 8.

102. U.S. Congress, Senate, *Television Decoder Circuitry Act of 1990*, 2, 5.

103. Sy Dubow, "The Television Decoder Circuitry Act—TV for All," *Temple Law Review* 64 (Summer 1991), 609.

104. Harry Jessell, "Captioning Capability for TV Sets Becomes Law," *Broadcasting* (October 22, 1990), 44.

105. Lawrie Mifflin, "Closed-Captioning Opposed for 'Springer,'" *New York Times* (March 5, 1998), E13; "Congress Opposed to Captioning Springer," *Weekend All Things Considered* (March 8, 1998).

106. Dan Trigoboff, "Senators Fight 'Springer' Captions," *Broadcasting and Communications* (March 9, 1998), 14.

107. "Closed Captioning Controversy," *Good Morning America* (March 6, 1998).

108. Trigoboff, "Senators Fight 'Springer' Captions," 14.

109. National Association of the Deaf, "Education Secretary Riley Responds to Senators on Springer Caption Funding" [letter, Education Secretary Richard W. Riley to Senator Joseph Lieberman (March 30, 1998)], http://www.nad.org (accessed February 21, 2004).

110. "Congress Opposed to Captioning Springer."

111. Joseph Pitts and Roy Blunt, "Send Dollars to the Class or Fund 'The Jerry Springer Show': It's Your Choice," *Congressional Press Releases* (April 9, 1998).

112. Pete Hoekstra (testimony), *Federal Document Clearing House Congressional Testimony* (July 17, 1998).

113. U.S. Congress, Senate, *Individuals with Disabilities Education Act Amendments of 1996*, Senate Report 104–275 (May 20, 1996).

114. "Department of Education, Office of Special Education and Rehabilitative Services; Special Education—Technology and Media Services for Individuals with Disabilities Program: Notice Inviting Public Comments," *Federal Register* (December 17, 1999), 70981–70983.

115. "Department of Education, Office of Special Education and Rehabilitative Services: Notice Inviting Applications for New Awards for Fiscal Year 2003," *Federal Register* (July 28, 2003), 44317–44328.

116. Zay N. Smith "Advocates for Deaf Charge Censorship in Closed Captioning," *Chicago Sun-Times* (February 20, 2004), 5.

117. National Association of the Deaf, "Television Captioning Censorship Hurts Family Values," press release posted to their Web site, http://www.nad.org (accessed October 2, 2003).

118. Smith, "Advocates for Deaf Charge Censorship in Closed Captioning."

119. National Association of the Deaf, "Television Captioning Censorship Hurts Family Values."

Conclusion: Education, Work, and the Culture of Print

Directions for Future Research

JAMES P. DANKY

Education and print go hand in hand, as this volume shows in so many fascinating ways. Yet the chapters in this volume only begin to illustrate the vast potential for scholarship on the connections between education and print. Many aspects of the historical sociology of print are not well understood, and more could be done to illuminate the complex interrelations between print and education, how these domains define one another, the nature of their mutual interdependence, and how their interactions have changed over time and in different contexts. In what follows I offer some possible directions for future research. The specific examples included are not exhaustive; they seek merely to provide starting points in what might be called a "needs and opportunities assessment." Moreover, these starting points are limited to the American scene; the global story of education and print remains perhaps the largest of the underdeveloped themes in this field.

At first glance, readers new to print culture history might wonder what a study of the interaction of education and print can add to our understanding of either education or print as historical phenomena. After all, it is hard to think of these domains as separate, or indeed separable. For centuries, education has involved print, and the links between education and print have increased exponentially over time. Yet the paucity of serious work on the historical sociology of print in the realm of education is startling. Consider the United States' Educational Resources Information Center (ERIC)—touted as "the world's largest digital library of education literature." This database, for all its diversity, is almost completely devoid of historical studies on the relationship between education and print! While the chapters in this volume begin to redress this problem, they are only a first step.

How, then, might scholars organize their study of the relationship between education and print? One approach, of course, would be to imagine the different communities of readers that use texts for educational purposes—communities differentiated by various markers of identity: race, ethnicity, nationality, gender, sexuality (dis)ability, social class, and so on. Certainly, there is much more to be written on education and print among the many groups of Americans represented and not represented in this volume: African Americans, Asian Americans, Latino/a Americans, Native Americans, European Americans, and all the various subgroups that give these categories their historical significance. In addition to studies organized around markers of identity, the field would also benefit from work framed around the different kinds of *institutions* that shape American readers' encounters with "educational" print. As Adam R. Nelson explains in his Introduction, a vast array of modern institutions frame the interaction of print culture and education. Elementary and secondary schools come most quickly to mind, but many other educational institutions, both formal and informal, from the market to the professions to the state, have their own worlds of print. In fact, as this volume demonstrates, a tremendous amount of education occurs *outside* what we typically define as schools. I would like to highlight some of the alternate settings in which texts and readers interact with what we might call "educative" effects, starting with the world of *work*.

There are few fields of work in which practitioners do not participate in some form of ongoing education (or "professional development"), and a panoply of institutions provide specialized instruction for occupations from the oldest to the newest. Moreover, print has become a ubiquitous element in virtually every work setting. Think, for example, of the forms of education promulgated by training manuals for skilled workers, orientation kits for service employees, professional journals for white-collar workers, targeted magazines or newsletters for certain jobs (take, for example, *Roll Call* magazine for congressional staffers, created in 1955). The print used to educate a modern and ever-more-specialized workforce is almost limitless in range, and while many of these sources rarely find their way outside of their narrowly focused communities of workers, the relationship between education, print, and work—or, more accurately, the cultivation and discipline of specific groups of workers across all levels of a complex modern economy—bears closer analysis than it has received to date. How has print structured the values, attitudes, habits, and skills of workers in modern America? How, in other words, has print "educated" the American workforce?

To take just one segment of the American workforce—professionals—the link between print, education, and work reveals much about the nation's history: its labor history, to be sure, but also its social and cultural history. The wave of professionalization that swept the United States in the late nineteenth century brought new forms of educational print that reshaped the world of work. No profession escaped this trend. Indeed, one might even say that creating new forms of educational print was essential to defining a new profession *as* a profession. Doctors and nurses, teachers and journalists, architects and engineers, urban planners and park rangers, chefs and hotel concierges—even morticians and taxidermists—all created new forms of professional education with attendant forms of educational print. These new print cultures were instrumental in the production and reproduction of professional groups. Medicine, law, business, and other professions—including, of course, education itself—produced torrents of books and periodicals that structured the field, standardized its practices, socialized new members, secured their prestige, and built demand for services. What would the process of *professionalization* be without print? The question itself reveals the significance of the answers historians might find. We need much more research on the educational nexus between print and professionalization in modern America.

Meanwhile, blue-collar fields have developed their own forms of print to educate tradespeople in skills ranging from plumbing to masonry to home-appliance repair. Education in these arenas has typically occurred in vocational and technical schools, in union shops and apprenticeships, and, by the last quarter of the twentieth century, in so-called "temp agencies" that came to symbolize the growing insecurity of employment in the American labor market. These workers, too, had their own education-related print cultures. Often developed through a process of negotiation involving management, labor representatives, and business consultants calling themselves "educational professionals," instructional materials in blue-collar fields have typically stressed such goals as "product standards"—meant to overcome the variability or diversity inherent in a human workforce. Print, in a sense, has sought to standardize the manufacture not only of products but also of *people*. This process of standardizing worker practices—whether the worker is fixing airplanes or drawing up estate plans—has its counterparts in earlier efforts in a modernizing economy to standardize everything from accounting methods to machine-tool design to any other task associated with producing goods or services for a "mass" (and therefore inevitably standardized) market. We need more historical research to understand how print fostered this process of standardization—a process that did not equalize but, rather, *segmented*, *stratified*, and *specialized* the world of work, the world of education, and the world of print itself.

Of course, the range of work-related educational print is practically infinite, covering everything—or almost everything—that people have done to make a living. And while, on the one hand, such print has a certain universal or generic quality to it, much of it can also be extremely specialized, thus creating significant (and at times intentional) barriers to wider dissemination. For this reason, the books, serials, and other materials produced for different sets of workers can be difficult for outsiders (including historians and other researchers) to acquire, let alone to understand. One need only consider the training manuals that have been produced for, say, derivatives traders or diamond cutters to grasp the ways in which the specialization of knowledge contained in these materials shapes the community of readers (or "learners") who use them. Because these work-related educational materials often have very targeted production and distribution, they can be hard to find, collect, and study. Nonetheless, work-related educational texts offer potentially valuable avenues for exploring the ways in which readers, as "students," become "workers" who internalize (and occasionally question, challenge, or change) the institutionalized norms of their jobs. If we are to build compelling interpretations of the broader ways in which print, education, and work become mutually reinforcing, we need far more studies of the specific interactions of print and education that occur in the world of work.

To illustrate the potential of such analyses, let me highlight one case, chosen more or less at random: the work-related educational print of religious professionals. The education of religious professionals in seminaries, yeshivas, madrassas, and other faith-specific bodies puts a premium on textual training that often dates from the religion's beginnings. While believers see some of the texts in terms of holy books, such as the Bible or Koran, there is a world of specialized print including youth educational volumes, hymnals, catechisms, handbooks for church organization, theological journals, and magazines of all sorts that provide the educational underpinnings for each faith. Such print is little collected beyond the libraries associated with the education of religious professionals and is, thus, little analyzed as print culture. The interactions between students and print provide the faith experiences for most of the world's population and yet are little understood by those "on the outside," be they scholars or believers. Surely, it would be desirable to see the results of comparative historical studies that reveal how well-established groups such as Roman Catholics or Methodists differed in their use and deployment of print from each other and from religious groups somewhat newer to America, such as those practicing Buddhism, Hinduism, Confucianism, or Islam or those committed to various New Age beliefs. As with much contemporary history, a lack of comparative analysis often results in work that speaks to the singular instead of the general. Scholars of print culture have a chance to illuminate this common heritage of print in service to education in the sacred that other disciplines too often overlook.

Beyond the worlds of work—and faith—other less-often-considered settings may also provide rich opportunities to study the relationship between education and print. To cite just one possible example, take the military, or military education, both of the West Point variety and education for the regular military. Following the sort of work that Christopher Loss has done in his examination of Armed Services Edition paperbacks for U.S. soldiers during World War II, close studies of education-related print in the military can reveal a range of sources ripe for investigation: not only textbooks or technical manuals to train military engineers to repair tanks and helicopters, but also materials for soldiers that teach methods of armed conflict, codes of military conduct, and the international rules of war. Along similar lines, the role of military organizations in developing a patriotic citizenry merits closer examination, as do print sources associated with patriotic groups such as the American Legion and Veterans of Foreign Wars. Such groups (and hundreds of similar, if lesser known groups) have their own armada of texts that seek to educate and politicize members. What kinds of citizens do these texts aim to produce: the question cannot be answered without close readings of the specific print employed in this task. (Of course, in a related vein, print-based instruction for citizenship, a process that has involved millions of immigrants over the last two centuries, raises similar questions about print, education, and national identity and inclusion. This arena, too, would benefit from more research in an ever-more-diverse America.)

The range of settings in which print and education coexist is literally endless, and this brief epilogue can suggest only a few in the hope that such a list will generate other ideas. In keeping with the notion that educational print often aims to structure values, habits, and attitudes, it seems, for example, that the role of print in educating for moral improvement is another area that calls for examination. In the history of the United States, redemptive print is most identified with the Bible and other religious tomes, but other arenas, perhaps not overtly religious, offer similar paths to personal reform through print. Self-help books constitute one form of "educational" print; the stacks of pamphlets made available at any half-way house or rehabilitation center represent another. Prison life (and, more directly, the prison library) is a setting suffused with print offered as a route to a new life. Similar in their strictures to the military and other constraining institutions, correctional facilities use print to inculcate standards of behavior and to offer inmates an opportunity to garner needed vocational and life skills for the "outside world." The incredible variety of print associated with youth centers, retreat venues, or even luxury spas does the same (albeit in very different ways). As historians and other scholars think of "life-long learning" and the pursuit of education through all stages of the life course, such alternate educational settings—and the specialized print that accompanies them—should begin to attract more attention. How has print educated Americans?

There are countless other arenas that might be identified in a "needs and opportunities assessment" exercise such as this—the bookshelves at women's shelters; the reference sources at health clinics; the guidebooks at parks, gyms, and other recreational facilities; and even the magazine racks in psychiatrists' offices or retirement homes (if such sources were historically recoverable in any systematic way)—but in each of these examples the message that comes through loud and clear is this: the numerous ways print functions in education is so little studied that we need to ask these seemingly obvious questions, not just to create a more orderly past but to foster more inclusive and useful scholarship on education and print culture in the future. The range of settings in which print and education interact is vast and should not be limited to schools.

That said, schools should not be overlooked in the history of education-related print. Of all forms of education, schools are far and away the largest and most significant print-driven institutions, trading in print on a scale that dwarfs those mentioned to this point. While new educational history and analysis is changing our views of the school, the print products designed for and consumed in these settings have remained remarkably understudied. We have, of course, several excellent studies of the history of textbooks and the history of school libraries (starting with Wayne Wiegand's outstanding work on this subject), but the uses of print in schools is rapidly changing. Such print today reflects the growing corporatization of American life in the form of "consumables" such as workbooks and other packaged learning systems, often with associated DVDs and, now, online components. Higher education at both the undergraduate and graduate level has seen similar developments in its textbooks, custom-crafted course packs, and online readings, all of which change at a pace that ensures a sort of planned obsolescence that maximizes industry profits.

Behind the texts at the precollege level lay the curriculum-specific instructional scripts, their own form of print that offer education in the guise of being "age-appropriate" or "cognitively appropriate." Such materials exist for nearly every subgroup of pupils: each category of disability (or "giftedness"), each set of English language learners, each age, ethnicity, or geographic location. Here the role of the teacher as intermediary in the chain of print desperately needs greater scrutiny. How has the presence of the teacher affected the interpretation of meaning? The reader, often but not always a child, lies between two authority figures—the teacher and the text—a situation that students in high school and college literature classes should easily recognize. How have students used print itself to challenge or defy their teachers or the institutional authority that teachers represent? In addition to these examples of "print from above," more attention ought to be paid to the role of student-produced print—things such as poetry magazines, school newspapers, and class journals, not to mention special-interest publications for students involved in sports, theater, community service, or special-interest clubs. Such materials, studied historically, allow us to see the creative reception of the experiences of print in education through a form of reproduction by the student, however closely monitored.

Just as each field of work has its attendant educational print needs, school-related print takes a myriad of *forms*. From technical diagrams to end-of-chapter "self-tests," "problem sets," or "questions for thought and/or discussion," textbook learning has been structured in various ways. From hip-pocket "field manuals" to detailed "case studies" made famous by the Harvard Business School in the early 1900s, the relationship between form and function in print has long influenced the nature of the educational experience. One of the most significant shifts in textual form has occurred recently as electronic text has begun to supplant print materials. The end of the codex format has been predicted for a number of years, and clearly the Internet has changed the world of reading and learning more than any other development in the recent past. For education, this change has meant a rise of new institutions such as "virtual schools," where an array of online print, e-learning, and blogging have redefined the educational experience. These electronic sites for education have radically changed the geography of education, potentially globalizing the classroom and rendering the brick-and-mortar classroom a historical curiosity. Literacy software, educational video games, and other programmed learning materials that are now for sale online have their origin in printed works from the early nineteenth century: workbooks for math, science, geography, spelling, and grammar, among others. Historians might address these recent changes by studying earlier versions of "distance education," from correspondence courses to mail-order encyclopedia sets to the "Great Books" or "great lecture" series advertised in the back pages of popular magazines. The increasing *mixture* of print-, audio-, and video-based learning in the electronic age has made the relationship between education and print all the more complex.

The editors of this volume have gathered contributions from a wide variety of scholars who, though each bringing a unique disciplinary focus, have in common the role of the intervenor in this Darntonian circuit, namely the teacher. Whether the beginning of this circuit lies in the moral imperatives voiced by Horace Mann or in the relentlessly practical ethos that defines so much of present-day education, the key figure is the teacher. Teachers are everywhere, especially when they are not termed teachers. Teachers exist in the interstitial spaces between readers and texts and exercise their power to guide readers toward ideas that "need to be understood." Clearly such ideas of "understanding" involve a regression that ultimately returns us to *texts* (consider the role of Teacher's Editions), but the consumption of texts has consequences that cannot always be predicted. Some books are now taught deliberately and intentionally *against* the text—say *Mein Kampf*. Further, some readers come to a text and work against the mediation that teachers offer. Such transgressive reading reveals individuals reacting to the institutional power inherent in teachers and "teaching." Often, these independent interpretations mark the very sort of "critical thinking" that teachers encourage. When this contest between teachers and students, readers and texts, is expanded beyond the classroom setting, we observe teachers, readers, and texts engaged in similar negotiations almost everywhere we look. Consider bosses at work, drill sergeants in the military, or prison wardens. The list could go on and on. All are engaged in interpreting texts for—and with—students.

In this model for understanding the encounter of "education" and print the various roles of the teacher as intervenor, the text is the final product of a long process of authorship, publishing, dissemination, and interpretation. Few if any readers ever blindly accept the interventions of teachers or recognize the authority of texts. Rather, readers encounter the text alone (even in the classroom) but come to understanding with the teacher and the society that surrounds them. It is this collective process of *learning* that defines education and represents the relationship of the individual to the society. In the end, the negotiation of meaning is not merely an autonomous act; it depends on a variety of institutions and communities that are so deftly illuminated by the chapters in this volume.

Contributors

RYAN K. ANDERSON is an assistant professor of history and coordinator of the American studies major at the University of North Carolina at Pembroke. His current project is tentatively titled "What Would Frank Merriwell Do? Middle-Class Readers, the Business of Popular Literature, and the Progressive Era Roots of All-American Boyhood."

MICHAEL BENJAMIN is an independent teacher-scholar. He holds two doctorate degrees, a JD and a PhD in modern history and literature, and an MBA and an MA in book history in America. As a cultural historian he teaches and writes in the fields of African, African American, and American history and literature. His current project is tentatively titled "In Search of the Grail: The Origins and Meaning of Murray's Encyclopedia of the Colored Race throughout the World."

JAMES P. DANKY is the cofounder and past director of the Center for the History of Print Culture in Modern America. Although recently retired from the Wisconsin Historical Society, he continues to teach at the University of Wisconsin–Madison's School of Journalism and Mass Communication and is the author and editor of several articles and volumes related to print culture.

GREG DOWNEY is a professor at the University of Wisconsin–Madison in the School of Journalism and Mass Communication and the School of Library and Information Studies. He is the author of *Telegraph Messenger Boys: Labor, Technology, and Geography, 1850–1950* (Routledge, 2002) and *Closed Captioning: Subtitling, Stenography, and the Digital Convergence of Text with Television* (Johns Hopkins University Press, 2008).

JANE GREER is an associate professor of English and women's and gender studies at the University of Missouri–Kansas City. She teaches composition courses as well as courses on the rhetorical practices of women and girls. She is currently completing a manuscript on working-class women's opportunities for rhetorical education from the 1840s through the 1930s.

FRANK TOBIAS HIGBIE is an associate professor of history at the University of California, Los Angeles. He is the author of *Indispensable Outcasts: Hobo Workers and Community in the American Midwest, 1880–1930* (University of Illinois Press, 2003).

KATE MCDOWELL is an assistant professor at the Graduate School of Library and Information Science at the University of Illinois, Urbana-Champaign. Her research interests include the history of children's librarianship, women's contributions to librarianship, and new forms of traditional storytelling in libraries. Her work has been published in the journals *Book History*, *Library Quarterly*, *Storytelling, Self, Society*, and others.

ADAM R. NELSON is an associate professor in the Departments of Educational Policy Studies and History at the University of Wisconsin–Madison. He is the author of *Education and Democracy: The Meaning of Alexander Meiklejohn, 1872–1964* (University of Wisconsin Press, 2001) and *The Elusive Ideal: Equal Educational Opportunity and the Federal Role in Boston's Public Schools, 1950–1985* (University of Chicago Press, 2005). He is currently working on a history of nationalism and internationalism in the American research university.

ROBERT ORSI is Grace Craddock Nagle Chair in Catholic Studies at Northwestern University and most recently the author of *Between Heaven and Earth: The Religious Worlds People Make and the Scholars Who Study Them* (Princeton University Press, 2005).

JOHN L. RUDOLPH is a professor in the Departments of Curriculum and Instruction and History of Science at the University of Wisconsin–Madison. He is author of *Scientists in the Classroom: The Cold War Reconstruction of American Science Education* (Palgrave Macmillan, 2002) and is currently writing a book on classroom portrayals of scientific epistemology since the late nineteenth century.

ADAM R. SHAPIRO is the Dibner Fellow in the History of Science at the Huntington Library in San Marino, California. His research focuses on the historical intersections of science, religion, and education. He also worked as an editor of mathematics textbooks for the University of Chicago School Mathematics Project from 2005 to 2007.

CATHERINE TURNER teaches in the English department and is Associate Director of the Center for Teaching and Learning at the University of Pennsylvania. She is currently completing a book on literacy and public policy during the New Deal.